The Secret World of Stamps

An insider's behind-the-scenes look at how America's stamps are created

Terry McCaffrey

Small Art Press—New Braunfels, TX
ISBN: 979-8-218-33356-0
Library of Congress Control Number: 2023923152
Title: *The Secret World of Stamps: An insider's behind-the-scenes look at how America's stamps are created*
Author: Terry McCaffrey
Digital distribution | 2023
Paperback | 2023

All stamps discussed in this book are available for viewing on the internet.

Dedication

This book is dedicated with love to

Ann
My rock and foundation

Table of Contents

Prologue: My Initiation into the World of Stamps vii
How from childhood on I was destined to become a part of the stamp world.

Chapter 1: Where *Do* Those Stamps Come From?......................... 1
Explaining how those miniature works of art called stamps come to be.

Chapter 2: The Customer is Always Right 5
Responding to customer complaints, concerns and suggestions, not to mention unsolicited artwork.

Chapter 3: Adding Their 'Two Cents' 22
Coping with and appeasing influential individuals and groups both within and outside the Postal Service.

Chapter 4: Let's Make a Deal 78
Balancing integrity versus marketing potential when developing stamps.

Chapter 5: Design Challenges... 93
Tiptoeing through the minefields of mistakes, right decisions, unforeseen problems and altering art.

Chapter 6: The Rights Stuff.. 129
Making sure the stamps pass the legal test.

Chapter 7: It's All in the Family 137
Whether it was Presidents, Musicians, Monsters, or Movie Stars, the families all had their say.

Chapter 8: The Big Show 176
Stamp dedications whether large or small, were always eventful.

Chapter 9: The Ones That Got Away 193
A behind-the-scenes look at some subjects that never made it to the Post Office.

Chapter 10: Around the World in 8,000 Days 205
Adventures and misadventures of trips both far and wide over 20+ colorful years.

Epilogue: The Long and Winding Road 233
Summing up a colorful, exciting life of great experiences

Acknowledgements 239

About the Author 240

Prologue

My Initiation into the World of Stamps

Postage stamps have been part of the American scene for more than 170 years.

In today's society of high tech and high-speed information, many people rely increasingly on email, social media, and other forms of communication rather than the U.S. Mail, which has diminished the demand for and use of postage stamps. But if one were to look at the U.S. stamp program since the first stamps were issued in 1847, one would find a record of its history, accomplishments, and the individuals who helped create the great country that we have today.

Stamps have frequently been referred to as "Our Nation's Calling Cards." Those little pieces of paper help celebrate its diversity and accomplishments. Being commemorated on a stamp is one of the highest honors our country can bestow on someone. Over the years, the U.S. Postal Service has issued in excess of 5,000 designs commemorating everything from baseball heroes to bats, presidents to peonies, entertainers to eagles, monuments to the military, and a myriad of other subjects.

I have been honored to be a part of that program for more than twenty years. As the Manager of Stamp Development, I oversaw the design of more than 2,500 stamp designs between 1990 and 2010. Each of these designs tells a unique story, thus the reason for this book.

But first, I have a confession to make. I have never collected stamps, not even as a child. During my childhood, stamp collecting was a popular hobby. But my access to stamps and the hobby was limited for me. Born in the small town of La Crescent, Minnesota, which had a population of 3,000, I instead became interested in art of all types. As soon as I could hold a pencil, I began to draw. I drew everything I saw and on everything available to me, including the Formica-top kitchen table, which saw many a "masterpiece" wiped away with a washcloth in preparation for dinner.

My interest was not limited solely to drawing. I found film to be one of the most fascinating art forms of our time. At one point, I seriously considered a career in film, but I soon came to my senses. But film continued to play a significant role when I began developing stamps later in my life and was a major contributor to my eventual career path as a graphic designer.

While drawing was always a love of mine, I knew that I could never succeed as a fine artist. Sitting and starving in a garret was not my thing, but numerous trips to the local movie theater opened the door to a promising career. It was in those darkened theaters that I discovered a field of art unknown to me at the time: graphic design. Watching the film credits of Saul Bass intrigued me, and I began to explore the world of graphic design, known at the time as "commercial art." Immediately, I knew it was the path I wished to pursue.

It was after a move to Washington, D.C. to study graphic design in 1960 that I encountered stamps. At that time, the Bureau of Engraving and Printing's, referred to as the BEP, was the lone printer of all U.S. stamps and the agency that oversaw the majority of stamp designs. While studying at the Corcoran School of Art, my classmates and I, one of whom was Bob Jones, a BEP artist, were informed that the Postal Service was holding a design competition to commemorate the one-hundredth anniversary of the Battle of Gettysburg. Eagerly, many of us in class submitted designs but failed to make the final cut. How ironic that some thirty years later, I would be overseeing the design of the entire stamp program.

As I neared graduation, Bob suggested that I apply at the BEP for a position in their art department. But my hopes were soon dashed when I visited their offices. The atmosphere and offices were very bureaucratic;

dark, dingy, and dirty best described the working conditions. Even the art staff wore white lab coats! The security measures were what convinced me it was not for me. Having to sign out of your office, walk across the hall to another office, sign in, sign out again, and return to your office and sign in yet again was just too much.

It wasn't until 1970 that the world of stamps entered my life again. After being laid off from a job in the private sector after seven years, I found myself knocking on the doors of the Postal Service. I was offered a job in their communications department as the first graphic designer for the Postal Service. My job was to launch the new corporate design program that was authorized by the 1970 Postal Reorganization Act. I was responsible for magazines, brochures, and posters, but not stamps. There was a separate department for that.

In 1973, along with Pat McCabe, a staff photographer, I convinced the Office of Stamps to produce large lobby posters with the issuance of every new commemorative stamp. My connection to stamps was back in place. Over the years, Pat and I produced more than two hundred lobby posters.

I was then approached by the Office of Stamps in 1975 to submit a design for the world's largest stamp show, "Interphil 76," held in Philadelphia in 1976 for the U.S. bicentennial. Amazingly, my design was approved by the Citizens' Stamp Advisory Committee (CSAC), and my first stamp was issued in January 1976. The following year, I created two stamps touting Energy Conservation and Development.

No more stamp designs came my way while working in the communications department, but the Stamps group began to enlist my design services for various stamp-related products, such as catalogs and annual stamp albums. It was only a matter of time before I would officially make the move to Stamps after a twenty-year stint in the communications department.

That change came about in October 1990 and, for the next twenty years, stamps became an integral part of my life. During those twenty years, I worked on projects that were frustrating, educational, amusing, perplexing, exasperating, exciting, and fun to develop. But I venture to guess that the vast majority of the public has no idea what goes into stamp development. It's with that in mind that I decided to share the design process and the behind-the-scenes stories of these miniature works of art in this book.

Chapter 1

Where *Do* Those Stamps Come From?

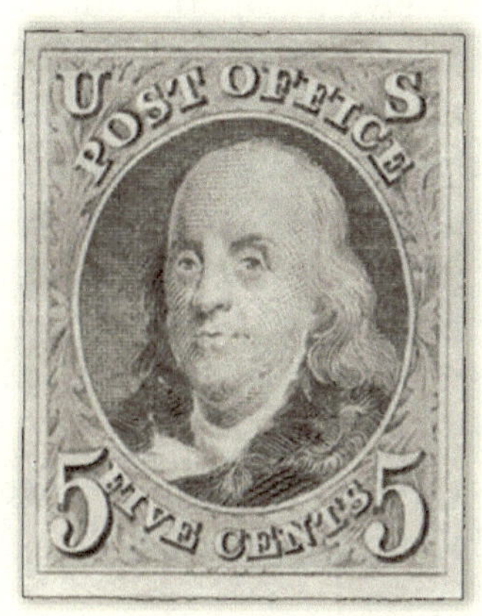

"I had no idea!" is the typical response when people hear about the complex evolution of postage stamps.

Stamps are a unique commodity. Like currency, they are considered a form of U.S. security. When the colonialists adopted the British concept of affixing paper images to envelopes as a form of payment for services, i.e., delivering their correspondence, it became the second form of U.S. security, and it remains so today. So, you could say that designing stamps is akin to designing currency. Or not. While currency design is complex, requiring multiple forms of security features to avoid counterfeiting, the postage stamp is a simpler palette on which to illustrate our nation's heritage. Stamps have far more latitude in design, color, shape, and subject matter than currency has in what is depicted.

Since the first U.S. stamps of 1847 were issued and for the next eighty years or so, stamps mimicked currency by depicting our greatest presidents, politicians, and statesmen. Gradually, other subjects began to find their way onto stamps, such as scenery and icons. It wasn't until the early 1960s that the first full-color stamp was issued in the U.S. Speaking as a designer, it's difficult to comprehend that it took that long for full color to be utilized on postage stamps. But, as I said, the stamp process is complicated, and it took a while for the technology to catch up with the rest of print and design.

Because of stamps' high visibility, they are subject to public opinion. Because of the monopoly the Postal Service has over the mail system, customers have no options for mailing letters. In recent decades, competition from FedEx and UPS has drastically cut into United States Postal Service (USPS) parcel shipments, but the USPS still maintains a monopoly on mailing letters, which require stamps, and the public wants a choice when purchasing stamps. Not only does the public make its wishes known, but the Stamps office must continually respond to requests from Congress, the White House, USPS management, the USPS Board of Governors, and numerous other interested parties.

Multiple steps are required to produce a stamp, so the following steps will give you a brief overview of how they are created.

Subject Selection

Many Americans do not realize that they can submit a subject for consideration as a postage stamp. Nonetheless, an average of 40,000 letters were received annually by my staff from citizens requesting consideration of particular subjects. The vast majority of these were ineligible either because the subject had already been featured on a stamp, the proposed individual had not been deceased long enough to meet USPS criteria, or the subject was prohibited by Postal Service policy from appearing on a stamp, i.e., organizations, religious groups, etc.

Subjects that did survive the initial review were then forwarded to the Postmaster General's Citizens' Stamp Advisory Committee (CSAC) for consideration.

Development

Upon review and selection by the CSAC's Subject Subcommittee, the assignment was then given to my staff to begin development.

Initial research was done to identify visual material from which to create the image as well as background information for use in developing press releases, products, and promotional materials. Each stamp was assigned to one of six art directors under contract to the Postal Service. They, in turn, would explore ideas on how the subject could best be depicted.

Because the CSAC now meets every quarter, the design development process typically took twelve to eighteen months. Concepts would be presented to the Design Subcommittee and then returned to the designer or illustrator for further development. Once approved by the design group, it was shown to the full committee, who then took a formal vote on approval.

Designs were then selected for a proposed year of issuance. The Committee would deliberate on the balance of subjects and designs for an upcoming year, ensuring that the program was well-balanced with popular subjects, historical commemorations, and diversity. Upon approval of the program, it was presented to the Postmaster General for final approval. He alone had the final "yea" or "nay" on any subject or design.

Printing

At the stamp printers a minimum of six months prior to the first day of issue. Millions of stamps are produced for every design. Some have smaller runs of around twenty million, but more-in-demand stamps would be produced in the billions. Stamps were then distributed to each of the more than 30,000 post offices nationwide.

Issuance

A philatelic tradition is that each stamp has a first day of issue and, in many instances, a first-day ceremony. These events had to be planned many months in advance, and a special group of staff members worked full-time to plan these events. Dignitaries, families, and supporters of the stamp subject were invited to partake in this unique ceremony, which was always well attended by the local philatelic community.

Collateral material plays a key role in each stamp issuance. Press releases for each first-day event, as well as a preliminary look at the entire year's program, were critical to promoting awareness of what stamp designs were currently available. For major issuances, press kits were assembled, and first-day ceremony programs were produced as handouts to attendees.

As one can see from the process I've described the idea that a stamp "just happens," as many people assume, is not the case at all. In fact, it is a very involved evolution requiring a large group of very talented people to pull it off.

Because stamp development is so complex, it demands that each stage of the process be addressed as its own entity. Rather than offering anecdotes in chronological order, I think it would be best for me to address the steps, missteps, problems, challenges, and solutions that I encountered in my twenty-year journey through the wild, wonderful, and wacky world of stamps by their various functions. The following chapters should provide proof enough that stamps are a unique, one-of-a-kind product, rich in art, information, and interesting individuals—and with plenty of wonderful behind-the-scenes stories.

Chapter 2

The Customer Is Always Right

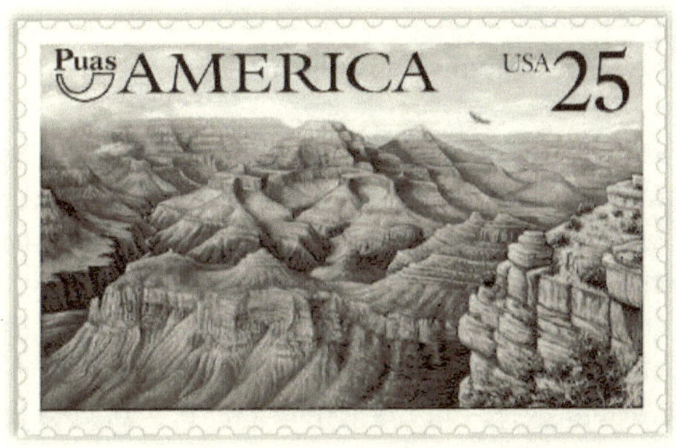

In 1956, popular recording and TV crooner Perry Como used to sing "Letters, we get letters. We get stacks and stacks of letters." Well, that could be the theme song for the U.S. Stamp Services office.

One of my responsibilities as Manager of Stamp Development was to oversee the mail we received from the public regarding stamps. Over the years, the ranks of letter writers swelled to a point where we were receiving more than 40,000 letters recommending a subject, complaining about a subject or an objectionable design, or anything else they felt was wrong with stamps. Rarely did we receive a complimentary letter.

Each letter was dutifully opened, sorted by subject, and recorded. For years, we had a secretarial support staff of three to four individuals whose sole responsibility was to do just that. Toward the end of my twenty-year tenure, the staff dwindled to just one person, Joyce Wahoski, who managed the mail in addition to numerous other responsibilities. By then, the number of letters had dropped by 10,000, but that still meant 30,000 letters needed to be read and sorted.

I had a standing request for Joyce regarding the letters. If she came across one that was unique, funny, or just plain outrageous, I wanted a copy of it for my "keeper" file. Over the years, this file grew in volume. Looking back over those letters has provided many laughs. While the letter writers were very serious in their comments, requests, or complaints, it was difficult sometimes for us to take their comments seriously.

'Questionable' Imagery

Three key aspects of developing stamps are to avoid controversy, ensure accuracy of the image, and monitor the public response to the issuance. Letter writers complained about "suggestive" imagery, politically incorrect subjects, religious or nationality biases, and everything in between, right down to the gap between an individual's front teeth being inaccurate. The Richard Nixon stamp was just one of many during my tenure that provoked a public outcry (more about that later). These controversies made life very interesting for the Stamps group.

"Suggestive" material, you ask? How did you miss that on stamps? We could ask the same question when we received the letter or phone call. After listening patiently to the customer's complaint, we were usually amazed to discover just what they were referring to. Here are just a few examples.

The Olympics stamps we usually issued every four years were always a source of raised eyebrows from our more conservative customers. The 1996 Atlanta Summer Games proved to be too much for a few grandmothers. Individual letters came in complaining about the disgusting display of the female bodies on the stamps. "Why, you could actually see the outline of the woman's nipple on her breast," wrote one grandmother. Another wrote that the poses of the female gymnast and beach volleyball player were lewd and suggestive. "I had planned to purchase panes of these stamps to give to my grandchildren, but upon closer inspection I found the stamps to be objectionable. You all should be ashamed of yourselves."

In 2004, we issued a single Olympic stamp honoring the Games in Athens. Our design resembled a Greek runner as often depicted on ancient urns. Unfortunately, some people felt that the image went a little too far by depicting a "specific part of the male anatomy that was indeed shocking," as one customer wrote. Upon reviewing the design after receiving the letter, it left us scratching our heads as to what she was referring to. It's truly amazing how people interpret images.

Even nature is subject to scrutiny, as we found over the years. In 1990, our office received a letter saying our depiction of the Grand Canyon in a stamp was "vulgar and crude." This customer had a very imaginative mind. He discerned that the rock formations on the cliff walls depicted an erect penis. After intense scrutiny, our staff finally located what we believe he was referring to. It certainly was not our intent to get "pornographic" about it, as he intimated. A second rock formation "inspired" a philatelist to single out the Postal Service's subliminal erotic imagery on another stamp.

In 1996, a letter was published in *Linn's Stamp News* commenting on the Utah Statehood image. The gentleman, who appeared to have a very fertile imagination, saw the famed Delicate Arch rock formation located in Utah's Arches National Park, with the moon rising behind it, as a "naked lady bent over backwards." That comment elicited numerous chuckles and head shaking throughout the office.

Nudity and sex have always been "no-no's" on stamps. In 2003, we issued a mail rate stamp depicting the "Wisdom" sculptural relief displayed at Rockefeller Center. This classic art deco relief had been on display for many years and enjoyed by everyone who saw it. Unfortunately, when we had the audacity to reproduce it on a postage stamp, we were accused of displaying male nudity.

The previous year, we had issued a stamp honoring Ogden Nash, the great poet, as part of our "Literary Arts" series. Some very observant individuals discovered the word "sex" in one of the lines of Nash's poem, entitled "The Turtle," depicted behind Nash's portrait.

For discussing the sex life of a turtle, we were chastised, once again, for our "lack of judgment."

My assumption is that the majority of the public would not consider postage stamps to be "sexy" by any stretch of the imagination. But there are individuals out there who seek out such a connection.

The annual "Madonna and Child" Christmas stamp has occasionally elicited negative comments about nudity, specifically, regarding the baby Jesus. For years, the traditional Madonna and Child stamp featured masterpiece paintings from major museums, a fact that often escaped the minds of the complainers. They ridiculed everything from the size of the baby ("too old and too muscular") to the shocking depiction of a nude baby complete with genitalia. Obscenity was a term used often to describe those stamps.

Even cherubic angels didn't pass muster for some people. The "Love" cherub design I created in 1995 using the famous and oft-reproduced angelic images from Raphael's "Sistine Madonna" painting was considered "vulgar" and "lustful" by some offended customers. One customer wrote to us calling the Love Cherub "that naked kid" and accused us of child pornography. Yet he admitted to purchasing the stamp, only to express concern that he hoped he "wouldn't use them to mail to a man with the word 'Love' on it, for fear the man would think I'm queer and want to have sex with him." Needless to say, we chose not to respond to his complaint.

Stamps submitted to us by the public for consideration occasionally had their own sexual connotations.

One writer suggested that a stamp honor country-western singer Barbara Mandrell because, in his words, "That's one stamp I can't wait to *lick*." No comment.

Another subject suggestion was supposedly from the cousin of Marilyn Chambers, the famed porn star, who recommended Ms. Chambers for the "Great Americans" series because she was "a great figure who showed the world that women have prowess in the field of sexuality." She ended her plea by admonishing us: "Don't be Pigs. Consider my suggestion."

Some even submitted their own designs, such as "Famous American Drag Queens," "Female Impersonators," "Transvestitism" and "Transsexuals." The illustrations depicted Candy Darling, a drag queen who passed away in the 1970s. "Prostitution," a rather cynical submission, came complete with a stick-figure drawing of a female nude holding "the almighty dollar" in one hand and a condom in the other. To complete the design, the artist recommended a 69-cent denomination.

Even science entered the picture alongside stamps and sex.

Before self-adhesive stamps became the norm, customers were forced to lick the adhesive on stamps. Numerous letters over the years from concerned customers wanted to know if the glue was harmful or how many calories were in the glue (obviously from diet-conscious customers). But one mother wrote to us with another concern.

As an expectant mother, she was concerned about licking stamps, so she delegated the task to her husband. He told her that after taking over the stamp-licking task, it increased his sexual desires. She noticed how much more affectionate he had become since taking care of the mail. She went on to state, "In fact, he won't leave me alone." Her question was whether any adverse effects have been found in lab animals or people from licking stamps. She didn't mind that her husband had increased sexual needs, but she worried about the effects on her baby. We had a standard prepared response to questions regarding adhesives, reassuring them that there were no "harmful" side effects. We never tested for the amorous side effects though.

Doctors, too, have written to us, or about us, regarding stamps.

One doctor was seeking information about the chemical makeup of our self-adhesive stamps. He was engaged in trying to improve condoms, which in his words were "suitable for sensuality but not for the protection against AIDS and other sexually transmitted diseases." He thought our chemical mix might be what his new, improved condom might benefit from.

Erectile dysfunction has become a household phrase, seen nightly in ads promoting medications to address the problem. One magazine article recently had an easier and less costly solution to determine whether one suffers from the problem. The suggested solution: "Take a strip of three or four stamps and stick the strip around the penis just before going to sleep. In the morning, if the stamps are torn apart, you can be sure the body is still physically capable of producing an erection. If the stamps are intact, the cause is probably physical." No recommendations were offered for which stamp designs to use. Maybe some of the "erotic" or "lustful" designs mentioned previously might have helped the cause.

The advent of self-adhesive stamps brought a lot of entrepreneurs out of the woodwork who made suggestions on how to improve the stamps. One of my personal favorites was the gentleman who suggested placing a piece of non-stick paper between each pane of stamps in stamp booklets. He complained that he had a new billfold and "every time I've gone to the toilet, it falls in the toilet, getting the stamps wet. They stick together, ruining the whole book." I might have suggested to him a much simpler solution to his problem, but then I reminded myself, "The customer is always right."

Aside from the letters, we received many phone calls from disgruntled mail users. How did their calls find their way to my office? I had the very efficient telephone operators at Headquarters to thank for that. Despite the presence of about 3,000 employees in the Headquarters offices, I somehow gained the reputation of "Stamp Man" over the years. So, whenever a caller wished to speak to someone about a stamp, the Headquarters operators immediately forwarded them to my office.

Political correctness plays a significant role in stamp development. Even the best of intentions is subject to chastisement. Issuances such as *Malcolm X* (1999), *Frida Kahlo* (2001), and *Paul Robeson* (2004) received criticism in the press, in Congress, and from outraged customers. We anticipated controversy when we honored Malcolm X as part of the "Black Heritage" annual stamp series. Controversial stamp subjects were usually manageable, but these three stamps were more controversial and often referred to as "Communists on U.S. stamps."

The inclusion of Frida Kahlo in the "Famous Artists" series of stamps generated criticism all the way to Capitol Hill. Senator Jesse Helms denounced the Postal Service on the floor of the U.S. Senate for our lack of judgment in honoring a known Communist and "hater of America." I personally received a letter from an outraged customer who enclosed a newspaper clipping depicting the Kahlo stamp image. He took the liberty to stamp, in red ink, "BULLSHIT" numerous times over the image. I assume he didn't care for our decision.

Three years later, we revisited the same controversy when we issued the Paul Robeson stamp, another in the "Black Heritage" series. Refusing to acknowledge the major arts contributions Mr. Robeson made to our country, some customers couldn't get past his supposed Communist leanings. There were no denunciations from the floor of the Senate that time, but some calls of concern from Capitol Hill were received by our Government Relations office.

Collecting stamps by themes is one way to build one's collection. I often jokingly said that we should create a "Great American Communist" series of which there would be many additional stamps from past years that could be included. No one wanted to touch that idea.

Politics of another sort reared its head in 1994 when we unveiled the designs for the fifth and final set of ten stamps honoring seminal events of World War II upon its 50th anniversary. The series started in 1991 with the first set of ten designs, reflecting events of 1941. In each of the following years, another ten subjects commemorated the events of the war in each subsequent year, culminating with the 1945 set. Obviously, one of the stamps would commemorate the dropping of the atomic bomb on Hiroshima.

Art director Howard Paine collaborated with illustrator Bill Bond to create all fifty stamp images. They chose to depict the iconic mushroom cloud in the background with the watch stopped at the moment of the blast. The CSAC members all felt it was an excellent choice and approved the design, which was subsequently approved by the Postmaster General, as all stamps are.

When the ten designs for the 1945 set were unveiled, a firestorm of controversy ensued. The media chose to isolate that one stamp from the other nine and published articles stating that the U.S. Postal Service was issuing a stamp commemorating the bombing of Hiroshima. They neglected to add the reason for the stamp, making it appear that the U.S. Government was, in effect, honoring this horrific tragedy. Subsequently, we began receiving numerous calls and letters, and about a week later, we were told that protests were mounting in Japan regarding the issuance. This action prompted the White House to contact our offices to insist that the stamp be dropped.

We explained that we couldn't drop the subject as we would look foolish for not including arguably the biggest moment in the history of the war. We were instructed to somehow find another solution. A much "safer" image depicted President Truman signing the order to drop the bomb, which for some reason was acceptable to everyone.

Speaking of bombs, our office was not even immune to criticism from our own employees. A few window clerks who routinely sold the stamps called to complain about the 2003 Holiday stamps. One of these whimsical illustrations of Santas and reindeers dancing across the pane of stamps raised eyebrows. It seems that the reindeer carrying a pan pipe (a musical instrument) gave these employees the impression that the reindeer was carrying a stick of dynamite. I suspect that the sensitivity of the 9/11 terrorist bombings played a role in their thinking.

An international mail rate stamp was issued in 2001 that utilized an existing photograph of Mt. McKinley. This series, entitled "Scenic American Landscapes," featured nature scenes from different areas of the United States. Mt. McKinley would represent the far northwestern section of the country. Unfortunately, we did not confer with the original inhabitants of that region. Mere days before the official first day of issuance ceremony, we were informed that the Native Americans of the region were demanding the withdrawal of the stamp. Their reason? The stamp was incorrectly named. Instead of Mt. McKinley, which in their words was the white man's name, it should have read Mt. Denali, the original Indian name. While I agree, in principle, that they were correct and that we probably should have used the original name, it was far too late to change it. (Note: The peak was officially renamed "Denali" in 2015.) The stamps had been produced months prior to issuance, and the design had been unveiled earlier. But that didn't stop the Native Americans from protesting. They arrived at the first-day ceremony along with the dignitaries and guests and formally protested the issuance.

Sensitivity is and has always been an issue in stamp development. Our job was to attempt to analyze all aspects of the subject to ensure that we were sensitive to all parties. Not an easy task. To say that we "failed" on occasion wouldn't be too far from the truth. But I think that "failed" is a rather harsh word to use in those cases.

Whether it involves humans or animals, sensitivity is always an issue. In 1996, we issued a pane of Endangered Species stamps using the brilliant photography of James Balog, one of the world's preeminent wildlife photographers. Using his existing photos saved the Postal Service from having to commission new photography, which would have been cost-prohibitive given our budget. Balog's photos had previously been reproduced in books and other media to much critical acclaim.

A unique feature of Balog's photos is how he photographs the subjects in a controlled environment rather than crawling through jungles and swamps to capture them on film. The beautiful close-up images depict crocodiles, ocelots, parrots, fish, and numerous other creatures. Included in this set was the ever-popular manatee. The photo we chose to use showed a reclining manatee, partly out of the water, which was in keeping with the other creatures depicted in close-ups.

The Postal Service traditionally unveils its designs a year before issuance, which gives us time to generate public interest. Occasionally, such public interest backfires. It seems that manatees have fans. A Floridian woman, an avid fan of these rotund creatures, was shocked and dismayed upon seeing the stamp image and began a campaign to get us to change it. Her claim was that the manatee shown in that uncharacteristic pose was, in effect, "mistreated." She began her lobbying efforts by contacting her local newspaper. Her demands spread nationwide, forcing us to reconsider our choice. In the end, we used another Balog photo of two submerged manatees. While still a good photo, it never really was in concert with the other images from a design standpoint. But, as the old adage goes, the customer is always right. Right?

Ethnicity plays a critical role in the stamp program as well. The Postal Service never developed its annual program by filling quotas, as some people have suggested. We attempted to show the diversity of our country by commemorating not only famous individuals but diverse cultures as well. And there was one person who spent a great deal of time ensuring that his heritage was reflected in our annual program. He was a member of a state chapter of the Commission for Social Injustice, the anti-defamation arm of the Order of Sons of Italy in America.

This gentleman emailed me to register a strong protest, contending that the upcoming year's stamp program did not include an Italian subject. His lengthy letter cited the previous year's issuances, which showed Italians. Many of those subjects happened to be the Madonna and Child Christmas stamps which often reproduced Italian Renaissance masterpieces. For the year in question, we not only did not use an Italian artist's Madonna and Child but neglected to honor Italians in any other stamp categories.

I politely wrote back stating that we did not select our subjects by nationality or ethnicity and thanked him for sharing his thoughts with us. The year passed, minus an Italian stamp subject, and I thought I had heard the last of him. Little did I know!

The use of an Italian Renaissance Madonna and Child masterpiece a year later seemed to appease the gentleman. But when the following year came and no Italians were slated, I again heard from him, this time in very forceful language. He was so adamant that all of his letters were cc'd to the Postmaster General, *Linn's Stamp News*, his Congressman, two U.S. Senators, and last but not least, the President of the United States. Now, for those of you who know the workings of bureaucracies, these cc's meant that each of these offices in turn contacted us to request an explanation and language on how to answer this person. Despite my pleas that I could manage it, they insisted on being in the mix, requiring me to spend an inordinate amount of time explaining and writing responses for the various offices. The same general response was formulated and mailed to him. But we all knew that he was not to be satisfied.

When the 2004 program was unveiled, I felt confident that I wouldn't have to deal with our Italian American patriot. Plans called for a stamp commemorating Henry Mancini, the talented Italian American film composer. You couldn't get much more Italian than Mancini. But our friend was not to be placated by this addition. He sent me (with the usual cc's) a scathing letter demanding we change the image. It seems that to his way of thinking, we were defaming Mr. Mancini. His letter started off by thanking us for honoring a fellow Italian American, but then he launched into a litany of "mistakes" in judgment regarding the design.

The image depicted Mr. Mancini conducting with both arms raised, complete with baton. He was attired in a turtleneck sweater, as shown in the original source photo of a recording session for one of his films. Our friend stated that Mancini's attire was demeaning. He questioned why fellow musician Leonard Bernstein, three years prior, was depicted on a stamp in a tuxedo. He demanded that Mancini receive the same treatment and that the illustration depict him in a tuxedo.

Secondly, he was offended by the placement of the Pink Panther cartoon image. Our design depicted an audience in silhouette at the bottom, which included a proud Pink Panther gesturing toward Mancini. Our disgruntled friend said that it appeared that the Pink Panther was "tickling Mancini's armpit."

Thirdly, he felt we were attempting to send a message to purchasers that Italian Americans are linked to crime. On a silver screen behind Mancini's portrait, we showed a list of many of his most popular film scores, which included "Experiment in Terror" and "Touch of Evil." As if the inclusion of the latter wasn't bad enough, the word "terror" appeared under Mancini's arm, separating it from the first part of the title and thereby sending a subliminal message to customers that Mancini's ancestry might be connected with crime and the Mafia. Or so our friend believed.

Once the laughter subsided in our office, we reviewed his protestations. We agreed to move the Pink Panther slightly to the left to make it look less like he was tickling Mancini. We chose not to act on any of the other complaints. Not only were we convinced that we had done right by this stamp design, but we had met personally with Mancini's widow, Virginia, who worked closely with us as we developed the art. She approved the final image and expressed her pleasure with the results. All of this was shared with our Italian American friend. We didn't hear from him again until after the stamp issuance when he again protested that we didn't change the "tickling" scene. We reassured him that as the millions of stamps were run through the press, the colors might have shifted ever so slightly so that the Pink Panther moved a little too close for his comfort. Not surprisingly, he chose not to accept our explanation. I suspect that he is still out there monitoring the annual stamp program.

All of this brings me to a widely discussed issue: The Vince Lombardi stamp that was among the four 1997 Legendary Football Coaches stamps. The photograph we chose to use for the stamp painting featured Lombardi being lifted in the air by his players after a victory. The controversy? We depicted him with a gap between his two front teeth. I thought I had seen and heard it all, but when that one surfaced, I threw up my hands in despair.

He did, indeed, have that gap, but it seems it was too exaggerated for his many fans. News articles were written about it. Official media responses were released. But the controversy continued for as long as there was interest in the subject. Eventually, as with the majority of "errors" on stamps, interest waned, at least among the general public, though not necessarily among some stamp collectors. Such issues tend to be remembered by the collectors.

Many of these questions, complaints, and comments were played out in personal correspondence between the customer and the Postal Service, but some reached a wider audience when the media took notice. Much of it was relegated to the stamp media—small in circulation, but vocal in their criticism. As noted earlier, some issues made their way to the halls of Congress and subsequently the national media. Many issues that received attention of that magnitude involved errors of a different nature. Most correspondence from the public, while they may have felt they found an error, merely reflected differences in opinion. One issuance that generated conflicting opinions made national news. To make matters worse for me, it was one of my designs.

One of the design challenges for the Stamp Development group and its art directors was to continually create new, fresh concepts for the annual "Love" stamps, which were extremely popular with the public. The same held true for Christmas stamps. But the issue at hand revolved around the Love stamps issued in 1995.

We have all seen the two cherubic angels lifted from the larger painting "The Sistine Madonna" by Raphael. Their heads are resting on their hands with a languid, almost bored look on their faces. They proved so popular that they have been used on Christmas cards, coffee cups, magnets, posters, postcards, etc. over the past century. Like many, I always enjoyed those images.

One day in 1993, I was antiquing, a favorite pastime of my wife and me. In one shop, I came across postcards depicting the Raphael angels. Despite having seen them countless times before, something struck me this time. Why not reproduce them as "Love" stamps? I bought the two cards and returned to the office to begin developing the stamps.

After obtaining the rights and procuring a high-quality reproduction of the image, I set about creating companion Love stamps, one for the first-ounce rate and the second for the two-ounce rate. Love stamps were used not only for Valentine's Day cards but for wedding invitations as well. The first-ounce stamp was typically on the invitation's reply envelope and the two-ounce stamp on the outer envelope of the invitation. Depicting the two angels on separate stamps with the word "Love" above their heads was a natural and easy design decision. The CSAC members approved the designs, as did the Postmaster General, in early 1994.

More than one billion of these stamps were produced, a normal number for Love stamps. The first day of issue was held on February 1, 1995, in Valentine, Virginia, a small community in the southwestern corner of the state near the North Carolina border. My wife and I attended and were treated like royalty. I must admit that my head was a bit swollen by all the adulation, but that balloon was about to pop.

A few weeks after the issuance and all the attending media releases surrounding it, my wife and I were reading the *Washington Post* one morning. Ann muttered, "Oh, no!" I asked her what the matter was. She replied that I shouldn't read the Letters to the Editor, which meant, of course, that I just had to. There, larger than life—well, larger than the actual stamp anyway—was my Love stamp alongside the letter to the editor. My first reaction was elation, but then I remembered Ann's foreboding "Oh, no!"

The letter, written by an art historian, chose to comment on my choice of images for the Love stamp. The media release had referred to the angels as cherubs. Wrong, said the art historian. In fact, they are putti, or translated, "Angels of Death." It seems that in the Raphael painting, they are depicted at the base of the painting, and the object they are resting on is the coffin of Pope Julius II. They are awaiting instructions to transport his soul to heaven. The historian went on to say that it was a serious error in judgment for me to use these putti on a Love stamp. In effect, he then called me a fool for doing so. Needless to say, I was mortified. I had never been told this. Nor had I been called a fool in print. Stamp designing just got more personal!

The historian never referenced the fact that the same putti had appeared on Christmas cards, numerous Victorian-era romantic images, and hundreds of other romantically linked commercial products. It was only when *I* chose to use it that he called attention to my alleged poor judgment. I soon found that when an "error" of any sort is made by the Postal Service, it is a grievous one, even if the same error had been made by other agencies, organizations, or companies. I knew then that I would have to develop a much thicker skin if I was to survive in the stamp world.

To make matters worse, within a week, a second letter appeared on the same pages. This time, yet another art historian commented on the first historian's missive. He corrected some of the facts laid out by the first gentleman but then ended with a caveat, stating that I was still a fool for having used the putti in this manner.

Yet another week passed before a third art historian's letter was published. Obviously, business in the art history world was so slow at the time that they could spend time critiquing stamps. The third writer, a woman, took both of the other historians to task, in effect saying, "Get a life! It's a beautiful stamp regardless of how the image was used." Now that was a critique with which I could live.

What I didn't realize as these back-and-forth letters were playing out in the *Post* was that other newspapers saw them and wrote stories about the "Angels of Death portrayed on Love Stamps." As with most controversies, it eventually died down, and the world continued to revolve on its axis. Or so I thought.

Just as the story began to fade from the media, I began receiving calls and letters from customers. This time it wasn't art historians but brides-to-be and mothers of the bride. They were very distraught that they had sent out wedding invitations bearing "Angels of Death." One mother's plaintive plea read: "How could you do that to them?" Another mother of the bride was so furious that she insisted I had jinxed her daughter's wedding. I keep waiting for the day I get a call or letter saying I have been named as a party to a divorce case.

Not only were we accused of the inappropriate selection of subjects or artwork, but we were accused of reproducing customers' images on stamps without their permission. The classic example of that was the man from Pennsylvania who filed a complaint with the Office of the Attorney General of Pennsylvania demanding compensation for having been insulted for using his likeness on a postage stamp without his permission. He included with his complaint a copy of the stamp.

The complaint was forwarded to our office for a response. Whether the "passing of the buck" was merely bureaucratic or idiotic, it never should have gotten further than the AG's office. Why? Because the stamp he submitted as evidence was the 25th Anniversary of the Moon Landing, which depicted Neil Armstrong in his space suit with the surface of the moon reflected on his face shield.

Needless to say, the gentleman never received compensation or an apology from the Postal Service.

Not all letters were negative—only 99.9 percent! Receiving a complimentary letter was rare but much appreciated. My favorite was from a young student who had requested information on stamp collecting. After receiving the materials, we sent back, I received a thank you letter from her which included, and I quote: "Thanks a bunch for the stuff. YOU ROCK! YOU RULE! YOU R DA BOMB! Love all the stuff you gave us. YOU ARE SO KEWL!" It's letters like that that made the job a little easier.

Who would ever expect such little pieces of paper could elicit such fervor. When joining the Stamps Department in October 1990, I had little knowledge of just how important it was to ensure total accuracy while being mindful of various sensitivities, ethnic groups, and individual tastes and perceptions of the American public. Over the twenty years I spent working on the stamp program, I was continually amazed at how people thought and reacted to things. Whether it was sex, religion, nudity, Communism, ethnicity, bombs, death angels, or even spaces between teeth, those little pieces of paper have more power to move and stir the passions of people than one could ever imagine.

As if there weren't enough critics out there who were ever vigilant in making sure we were doing things right, we received mountains of correspondence over the years offering their own ideas for what constituted a "winning" stamp design.

Each year, my office received in excess of one thousand design suggestions, sample portfolios for stamp design consideration, and requests for information about the design process. Sadly, the vast majority of design submissions ranged from extremely crude scribbles and pencil drawings to incoherent art rendered in colored pencils, watercolors, and magic markers.

Both online and in free pamphlets mailed to interested parties, we provided information on the design process and how to go about making subject suggestions, but we discouraged individuals from submitting their own designs. One sentence in particular always seemed to pique the interest of the inquirer: the line about money paid to artists under contract to the USPS. These payments were $1,500 for the initial concept and, upon approval, $3,500 for the final art for a total of $5,000 per illustration. With dollar signs dancing in their heads, many would-be artists wrote seeking commissions.

Some individuals, though, failed to grasp the process and chose instead to write to me, sometimes scribbling on postcards their ideas for stamps (virtually all of which had previously been issued). They diligently suggested the amount of money owed to them for their suggestions and provided instructions on where to send the money.

One person, who listed her credentials as a doctor with a Ph.D. and R.N., submitted her own contract for me to sign. Details of her contract stipulated that she was available 24/7 to work on designs. She listed her annual salary for professional work at $900,000. Oh, and she wanted to be paid weekly. I guess her medical practice must have been hurting for her to solicit stamp design work.

Of the thousands of unsolicited "designs" I reviewed over the years, a few really stood out. Not for their quality of design but more for their uniqueness or creativity. Having said that, I can assure you that none of those designs could ever be produced as a postage stamp. But their creators must be credited with displaying passion for their work. Two such examples come to mind.

The first arrived in a large manila envelope stuffed with ten pages of small colored scribbles, thirty to a page, all individually labeled and numbered. Accompanying those three hundred "drawings" were twenty pages of detailed, typed instructions on how to "interpret" the stamps and how to use them on letters. As you might well imagine, the instructions rambled on incoherently, page after page. I had immediately suspected the package I was about to open would contain some strange material. The return address was, in part, "Montana, United States of America, Earth and Elsewhere." My thoughts went immediately to the recently arrested Unabomber, living in the backwoods, hiding from the world. I immediately filed the artwork without responding, not wishing to open what could develop into an ongoing dialogue with someone with serious issues. Indeed, if my Unabomber theory had been right, the envelope might have exploded when I'd opened it.

The second one was far more harmless. Yet another large manila envelope, mailed from Louisiana, was stuffed with thirty pages containing seventy-seven stamp images each, totaling 2,310 designs. Also included was the artist's resume, whose career ranged from a stint in the Korean War to auto repair and upholstery, among other professions. The vast majority of the designs, arranged on each page to simulate a pane of stamps, were very similar in content: a single squiggled line, in color, with a small line of green grass rendered in watercolor and a printed line of type that read: SEGMENTS 32 USA. Most of the stamps had the single squiggled line in the shape of letters of the alphabet—no actual words spelled out, only letters.

Busy that day and perplexed by the purpose of these designs, I initially set the submission aside for later review. Days later, I filed the submission, forgetting to have my staff respond to him. Months later, I received a call from an individual with a heavy Southern drawl wanting to discuss his submission. When such calls got through to me, I had to take a deep breath and show as much patience as I could muster to listen to them. I had learned over the years that they were all very sincere in their efforts to help the Postal Service. This gentleman wanted to know when he could expect to see his designs produced and sold in his post office. As I patiently listened to his concern, it struck me that I was speaking to the gentleman that had submitted all of those cryptic designs. While listening to him, I dug into my files and pulled out his submission. In his most Southern Louisiana drawl, he was perplexed as to why we couldn't produce his designs. As we discussed the designs, it finally hit me. Those squiggly single-line shapes on every one of those 2,310 stamps were worms. I immediately turned back to his resume to discover that I had overlooked, in my haste, one of his many professions: worm farmer.

It seems that a lot of his worms must have sacrificed their lives in the pursuit of art. It became apparent that he had taken individual worms, pressed them against either red or blue inkpads, and pressed them carefully in the shape of letters onto each little stamp.

It took me half an hour to convince him that he shouldn't hold out hope for his unique designs to appear in his local post office. Like a true Southerner, he was very gracious about it all despite his disappointment. In the twenty years I received stamp art submissions, none reached the level of ingenuity, nor the level of time devoted to development, as my favorite Louisiana worm farmer.

Chapter 3
Adding Their 'Two Cents'

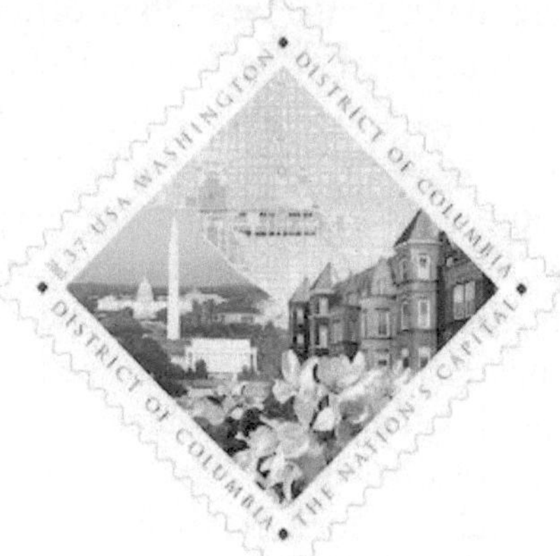

Prior to 1957, stamp subjects were either chosen by the Stamps staff at the Post Office Department or, less fortunately, by members of Congress or occasionally the President of the United States. This explains why the majority of stamps depicted politicians, organizations, and an occasional historical event. As the twentieth century progressed, so did subject selection. We began to see more interesting subjects such as national parks, authors, artists, and composers. But the annual program was still dominated by very serious subjects.

In 1948, a particular stamp struck the consciousness of the American public. It was when the Post Office issued a three-cent stamp honoring the Centennial of the American poultry industry. Now, it wasn't the actual wording that brought it attention; it was the design that depicted a very large chicken. The public began to ask, "What is a chicken doing on a postage stamp?"

A subsequent *Life* magazine article in 1948 displayed the entire year's stamp program, questioning why so many of the stamps were politically motivated. There were stamps for numerous organizations as well as the usual politicians. The article seemed to be asking, "Why can't we have some good-looking, interesting stamps?"

As is usually the case in a bureaucracy, it took years to respond to that question with a satisfactory solution. But in 1957, a mere nine years later, the Post Office produced just such a solution. They created a committee. Shocking, I know. But what else would you expect from a giant bureaucracy?

CSAC Rules

Fortunately, in this case, a committee was actually a helpful solution to the problem. Then-Postmaster General Arthur Summerfield created the aforementioned Citizens' Stamp Advisory Committee (CSAC). One of the guiding principles and charters of the Committee was their responsibility for stamp subject selection on behalf of the Postmaster General. In effect, it took the selection process out of the hands of Congress. I'm sure there was plenty of political huffing and puffing on Capitol Hill when the announcement was made. But it seemed to work. Congress did back off, for the most part. They still recommended subjects, but they didn't have the clout to force the issuance. They merely used their influence to get the subjects before the Committee for consideration.

Initially, it was a small working committee that met only a few times annually. As the years passed, the Committee decided that it needed artistic guidance as the stamps were developed. They turned to Stevan Dohanos, a leading illustrator out of Connecticut, who had achieved fame for his numerous *Saturday Evening Post* covers. Over the next few years, the program began to grow, and Stevan requested additional help for the design of stamps.

Prior to Stevan's appointment, virtually all stamps were designed and printed by the Bureau of Engraving and Printing (BEP), in addition to currency for the nation. The BEP staff was comprised largely of illustrators and engravers. To my knowledge, however, they did not employee graphic designers. The Bureau seemed to have a lock on the look of the stamp program, so much so that they attended the CSAC meetings and presented not only their designs but suggestions for stamp subjects. Dohanos and his new designer, Bradbury Thompson, were about to change all that.

Bradbury brought with him a reputation as one of the most prominent and celebrated graphic designers of the twentieth century. His forte was typography, and during his many years of service to the stamp program, he changed the typographic landscape in addition to displaying his sophisticated taste in choosing appropriate imagery for many subjects.

Dohanos and Thompson forged a path through the staid, very conservative, limited-color program. Through their efforts, they brought the program kicking and screaming into the twentieth century. Or was it the screaming and kicking of the serious stamp collectors that we heard? If you were to ask a serious stamp collector which stamps are their favorites, odds are that it would be a single-color engraved stamp from the first half of the last century, if not earlier. Let me be the first to say that many of these engraved stamps are among the classic stamps of all time and are of great beauty. But there is room in the annual program for bright colors and more contemporary subject matter. That is a battle that has been fought for years and will continue to be fought for years to come. Serious collectors are a strong-willed, conservative group. I can't tell you how many letters from those collectors I received in my twenty years with the stamp program taking me to task and accusing me of destroying the U.S. stamp program.

I'm sure that both Stevan and Bradbury heard the same complaints I did, but we all persevered. Stevan left the program in the early 1980s for health reasons and passed away in 1994. Bradbury assumed full responsibility for the design program until he realized he needed assistance. It was then that he turned to a then-current member of the CSAC for help. Howard Paine, art director for *National Geographic* magazine, had been appointed to the Committee in 1979. Bradbury convinced Howard that he could be of more assistance and value as his assistant. Howard accepted Bradbury's offer and stepped down from the Committee.

Howard's CSAC replacement was Derry Noyes, a Washington, D.C. designer of note who had studied under Bradbury at Yale University's design program. Her father was the famous industrial designer, Eliot Noyes. Derry's tenure on the CSAC was to follow the same course as her predecessors. Bradbury and Howard had turned to Derry because they felt they needed help, and after a year, she too accepted the role of stamp designer and resigned from the Committee. Both Howard and Derry's contributions would be felt throughout the program over the next thirty years.

While the program grew in size, the CSAC membership experienced the same growing pains. Over the next few years, the

Committee grew to an average membership of twelve. To lend credibility to the selection process, additional prominent individuals were selected to serve. My belief, despite my not being a part of the program at the time, is that it was done to keep Congressional pressure off the program. Senators and Congressmen would be more reluctant to exert pressure or question subject selections made by prominent professionals who were well respected in their fields.

Over the years, the membership has seen the likes of Andrew Wyeth, the famed artist, who was followed by his son, Jamie, another gifted artist; author James Michener; Academy Award-winning actors Ernest Borgnine and Karl Malden; I. Michael Heyman, Chancellor of the Berkeley Law School and former Secretary of the Smithsonian Institution; J. Carter Brown, Director of the National Gallery of Art in Washington; C. Douglas Lewis, Head Curator of Sculpture at the National Gallery of Art and former CSAC Chair; Jean Firstenberg, President and CEO of the American Film Institute and former CSAC chair; Richard "Digger" Phelps, the famed Notre Dame basketball coach and ESPN sports commentator; Jerry Pinkney, the award-winning children's book illustrator; Joan Mondale, the former Vice Presidential First Lady and patroness of the arts; and Dr. Henry Louis Gates, Jr., the preeminent African-American Harvard scholar and creator/host of the popular PBS series, *Finding Your Roots.*

Those are some of the individuals with "name" recognition. But the Committee's ranks have been graced with many other gifted and talented top professionals. A few of the past CSAC chairs are Dr. Virginia Noelke, professor of history at San Angelo (Texas) State College; Jack Rosenthal, part-owner of the Chicago Cubs, owner of multiple radio stations, and owner of one of the world's best stamp collections; Ron Robinson, co-owner of the largest advertising agency in Arkansas, an Arkansas Man of the Year, and state campaign chair for both of President Clinton's campaigns; and Belmont Fairies, a national stamp columnist.

The rank-and-file membership was and is equally prestigious. I was honored to work beside a number of graphic designers who either served as Design Subcommittee chairs or spent many hours carefully deliberating over designs. Phil Meggs, a professor of design at Virginia Commonwealth University and the author of *The History of Graphic Design* (considered to be the designers' "bible" and required reading in many design courses); Jessica Helfand, a Yale graphic design professor; Sylvia Harris, a preeminent African American informational graphic designer out of New York; and Maruchi Santana, a New York branding specialist who helped to rebrand the Barbie doll. The list goes on and on with the names of individuals whose contributions to the program are invaluable whether they represented stamp collecting, the business world, history, or the arts.

So, as you can see, from this very august list of individuals, the Committee brought to the table a vast wealth of knowledge and experience, and they put it to effective use by developing a well-rounded annual stamp program.

For many years, the Committee worked in near anonymity. Few people outside the stamp collecting world knew of the existence of the Committee, nor do most people even today. But as the Postal Service began to market stamps more aggressively in the 1990s, more people became aware of its existence. That meant letters! Most who wrote asking to be appointed to its membership were disgruntled stamp collectors who wanted to "get on the Committee and knock some sense into the other members and go back to producing single-color engraved stamps honoring patriots and historical events," as one frustrated collector wrote. Our office received hundreds of applications for membership, only a few of them quite as blunt as that collector. Each application was considered, but when decision time came, the choice was made on the particular field of interest needed, whether in art, history, sports, or whatever.

It was my role as Manager of Stamp Development to search nationwide for individuals whose talents would be of service to the program. I was ably assisted in this search by the PhotoAssist research team. But the final decision on offering an invitation to join the CSAC always rested with the Postmaster General (PMG). Occasionally, a decision to add a member was made personally by the PMG without consultation with our office. One such instance comes to mind.

PMG Bill Henderson attended a first-day ceremony in 1999 where he was introduced to Larry King, the talk show host. I had met King at the *Celebrate the Century: 1900s* stamp dedication at the Old Post Office Pavilion in Washington in 1998. During my conversation with him, he told me that he was interested in stamp collecting and was himself a collector. It surprised me a bit, but I had heard similar comments from other prominent individuals over the years, and the truth of the matter was that they collected when they were kids and had long since given up on the hobby. So I took King's observations with a grain of salt.

When Henderson met King in 1999, they had a similar conversation. At that point, Henderson inquired whether he would be interested in serving on the CSAC, and King said he would. Upon returning to Headquarters, he sent word down through Government Relations V.P. Debbie Willhite and Stamp Services Director Azeez Jaffer instructing me to immediately prepare the commissioning papers to appoint King to the Committee. My initial reaction was one of skepticism. How on earth was a popular TV talk show host, who hosted a live show five nights a week, going to find the time to attend two days' worth of meetings four times a year? Not to mention that the meetings were being moved out of Washington and held in different cities nationwide. The response I received was to "shut up and make it happen," which I did.

Working through Mr. King's administrative assistant, we shared the schedule for the next year so that appropriate travel and schedules could be coordinated. All went well until the day before his first meeting, which was still being held in D.C. His assistant called to say, "Mr. King will be unable to attend the meeting due to a scheduling conflict. He will be preparing for his nightly TV show." Duh! As if I hadn't seen that one coming. I thanked her and said I hoped he would be able to attend the next meeting three months later. I was assured he would "consider" it. As you might expect, the same scenario and excuse repeated three months later, and again three months after that. Despite Azeez putting out a major press release extolling the virtues of such a stellar celebrity serving on the Committee, he was a no-show every time. It was my belief that each member of the Committee plays a vital role, so to have a seat on the Committee that was unused was doing a disservice to not only the other members but the Postal Service and the stamp program as well.

With that belief in hand, I recommended to Azeez and Ms. Willhite that they reconsider King's appointment and ask him to step down. Both said they didn't want to have any part of asking King to resign, but after talking with them further, they reluctantly agreed to bring it up to Henderson at their next meeting. Henderson, who had never shown much interest in the CSAC, accepted the idea readily and said that we should call King and ask for his resignation. "We" turned out to be "me." Both Azeez and Willhite said that they weren't doing the deed and that it was my responsibility. So, I called his office, and as usual, had to deal with his assistant. I made my case and asked that Mr. King carefully consider resigning his position. I received a call the next day. Mr. King agreed and was sorry that he was unable to participate as an active member. So much for PMG's personally picking out new CSAC members!

Over the years, there were a few other appointments that "came in through the back door," most of which resulted in less than stellar results. But those individuals shall remain anonymous primarily because their contributions were of little value to the overall program.

While the Committee was formed to control the stamp selections recommended by Congress, some members of the Committee influenced stamps that satisfied their own interests. I once did an analysis of where the stamp subjects came from. I asked the following questions: Did they originate from the thousands of letters from the public? Did CSAC members bring those subjects to the table? Did Postal staff and management recommend subjects? And lastly, did Congressional or other political pressures influence the creation of certain stamps? The results proved interesting.

Despite those thousands of letters, less than twenty percent of the stamps were suggested by the public. CSAC members and Postal staff were responsible for more than sixty percent of all subjects, while senior Postal management provided about ten percent and the remaining ten percent came from political entities. While not a scientific assessment, it did show an interesting pattern of selection. One might ask, with thousands of letters coming in annually from the public, why was their percentage not higher?

There was good reason for reality. Almost all of the letters fell into one of three categories. The first category included letters that were part of write-in campaigns when thousands of letters from participants in grassroots campaigns requested one particular subject. The second category included the letters that proposed subjects that were ineligible. The CSAC established a set of criteria years ago to provide a balanced program. One criterion, for example, was that an individual had to be deceased ten years before being commemorated on a stamp. (This rule has changed over the years.) Another is that organizations are not honored (keeping future poultry industry chickens off stamps!). The list goes on, but many subjects were rejected based on that criterion. The third category included subjects that simply didn't make the cut to be eligible for consideration before the Committee. That third category was a much smaller list from among the thousands submitted, thus making the Committee's review role much easier.

The Committee has always been allowed to suggest subjects in addition to reviewing subjects submitted to them for consideration. That's why the makeup of the membership is critical to a successful program. Having diversity in their professional backgrounds, coupled with a vast wealth of knowledge and experience, made for interesting stamps, not to mention interesting discussions during the meetings.

On occasion, a member's suggestion appeared, on the surface, to be a bit self-serving. But usually, the end result was a win for the program.

Former CSAC Chair Jack Rosenthal was passionate about his home state of Wyoming. When the fiftieth anniversary of statehood approached in 1990, he ensured that he would be involved in the design—so much so that he insisted a fine art painting of the Wyoming landscape be used. When reproduction rights were sought, it was discovered that he personally owned the painting. Postal officials expressed concern about the appropriateness of a member reproducing their personal property on a postage stamp. After much discussion, Jack agreed to donate the painting to a gallery, which made the scenario more legitimate.

In 1993, Jack again used his influence when he insisted the Oregon Trail anniversary depict a map of the territory, which included guess which state? The design group fought to create a more colorful representation, but Jack's clout as chair won the day. A simple map with a red line showing the trail was selected. One of our lesser design efforts, I must say.

Another chair who displayed some clout was Ron Robinson from Arkansas. In 2001, he recommended fellow Arkansan Hattie Caraway, the first woman elected to the U.S. Senate, for inclusion in the Distinguished Americans series in 2001. While she was certainly deserving of a postage stamp, it took a fellow Arkansan to make it happen. In 2004, Ron promoted the concept of issuing a stamp commemorating Presidential Libraries. And, oh, by the way, the Clinton Library in Little Rock was set to open in 2005. What a coincidence. It showed Ron's ability to think large. As an advertising executive, he knew how to capitalize on a product. Tying the stamp issuance to the opening of the library made for better media, something the Postal Service was very keen to welcome.

Ron's predecessor as chair, Dr. Virginia Noelke from Texas, recommended the subject of Bats, which caught the members by surprise. The initial reaction was that they were too "ugly" to be put on stamps. Some members even greeted the idea with small shudders of disgust. Her presentation on the positive qualities of bats, however, won the members over. And, oh, by the way, each evening during the summer months, thousands of bats fly out from under the Congress Avenue Bridge in Austin, Texas, to the delight of tourists and locals alike, which would (and did) make a perfect first-day-of-issue event in 2002. They may have been ugly little critters, but the stamps proved to be very popular.

Probably the most interesting and entertaining subject recommendation from a member came from "Digger" Phelps, our resident sports authority. His recommendation was not to feature a sports figure but a very popular musician, Henry Mancini. Why Mancini? Well, it seems that at the time of "Digger's" recommendation, he was dating Monica Mancini, the composer's daughter, whom he eventually married. My assumption is that Monica questioned why her father hadn't been on a stamp, and "Digger" said he would take care of it.

His recommendation was discussed and approved by the membership for issuance in a "year to be determined." Everyone felt that Mancini was worthy, but they weren't sure where to place him in a future year's program. "Digger" was known to attend only two of the four annual meetings. Commitments during basketball season usually prevented his attendance. But then he didn't show up for three or more meetings in a row. We finally made a rule that if a member missed more than two successive meetings without a valid reason (sounds a bit like school, doesn't it?), they could be asked to step down from the Committee. After that, "Digger" made sure that he never missed two in a row. It was a running joke between the two of us.

At one of the meetings he missed, the Committee discussed the Mancini stamp and decided it didn't fit in, so they removed it from the program. At the very next meeting, "Digger" immediately noticed the missing subject and loudly protested that Mancini be reinstated. All of the blustering was done in good humor. The Committee caved, and Mancini was back in the program, only to be removed at the following meeting when "Digger" again was absent. The same scenario took place when "Digger" came back. I believe it happened yet again, a third time, before the Committee decided once and for all to leave Mancini's name in the program and assigned him to the 2004 program.

The stamp was designed; approved by the CSAC, the PMG, and Mancini's widow, Ginny; and readied for issuance. It was then revealed that "Digger" and Monica had divorced, less than a year after they left a CSAC meeting to marry. There was no going back now with the issuance, though, and no one suggested such a move. The Mancini stamp proved to be very popular with the public. Well, popular with everyone except a certain Sons of Italy Historical Society member that I discuss in another chapter.

Despite the breadth and depth of the Committee members' knowledge and experience, there have been a few instances when the CSAC relied heavily on experts in a particular field the members wished to commemorate.

One such subject was Comic Strip Classics. The centennial anniversary of America's first comic strip, *The Yellow Kid*, in 1995, was fast approaching, and the postal staff suggested to the Committee that they consider stamps to commemorate this popular subject.

While virtually everyone has at some time read daily comic strips, none of the members felt confident enough to make the final decision as to which twenty subjects to commemorate without inserting their personal preferences into the mix. It was for that reason that we turned to the International Museum of Cartoon Art for help. We had contacted the Library of Congress and sought the advice of Harry Katz, a leading expert on the history of comics, but we also wanted to get input and possible support for the issuance from the museum. Mort Walker, creator of the classic and still-running strip, *Beetle Bailey,* became our contact for the project. Mort polled the members of the National Cartoonists Society for their top twenty choices. Once the submissions were received and tallied, the results were provided to our offices.

One of the primary concerns of the Committee was that it not appear too commercial. How we were going to prevent that perception was going to prove difficult. In its infinite wisdom, some members of the Committee offered the solution of limiting the selections to the first half of the century, thus avoiding commemorating strips currently in syndication. A vote was taken by the members, and that suggestion gained favor, resulting in our going back to Mort and the Society and asking them to recast their votes based solely on the first fifty years, which they reluctantly did. Their new list was used to create the final set of stamps.

One concern the Committee shared was that the original strip creators either not be currently creating a strip or be deceased. It wasn't until the stamps had been unveiled and the release date close at hand that I received a phone call from one of the creators, whom I had been told was deceased. No, it wasn't a call from the dead. In fact, Dale Messick, the creator of *Brenda Starr*, was alive and well, as she so firmly assured me. She was eighty-nine at the time but still very active. Our research error proved to be a bit embarrassing, but Ms. Messing didn't seem to object. She was just thrilled with the recognition of her work.

As I previously stated, the development of multiple-design stamp sets required a great deal more time to produce. But sometimes, ideas surfaced that were almost too good to pass up, as was the case of the Celebrate the Century stamp sets. In retrospect, in some ways, I wish we had passed on this project, which was slated to celebrate the new millennium by honoring the major achievements of the twentieth century.

These stamps were the brainchild of Azeez Jaffer, our own "Stamp Czar" as the philatelic media referred to him. As the story goes, he came up with the idea while on a flight from California back to D.C. after one of his numerous trips to Los Angeles. When he presented the concept to the Committee in early 1997, the members were stunned. Not by the brilliance of the concept but by the mere thought that a project of the magnitude Azeez was suggesting was even conceivable. But Azeez was not one to be dissuaded from his mission. He informed the Committee that he had discussed the idea with the Postmaster General, who had endorsed the project, thus mandating the Committee to rubber-stamp it and move ahead.

The concept hatched at 34,000 feet was for ten panes, one per decade, consisting of fifteen stamps per pane, honoring seminal events, individuals, and the culture of each decade. The first set would be issued in early 1998 with subsequent decades issued every three to four months, culminating with the final decade, the 1990s, in early 2000.

At the next CSAC meeting, our newly formed research firm, PhotoAssist, presented a list of potential subjects for each of the first five decades. PhotoAssist was, in effect, the result of a mistake on the Legends of the West stamp set issued in 1994. As a result of that mistake, which will be detailed at length in another chapter, an entire company was formed to avoid future errors on stamps.

Reviewing these lists, the Committee spent time deliberating how to best categorize the myriad of topics recommended by experts whom PhotoAssist had consulted. Stamps chosen for each decade would be represented within one of eight thematic categories the Committee identified: art, sports, historical events, technology, entertainment, science, political figures, and lifestyle. But before art could be developed, the subject matter needed to be chosen.

Azeez's other airborne idea was to have the American public choose the subjects. Talk about going to the experts! The mind reels. It was one thing to have leading experts within a chosen field, e.g., comic strips or the Civil War, make subject selections. But to now ask for input from the average citizen invited undisciplined chaos on a scale we couldn't fathom.

The Committee convinced Azeez that there wasn't enough time to seek public input and still begin to issue the first sets of stamps in 1998. Thus, taking on the daunting task of making selections, the Committee devoted an entire meeting to selecting subjects for the first four decades. They agreed with Azeez to allow public input beginning with the 1950s and then beyond. The first four decades proved easier to select based on how they have withstood the test of time. The remaining decades would prove to be far more difficult as many subjects in the more recent decades were still subject to questions regarding their place in history.

It's at this juncture that the Committee was reluctantly forced to ask for assistance in subject selection. A major national promotional campaign was launched by Azeez's marketing group to solicit ideas. But because the Committee feared the number and range of subjects might prove uncontrollable and questionable, they convinced Azeez that they could compile a list of potential subjects on which the public could vote. This allowed the Committee to better control which issues made it as stamps.

The ensuing voting campaign was well received, and the public reacted by encouraging others to "stuff the ballot box" with their particular favorites. My favorite recollection is regarding the Sons of Italy organization whose members were dismayed to see the classic film *The Godfather* as one of the subjects within the entertainment category of the 1970s stamp set. They mounted a vigorous campaign to encourage voters to vote for "anything but" *The Godfather*. It obviously worked. One of my favorite films and a film that has consistently been on lists of the top ten movies of all time never made the final cut. So much for democracy!

While the great preponderance of stamp subjects was, indeed, personally selected by the Committee, drawing on their broad knowledge, other stamps required some degree of input from outside experts.

Some of those stamps receiving expert guidance were in the set of fifty stamps commemorating the seminal events of World War II, a set of five sheets with one issuance each year on the fiftieth anniversary of the war. Numerous military experts were consulted prior to the selection; The Legends of American Music series (1993-1999), with seventy-eight selections chosen from a broader list of potential subjects within each music genre, were provided to the Committee by the Smithsonian Institution's musicology group. The Four Centuries of American Art set enlisted the expertise of art historian John Wilmerding. The twenty American Illustrators in 2001, commemorating the centennial of the Society of Illustrators, were selected by the Society's membership. Subjects for the 2002 issuance of Masters of American Photography were selected with assistance from Princeton Photography Professor Peter Bunnell. And the ten film industry artists whose crafts and disciplines were honored in The Art of Filmmaking: Behind the Scenes issuance were chosen for us by the Academy of Motion Picture Arts and Sciences (the organization that produces the Oscars).

Without the assistance of these and numerous other experts, the

Committee would have had to rely solely on their personal likes and dislikes, putting themselves in a position to be criticized for their selections. Not that there weren't anyway, but it could have been far worse. It seems that virtually every stamp that was issued received some criticism. We all grew to accept these critiques with a grain of salt. The Committee and the Postal Service staff owe a great debt of gratitude to all of these largely unsung experts who have toiled behind the scenes.

The Capitol Viewpoint

While the CSAC participated in both selecting subjects of personal interest and seeking outside expert assistance, another large, forceful group continued to exert its influence on the stamp program: the U.S. Congress.

While one of the primary purposes for establishing the CSAC was to regain control of the stamp program from Congress in the late 1950s, Congress had been "recommending" subjects of interest to appease constituents, especially those from the business world and special-interest organizations. While the number of stamps recommended by members of Congress did drop off dramatically, there were often instances where they just couldn't resist the opportunity to press for a stamp. Congressional requests would be funneled through our Government Relations group to our office with the distinct caveat that a certain influential member of Congress wished to see this stamp happen.

Originally, such subjects were normally added to the overall list of subjects received by the public, without identifying the proponents. This ensured the subject would be evaluated on its own merit instead of being influenced by the Congressional proponent. This was standard procedure until the Stamps group was placed under the Government Relations department, at which point the Vice President of Government Relations insisted that Congressional proponent subjects be identified as such. Prior to the Stamps office's move to Government Relations, the proponent was eventually identified but not until the subject was approved and placed in the "Under Consideration" category of potential stamps.

One member of Congress who would not take "no" for an answer was Senator Dianne Feinstein of California. Her request in 1994 for a stamp commemorating the seventy-fifth anniversary of the Women's Suffrage movement in 1995 was turned down by the Committee on the basis that they only honored anniversaries in fifty-year increments. Not to be denied, she insisted on a personal meeting with the chair of the CSAC to make her case. It just so happened that the chair at the time was a woman, Dr. Virginia Noelke. During the CSAC meeting, Dr. Noelke was summoned to the Hill to meet with the Senator. It had been a policy of the CSAC not to meet with proponents because it would only open the door for numerous meetings, nor were proponents allowed to attend the meetings to make their case. But it's hard to deny a U.S. Senator.

During the meeting, Senator Feinstein assured the attendees that the stamp would definitely become one of the bestselling and most popular stamps of all time. If we had a nickel for every time a proponent used that promise, we would have all been rich. Upon Noelke's return to the CSAC, she shared the Senator's request. With pressure from our senior management, the Committee voted to add the stamp to the next year's program.

It hardly needs to be stated that the stamp did *not* become one of the most popular or bestselling stamps of all time. While no one disputes the importance of the subject, the stamp gained little recognition during all the events surrounding the anniversary. Part of it may be due, very candidly, to the stamp design. We made a valiant attempt to utilize innovative techniques when developing the design. Upon receiving it from the designer, we knew instantly it would never reproduce well at such a small size. Numerous attempts were made to have her "simplify, simplify, simplify." But each time she returned the revised art, it was still too detailed. On the fourth attempt, we felt it might work. The operative word here is "might." But if we had been given more time to develop alternate designs, we might have been more successful. Whether the lack of success was due to the design or the lack of public interest in the subject we'll never know.

Other Senators who have used the influence of their office included Ted Kennedy of Massachusetts, who wished to commemorate Irish Immigration in 1999, and Alaskan Senator Ted Stevens, who just happened to be on a committee that had oversight of various postal operations. He was aware of his influence, as was senior postal management. So when Senator Stevens made a request, it was given serious consideration. Among his numerous suggestions for Alaskan stamps was the 2001 Mt. McKinley stamp.

Sometimes, stamps were developed to gain favor with members of Congress. The Committee has always struggled with social awareness issues as stamps. Despite the difficulty of creating attractive stamps based on abstract issues such as diabetes, hospice care, Alzheimer's, etc., the Committee attempted to issue a social awareness stamp annually to promote awareness of such issues that affected the public.

In late 1998, a Hospice Care social awareness issue was announced as part of the 1999 stamp program. Shortly thereafter, it was brought to our attention that Senator Stevens had been diagnosed with prostate cancer. Senior management, through the Government Relations department, made a formal request that we quickly develop a Prostate Cancer Awareness stamp. My heart sank. Just how was I to develop a design for prostate cancer and make it look attractive? A thankless task.

I assigned Phil Jordan to be the art director for the project. I remember he gave me a blank look as if to say, "Why me?" But Phil stepped up to the plate and immediately called Michael Cronan, a brilliant West Coast graphic designer. As you can imagine, Michael's reaction was the same as Phil's. But his simple, strong graphic design met with quick approval, and Senator Stevens was asked to participate in the first-day ceremony, which of course he did. Ah, politics!

House members were not to be outdone by Senators. In 2002, a set of fifty designs entitled Greetings from America was issued. These designs were developed over a three-year period and were designed to resemble the popular and collectible 1930s and 1940s "Greetings from" linen postal cards. The suggestion had been brought to the Committee by staff as a potential subject that required the purchaser to obtain all fifty stamps, thus creating a reliable source of revenue for the cash-strapped Postal Service. Much to the chagrin of customers, they were unable to purchase individual panes of only their particular state. We had worked tirelessly to find a way to do just that, but the cost was prohibitive, and the collecting community that traditionally had to collect "one of everything" would scream about the cost involved.

But it wasn't the pane of fifty designs on one sheet that fired up a particular member of Congress. It was what was left *off* the sheet. Despite not being a full-fledged member of Congress as she was a representative without voting rights, Delegate Eleanor Holmes Norton was furious that the city of Washington, D.C. was left off. She had been worked tirelessly for years to obtain not only voting rights for the citizens of the nation's capital but statehood.

Despite being told that the pane of fifty stamps depicted *only* states and not territories or cities, she was not to be swayed from her mission to get a stamp for D.C. Not even when it was pointed out to her that the District of Columbia had been honored with a bicentennial stamp in 1991 was she dissuaded from her efforts. Her heated passion about the "omission" could not be cooled. She was so upset over the omission that she played it out in the media. Finally, senior management informed the CSAC that we would acquiesce to Mrs. Norton's wish.

I was duly summed to her Capitol Hill offices to discuss the design of the stamp. Upon entering, I was struck by the number of coffee-table photo books of Washington that she had scattered around her office. She and two staff members proceeded to "assist" me in identifying an appropriate image for the stamp. It was hardly the way stamps are designed, but she was a force to be reckoned with. She was adamant that the design not depict any monuments or museums that Americans readily identified with the capital city. Instead, it had to depict a typical street in Washington but definitely not Georgetown, one of the most scenic and recognizable areas of the city. Instead, she suggested showing an area of Anacostia. It took everything I could do to control my surprise at her suggestion. Anacostia, in its day, was one of the more beautiful row house areas of the city, situated on the other side of the Anacostia River, which divided the more well-known areas of the city. Unfortunately, Anacostia fell on hard times and became run-down, and many considered it a ghetto where people were reluctant to go after dark. Delegate Norton was sure that an appropriate Anacostia image could be found. But she did acquiesce to my request to allow us to explore a number of design possibilities.

The final design solution, issued in August 2003, was a diamond-shaped stamp that mimicked the actual shape of the D.C. boundaries. Within the diamond was a montage of photos depicting cherry blossoms, row houses, the D.C. skyline, and an old map of the city.

It took some convincing to get Delegate Norton to accept the skyline image. She agreed only after we pointed out to her that the other elements would not be instantly recognizable at such a small scale as a postage stamp.

Delegate Holmes was not the only non-voting member of the House of Representatives who was upset with the fifty Greetings stamps. Not to be outdone by another non-voting delegate, the Delegate from Guam demanded a meeting in his offices on Capitol Hill to be told why Guam, a U.S. territory, was not included in the Greetings from America series. Rational explanations were not always acceptable to members of Congress who felt their position and "power" was to be heeded despite common sense.

The meeting attended by the Delegate from Guam, two members of the Government Relations staff, and I did not go well. I cannot recall being treated so rudely in all of my discussions with individuals in my twenty years in that position. The Delegate proceeded to lecture us on how foolish we were to not include Guam in the set. To prove his point that the U.S. territories were collectively being slighted, he invited staff members from the offices of American Samoa, Northern Mariana Islands, the U.S. Virgin Islands, and Puerto Rico to support his position.

Unfortunately, neither he nor his staff had done their homework. He boldly proclaimed that Guam and the other territories had *never* been featured on a stamp. With great trepidation while swallowing a large gulp of air, one of the territory staff members corrected the Delegate by saying that his territory had been honored a few years before. Then, slowly, the other territory staff members all chimed in to admit that they, too, had been honored. The Guam Delegate then realized that his territory was the only one not to have received such recognition. This made him furious. A very strong lecture ensued. We stood our ground and refused to issue a "Greetings from Guam" stamp. Instead, I offered up the possibility of issuing a stamp in our Scenic American Landscapes series, which had kicked off in 1999. The series utilized international mailing rates and was very popular with the philatelic community. He initially insisted that the design be in the "Greetings from…" format. I assured him that would not happen and that I was developing a separate design for D.C. at the same time, and it would not be designed like the initial fifty state designs. Reluctantly, the Delegate agreed to the suggestion. But he insisted he would send us images from which we could choose for the stamp. I thanked him and indicated that we, at the same time, would initiate a search through stock photo houses for appropriate imagery. He continued to berate us all for half an hour, and then literally swung around in his chair, turning his back to us, and never said goodbye.

Months went by, and no images were received. Upon prompting by the Government Relations staff, he finally sent six photos, all of which were amateurish. We rejected them out of hand and proceeded to choose an image from a stock photography house.

It wasn't until 2007 that we finally released the Guam stamp as part of the Scenic American Landscapes series. By that time, the Delegate had already lost an election and was no longer a problem. We contemplated just dropping the stamp, but the Government Relations staff implored us to go ahead with the issuance to avoid any potential friction with the new Delegate.

In the late 1990s, Congress chose to take their stamp suggestions one step further by passing a law mandating the Postal Service issue its first semipostal stamp. Numerous other postal administrations worldwide had been issuing these special stamps to raise funds for needy causes, but the U.S. Postal Service had tried to avoid such issuances. It wasn't that they didn't believe in the causes seeking semipostals, but the logistics involved would be daunting, especially for the world's largest postal administration in the world, which processes more than half of the world's mail volume.

Our office was required to solicit worthy causes from organizations whose criteria met our requirements as legitimate national organizations. Once received, each organization's proposal had to be reviewed by the CSAC, and decisions were made as to which organizations would receive a stamp. The semipostal program was to run for a ten-year period with no limit on the number to be issued during that decade. But, in their infinite wisdom, Congress never specified when the program would start. This gave the Postal Service the loophole to avoid the program for a while.

Our office received twenty-six proposals that met the criteria. Submitting organizations were required to provide fifteen copies of their proposals. Then my staff had to recompile them into fifteen sets of all the proposals and mail them out to each member of the CSAC. Members were caught totally off guard by the huge box delivered to their offices or homes. Upon receipt of the behemoth boxes, we received calls of complaints from the members about the daunting task of having to read all the proposals. A majority of the proposals were in excess of one hundred pages each. Weeks were spent reviewing the rationales for stamp requests.

At the next official CSAC meeting, members were encouraged to make their selections. Members had very wisely left their boxes of proposals at home, not wishing to carry them on their trip to D.C. Copies were supplied to members during the meeting so they could review the proposals if necessary. Choices were made, and an agreement was reached that only one stamp every two years would be issued for a total of five semipostals during the mandated ten-year period. But, as I said, Congress never specified a date for the beginning of the program.

Not wanting to wait for the Postal Service to begin the program, a number of members of Congress introduced a bill to have the Postal Service issue a stamp promoting Breast Cancer Research. It passed both Houses of Congress and was immediately signed into law by the president. At that point, the clock was ticking. The law stipulated that the stamp had to be issued one year from the date of the law's passage.

Social Awareness stamps, as I previously mentioned, were among the most difficult to design. How to depict an abstract concept on such a small scale, all the while making it legible and appealing, is a very difficult task. But, having faith in the creative team, we began to work on it. I assigned the project to Ethel Kessler, the newest member of the art director team. I specifically chose her as she had confided to me a few years earlier that she was a breast cancer survivor. She tearfully accepted the assignment and began developing concepts. It took months to find the right design solution, but Ethel came through, as expected. Combined with a beautifully sensitive illustration by Whitney Sherman, the Committee approved the design, as did the Postmaster General, and it was rushed into print. Exactly a year later, in 1998, First Lady Hillary Clinton dedicated the stamp in the East Room of the White House.

The original law allowed for a two-year period of sale for the stamp. But as each deadline approached, Senator Dianne Feinstein passed another law extending the sale of the stamp for a few more years. As of this writing, it is still on sale more than two decades later, and I expect it will remain for sale for a long time to come. The stamp has been a proven success, generating more than $80 million thus far for breast cancer research.

Late in 2001, based on the success of the first semipostal, then-Senator Hillary Clinton, following the tragic terrorist attacks on the World Trade Center and the Pentagon, introduced legislation to create a semipostal to provide funds to families of victims of the attacks. They were to be known as Heroes of 2001. At that point, we internally began to wonder why Congress ever passed the original semipostal package if they were going to continue to circumvent the process and mandate individual stamps, the very thing they said they would get out of the habit of doing.

I tasked all six of the art directors to submit concepts for the stamp. Over the next six months, we reviewed dozens of designs. One of the more obvious design solutions was the then-famous photo of three firefighters raising the American flag over the rubble at the World Trade Center. Our consensus was that it had been reproduced so many times that it was becoming cliché, and we hoped to find a new design solution. And I thought we had. The Committee approved a new design and forwarded it to the Postmaster General for review and approval. The PMG, at the same time, received a notice to attend a meeting at the White House with President George W. Bush regarding the stamp. PMG Jack Potter took the recommended design with him, but he also took the famed photo solution as well. When he walked out the door with the two designs, we all knew which one would be chosen. Potter asked Bush's opinion, and he naturally chose the photo solution. We were disappointed that the new design solution never really had a chance, but we were just as eager to complete the process and issue the stamp regardless of the design.

While the Heroes of 2001 stamp did well in sales upon release in 2002, after a few years, interest waned, and the extension for sales was never exercised. It disappeared after five years. One of the major factors in the success of the Breast Cancer Research stamp was the support of groups such as the Susan G. Komen Foundation, a major supporter of research. The Heroes stamp never had such backing.

Despite not being able to duplicate the incredible success of the Breast Cancer Research stamp, the Heroes of 2001 inspired yet another Senator to circumvent the system. This time it was Senator Ben Nighthorse Campbell of Colorado. He was one of the major proponents of the Stop Family Violence stamp. His proposal was one of the original twenty-six subjects reviewed and accepted by the Committee a few years prior. Senator Campbell, spurred on by Senator Clinton's bold move to work around the system, decided he could do the same thing. He attached his bill for the stamp to another appropriation bill, which passed with little or no question. Thus, we were tasked with developing a third semipostal in as little as four years. And we hadn't even begun the official semipostal program mandated by the same individuals who were circumventing the system.

We thought that having to develop an appealing design for breast cancer research was difficult enough, but when faced with stopping family violence as a theme, it gave us great pause. Luckily, art director Carl Herrman stepped forward and offered to accept the design challenge. As was to be expected, numerous concepts were developed, but the final design happened almost by accident. Carl was working with a photographer and a child model. The child was off in the corner and did a stick drawing of people. Carl saw the merit in her work and asked her to draw a child outside her home crying. The resulting drawing proved to be a winner.

I took the design to Senator Campbell's office on Capitol Hill for his review and approval. His office was a virtual museum of Native American artifacts. Handcrafted, turquoise-encrusted silver jewelry, Native blankets, feathers, and paintings were among the many Native art pieces displayed throughout his office. His office was unlike any Congressional office I had ever set foot in. He enthusiastically endorsed the design we submitted for his review, and off to press we went.

The 2003 Stop Family Violence stamp was not as well-received as the other two semipostals. Unfortunately, it lacked backing from organizations and died a sad death, removed from sale after two years. A subsequent General Accounting Office (GAO) report on the sale of the stamps rendered an opinion as to why it was not successful. They laid the blame solely on the "poor" design. I would suggest that the brilliant staff of number crunchers at the GAO take a crack at designing a stamp about such a tragic subject to see if they could do any better.

Governor's Stamp of Approval

Interest and involvement in the stamps program was not limited solely to Washington D.C. and Capitol Hill. On numerous occasions, governors were influential in the design process. Unlike the Congressional interaction, which we rarely sought out, we specifically sought the approval of governors as we developed stamps commemorating anniversaries of their statehood. The Committee had an informal policy that the governor of the state in question should have some say in the design approval process. This policy was put in place as a result of a controversy over the 1989 North Dakota centennial stamp.

Until then, statehood anniversary designs were not routinely submitted for a governor's approval. Such was the case with the North Dakota Statehood stamp. The design featured a distinctive red barn on the open prairie. The subject matter was not the issue for the governor. It was who painted it. The Postal Service commissioned a prominent East Coast artist, Wendell Minor, to illustrate the stamp. The governor attended the first-day-of-issue ceremony. It was then that he discovered that someone other than a North Dakota artist was responsible for the artwork. He expressed his displeasure and publicly berated the Postal Service for its "wrong" choice of artists. Since then, we have been more aware of such nuances and concerns from the state level. Because of those concerns, we attempted to include the governor or his representatives in the design process. In some cases, it went very well, but in others, it became problematic.

In 1995, Texas was to observe its statehood sesquicentennial. Carl Herrman was assigned the project and chose to work with contemporary graphic illustrator Laura Smith. The final approved design depicted a cowboy on horseback holding a Texas flag, and the palomino was rising up on its two hind legs *Lone Ranger* style due to a rattlesnake at the bottom of the stamp.

Our initial attempt to share the design with then-Governor Ann Richards, who was campaigning for reelection, proved unsuccessful as she was unavailable. Instead, it was shown to the two Texas U.S. Senators, Phil Gramm, and Kay Bailey Hutchison, both of whom immediately responded, saying they would *not* accept a snake on the stamp. Back to the drawing board! Carl and Laura reworked the art, making it a horizontal stamp that eliminated the offending snake. The second time around was a charmer.

The following year, it was Iowa's turn for a centennial stamp. Carl again was assigned the project and, while teaming with an illustrator, produced a charming stamp depicting a very common scene on Iowa farms: a plump farm woman in an apron holding her prize-winning jars of pickles. At least it wasn't about pigs, which we felt would not be well received. Unfortunately, neither was the pickle-packing farm wife. It met with a resounding thud of disapproval from the Governor's office and members of the Sesquicentennial Commission, who felt it was demeaning to the state. They instead asked for alternate designs that would depict the scenic beauty and progressive nature of Iowa. It was back to the drawing board yet again.

The Wisconsin centennial was slated for 1998, and I had a personal affinity for the subject, having been born in La Crosse, Wisconsin. I assigned Phil Jordan as art director, and he chose to go the photographic route instead of illustration. Initial contact had been made with the Governor's office to determine if they had any concerns or ideas as to what they wanted to see depicted. This new approach of asking beforehand was to head off continual redesigns to appease the groups. It was felt it would be better to get their buy-in beforehand. This in itself could, and would, prove to be risky and problematic.

Governor Tommy Thompson, who would later secure a Cabinet position as Secretary of Health and Human Services in Washington, was known for being outspoken. I was soon to find out just how outspoken. In our initial meeting at the State Capitol, the Governor laid down the ground rules. "No cows, no cold, no cheese." So much for showing what has commonly been associated as America's Dairyland - a cow. And I suppose that showing the Green Bay Packers' rabid fans sporting "cheesehead" hats was out, as was the bitter-cold and snow-covered landscape.

That left us with bucolic scenes of rolling fields dotted with barns and not too much else. We were concerned that even showing a dairy barn might "violate" the Governor's edict. But barns proved to be acceptable.

Phil mocked up a number of scenic images, all of which were beautiful, but it was duly pointed out that they could have been in

Minnesota, Ohio, or any one of a dozen other states. Off to Madison I went to share the concepts with Governor Thompson.

Upon arriving in Madison, I made my way to the Capitol, one of the most beautiful of all State capitol buildings. The Governor's offices were being renovated and restored. It was a very warm day with no air conditioning, which proved to be very uncomfortable. By the time I was ushered in, I was sweating profusely—not the way I wanted to start an important meeting.

I had anticipated a very formal meeting, but it proved to be the opposite. I was ushered into the Governor's palatial office after stopping to rub the nose of the brass sculpture badger outside his door. It seems that's a traditional good luck gesture, so I readily took advantage of the opportunity to get a little luck going into the meeting. Once inside, I received a very enthusiastic greeting from the Governor himself. We spent time discussing the fact that I was Wisconsin-born. That seemed to set the tone for the remainder of the meeting. At one point, he asked me if I would like to accompany him on his motorcycle trip from Madison to Washington, D.C., which he was planning for later that year. I politely declined despite thinking that such a trip would be a real adventure.

I shared a number of design concepts with the Governor and his closest staff. All of the designs reflected scenic areas of the state. At that point, the meeting started to veer toward a designer's worst nightmare. The Governor liked the sky in one photo, the farm fields in another, and the barn in a third. He wanted to know if we could combine those into one photo. If it had been an illustration, it wouldn't have been a problem, but with photography, even with the aid of Photoshop, it would prove difficult. I offered the solution that I would search for additional stock photos that might fulfill all of their requests, which was agreed upon.

A second visit to Madison came a few months later. I took a range of new photo selections, all by Wisconsin photographers, a criterion that the Governor was adamant about. Again, he and his immediate staff were present. Their reactions to the new choices were very favorable. Not being able to decide on which concept to choose, he yelled for his Lieutenant Governor to come into the office and give his opinion. No clear choice was made, at which point the Governor jumped up and said to me, "Come with me." We went out into the outer office where a number of secretaries and staff members were diligently working away. He asked for their attention and then went from desk to desk asking every person's opinion. Again, it was a major nightmarish scenario for any designer.

After making a mental tabulation of which concept was "winning" the most votes, Governor Thompson decreed the winner, which just happened to be his first choice. No comment. I guess rubbing the nose of the badger really paid off because an image was chosen. In retrospect, those visits with Governor Thompson proved to be among the most entertaining of my many encounters with members of the political class.

To celebrate the fiftieth anniversary of the newest state in our Union, we developed an illustration by a leading Alaskan artist, John Fehringer, whom we were told was a favorite of the Governor. Winging my way north to Anchorage after a stop in Portland, Oregon to share the Oregon Statehood stamp with its centennial commission members, I felt confident that we had a winner with the Alaska Statehood stamp. It was a stunning illustration of a small plane, common to the state for its role in the transport of mail, goods, and people throughout that vast state. The plane was soaring over a meandering river with snowcapped mountains in the background.

Having hastily put the Oregon/Alaska trip together, I didn't have the time to prepare properly for the visit. My big mistake was that I didn't do homework on who the Governor of Alaska was. I failed to know it was a woman, the one and only Sarah Palin. My mistake!

I arrived in Anchorage late in the evening of October 30, 2007, and awoke the next morning to a very foggy, overcast, and dreary Halloween day. After finally locating her office, which was in a nondescript office building, I was met by the staff member assigned to the statehood anniversary events. I was told the Governor was busy and probably would be unable to meet with me. This excuse always rankled me. After taking the time and effort to fly clear across the country (and part of Canada), only to be told they were too busy was the height of rudeness. This happened more than once during my career.

I was shown into the conference room where the aide and a few others joined me to discuss the stamp. Already in the room was a distinguished-looking middle-aged man seated on a chair pushed against the side wall. He was reviewing a pile of papers on his lap. I found it odd that he wouldn't have spread the papers out on the conference table, but I gave it little thought. When he noticed us entering the room, he stood up and apologized, and said he would find another location to work. The aide insisted that it was fine if he stayed, but he insisted on leaving and shook my hand, saying "Good morning" as he left. I made some passing remark to the aide about him, and she responded with an incredulous look, informing me that I had just spoken to the Governor's husband. It was only then that I realized the Governor was a woman and that I had just met Todd, her husband, both of whom would go on to bigger fame and notoriety.

The meeting proved to be problematic. None of them knew exactly what they wanted, but they weren't convinced the solution being presented to them was something that would satisfy the Governor. To make matters worse, they had appointed a local stamp collector to be involved in the statehood celebration events, expecting him to lead the way on the stamp design. This collector had a totally different approach to stamps than I did, which made for a difficult discussion. His comments and suggestions to the group seemed to carry as much as, if not more than my recommendations

As I was leaving, after being reassured that the Governor was still busy, I was ushered out past Governor Palin's office. The aide did stop and show me that she did indeed exist and, at that moment, the Governor looked up from her phone call, smiled, and gave her now-famous wink and little wave. That was the total extent of my connection with the Governor of Alaska.

The following week, I received an email and follow-up call from the aide stating that the Governor did not like the art at all. She insisted on an image with a dogsled in it. It just so happens, as I found out much later when she was running for vice president, that her husband Todd was a dogsledder. What a coincidence. The Postal Service was trying to avoid depicting a dogsled because we knew that a certain animal rights group would protest as dog sledding was a major target of the group. But we acquiesced to the Governor and found a beautiful image of the mountains with a small, silhouetted image of a dogsled team in the foreground. And, yes, we were prepared for and did hear from the various animal rights group, but the controversy surrounding dogsledding never received the publicity we feared.

The General's Salute

Military subjects have always played a part in our national stamp program. I would be hard-pressed to think of a group that has received more stamps than the military. But that has never stopped military organizations from wanting more recognition. Not that they don't deserve it. They do.

Over the years, various military units and organizations have pressured the Postal Service for stamps. One of the CSAC criteria stipulates that aside from the major service units—Army, Navy, Marines, Air Force—no individual military unit would be recognized. The reason was that if we singled out one unit or division, it would be difficult not to commemorate all of the other units.

Probably the most prominent, not to mention aggressive, request came from the Jewish War Veterans. Their organization lobbied our offices, the PMG, and Congress to honor their group with a stamp. Our repeated denials did not deter them. They finally got a personal meeting with then-Postmaster General Marvin Runyon and very aggressively demanded a stamp. Runyon said he would confer with the CSAC, which he did. He listened to the members' explanation of the denials and felt confident enough to call them back and support the Committee's decision.

Various veterans' organizations lobbied us annually for stamps. There was continued pressure by those groups for a series of stamps honoring every major division of the Armed Services. That could have meant more than 120 stamps in the set, something we had no intention of considering. Our entire annual stamp program was usually limited to one hundred designs.

In order to stop this movement in its tracks, we requested a meeting of all major stakeholders at the Veterans Administration. The V.A. office hosted this summit in a huge conference room, and by the time the meeting began, every single chair was filled. The attendance odds were stacked against us: Postal Service, 4; veterans' groups, 36. The meeting was tense and filled with passionate individuals. But with the assistance of an old hand of the National Association of American Veterans we helped them all realize that their requests were not feasible. It then fell on my group to create a stamp that would satisfy everyone. The resulting 1999 Honoring

Veterans stamp was well received, but there were still grumblings about how they wanted their own stamp as this solitary stamp depicting the American flag was not cutting it.

The Postmaster General Delivers

Because the stamp program was technically the Postmaster General's, upon occasion we would occasionally receive word from the big suite on the tenth floor of Headquarters that he was interested in seeing a particular subject appear on a stamp.

Before I joined the Stamps group, I had heard stories of a previous Postmaster General and his "interest" in the stamp program. William Bolger, one of the longest-serving PMGs, had a fondness for attending Washington social functions at which individuals approached him with suggestions for stamps. Not wanting to say "no," he would, the following day, inform the Stamps group that we should develop a stamp for a particular individual. I say "individual" because, in almost every instance, it was for some little-know personage who had made a contribution to America in one form or another. Not that they didn't deserve it, but because of Bolger's inability to say "no," they were moved to the front of the line as new stamps were developed. In many cases, Stamps was able to put off issuing some of the subjects, using whatever excuse they could concoct. After my arrival and for years afterward, we would come across a completed design that Bolger had agreed to issue. Many of the proponents that made the original requests for these subjects had since lost interest, so a few of those designs still sit in the archives, awaiting their big day.

Officially, the PMG has the final say on all stamps. The CSAC makes its recommendations to him (or her—the first female PMG, Megan Brennan, wasn't appointed until 2015 after I'd left), and he does have the right to say "no" to any particular issue, whether it's because of the controversial nature of the subject or because the design doesn't suit him. Fortunately, over the twenty years I was involved with stamps, the PMG inserted his opinion into the program very rarely. Traditionally, he is shown the entire year's program in the summer preceding the year of issuance in a formal meeting held in his office suite. I attended most of these review meetings to provide background and insight as to the rationale for chosen subjects.

Those annual review meetings proved very interesting, to say the least. The interest level varied from PMG to PMG. Some sat attentively and asked questions about many, if not all, of the designs. Others showed little or no interest, and the meeting was over in ten to fifteen minutes. There were a few meetings that stood out in my mind as memorable.

The first time I was asked to accompany my boss, the Manager of Stamp Services, to the PMG's office was in the late summer of 1992, not long after Marvin Runyon had been appointed as Postmaster General. His reputation as a tyrant preceded him, and stories continually circulated in the building about different managers' run-ins with Runyon. Everyone lived in fear that he would summon them to his office, and they would return to their office with their head in their hand. I had never experienced a boss who elicited such fear in his staff.

James Tolbert, the Manager of Stamp Development at that time, asked me to go with him to show Mr. Runyon the 1993 program. The meeting was scheduled for 3:30 p.m. on that warm July day. Most of my day was spent going over the designs and subjects with James to ensure we were ready to answer any questions put to us. James was very nervous as this was his first meeting with Runyon, and it was also mine. We rehearsed and rehearsed, and as 3:30 drew closer, the phone rang. The PMG's secretary said that Mr. Runyon was unable to meet with us at 3:30 but asked us to stand by and he would notify us as soon as he was free.

Well, 3:30 came and went, and then 4:30 came and went, as did 5:30 and 6:30. It wasn't until 7:30 p.m. that we were finally ushered into the large, well-appointed PMG suite. But it was hard to see the fine furniture, photos on the wall, or any of the numerous awards displayed on the bookshelves. Mr. Runyon preferred to work under a single desk lamp, which gave off a slight warm glow, the only warmth in the room, as we were soon to find out. Out of that darkness and from behind the small spot of light emerged a very thin man dressed in a black suit and red tie, the only spot of color in his pale appearance.

Runyon himself was a striking man. Apart from his very thin frame and extremely white skin, coupled with his large shock of snow-white hair, his face appeared to be stretched side to side. It was as if someone had pulled a mask over his face and pulled it taut behind his ears, forcing his eyes and mouth to be stretched to the sides of his face. Only later, after much gossip about his appearance, was it determined that he must have had a facelift.

His demeanor was as cool as his somber appearance. He talked little, but when he spoke, it was short and to the point. Sensing our presence in the room that night, he grunted, "Sit over there," pointing to a very small round table in the corner of the darkened room. James and I dutifully moved to the table, and I looked at James as if to say, "Unless he turns on the lights, he won't be able to see the designs." James left it to me to ask Runyon if we could turn on a light over the table to better view the work. As he approached the table, he turned on a small ceiling spotlight, which shed just enough light over the table.

The three of us had to find room around a table built for two to lay out the folder of designs. James started the presentation in a very formal way, and Runyon just sat there staring at him. When it came time to present the designs, Runyon, who had been slouched down in his seat, sat up as if he were finally showing interest in the meeting.

Little response was made on Runyon's part as the designs were reviewed. As the review neared completion, we shared a set of twenty designs entitled the Legends of Baseball, which depicted the great baseball heroes of the past in their team uniforms. At that juncture, our office was still negotiating the rights to images of the players and the teams. As anyone who has ever had dealings with the Major League Baseball organization, obtaining rights is a very complex and frustrating experience. MLB is very demanding and money hungry as we were to soon find out. As this was our first experience with this organization, we felt we were close to finalizing the deal and thus felt comfortable in sharing the designs with the PMG. Having to hold back the designs and showing them at a later date when everything was finalized was not the best course of action. Or so we thought.

We explained to Mr. Runyon that we had not obtained the final rights yet and that there might be a possibility that we would have to remove the team names from the uniforms if it became an issue. It was at this point that Runyon came to life. He reached out to the table and forcefully shoved the artwork back at us, saying, "*Never* bring me a stamp for approval until it's done!" James became visibly nervous at this point, and my stomach wound up in knots. Runyon noticed the nervousness in James' voice and shaking hands and he went for his jugular vein. He lectured us about a number of things, but it soon became apparent that he was trying to make an impression on us. Over time, numerous visitors to Runyon's office discovered that if you displayed signs of nervousness, Runyon became antagonistic and cut you down to size. It was not a very likable trait but one we would have to deal with for the next six years. Annual stamp reviews for the next five years were usually met with fear and trepidation. But I must admit, none were as bad as that first one.

Ironically, the Legends of Baseball stamps hit a major snag in negotiations, and we were unable to issue them in 1993 as planned. It wasn't until 2000 that those stamps were finally issued.

The 1993 PMG review with Mr. Runyon passed with little or no issues. After the debacle of 1992, Azeez Jaffer, the Director of Stamp Services, stepped in and said he would conduct the reviews in the future.

The 1994 review would have passed with little or no notice, as well, if it weren't for one stamped envelope design. The presentation format developed for these reviews consisted of individual display boards showing the design at actual size and again as an enlargement for easier viewing. The same boards were then left with the PMG so he could affix his signature of approval to each design, as was the custom over the previous one hundred years. Azeez's concept was to make copies of each design and insert them into a binder so the PMG could flip from page to page at his leisure. But he wanted to display both versions in the conference room. That way, in Azeez's words, the PMG could make his own choice. Nothing like doubling the workload for the staff!

When Runyon entered the conference room, he was greeted not only by Azeez but James, three other managers, and me, for a new twist on a simple review. As Runyon shifted his gaze from the large group of people to the table, Azeez, gestured with a swoop of his arm that he, Runyon, could review the designs by looking at the display boards lined up in rows on the credenza or sit down at the conference table to review the book. Runyon chose the display boards.

As Runyon proceeded to the long side credenza, Azeez turned and snapped his fingers at me, indicating I was to follow along with him and Runyon in case the PMG had questions, which Azeez wouldn't be able to answer because he usually divorced himself from the process. Runyon proceeded to move from design to design, working his way down the long credenza, bent over at the waist, hands behind his back, with little or no comment to offer.

Near the end of the review, when we shared the stamped envelope designs, Runyon stopped, stared, and stood upright. He asked very inquisitively, "What is this?" Azeez turned, snapped his fingers at me, and prompted me to answer the man.

The design was entitled Graphic Design Eagle. It was a very simple line-drawing side view of an eagle's head with three angled stripes and the denomination. It was slated for use in Bulk Rate mail. Not too many months earlier, Mr. Runyon, who wanted to leave his mark on the Postal Service, chose to have the Postal Service logo redesigned. Replacing the full-bodied eagle outline, he approved a close-up of an eagle's head, which is still in use today. It was commonly referred to as the "sonic" eagle. It was a personal favorite of Mr. Runyon's. Our Bulk Rate stamped envelope was in no way intended to build off of the new logo; it just so happened that the envelope design was completed prior to the unveiling of the sonic eagle.

Azeez feared immediately that Runyon was expressing disapproval of the design, which was the reason he threw me into the center of it. His entire career was spent doing that sort of thing to his staff. When Runyon repeated the question for my benefit, I explained that it was a stylized eagle (which was obvious to everyone in the room). He was concerned about the eye of the eagle, which appeared to have an upturned, feminine-looking eyelash. It was at that moment that I said, in a casual, joking manner, "Yes, sir, it's a female eagle, and we plan to mate it with your new sonic eagle." To this day, I don't know why I said it. You could have heard a pin drop if it hadn't been for Azeez's quivering legs. At that point, I fully expected Azeez to reach out and strangle me. My throat dried up, and I thought my career was over.

But slowly, Mr. Runyon turned to me, looked me straight in the eye, and said, "Now that's funny." At which point I was able to breathe again. At the same moment, Azeez sought to capitalize on the reprieve we had just been granted by nervously laughing and, behind Runyon's back, gesturing for the others in the room to join in the laughter. I dodged a bullet that day, but it would prove to pave the way to a better working relationship with Runyon over the coming years.

Setting aside the annual review ritual, Postmaster Generals rarely got directly involved with design solutions. They usually left that to the CSAC to work out. But Mr. Runyon was unique in that sense. When a subject was near and dear to him, he exerted his influence on the process. Three such stamps come to mind.

One stamp not shown during the ill-fated 1992 review of the 1993 stamp program was the AIDS Awareness stamp, and for a very good reason. It was not selected by the CSAC, but Mr. Runyon shared with the Committee that he wanted to address the subject as one of our social awareness issues, and he didn't want to wait a year or two. Needless to say, we tackled this difficult subject immediately. The obvious design solution would be to use the red ribbon symbol synonymous with the cause. But our goal was to find a unique solution readily identifiable as the stamp design, not merely the symbol already in use in a plethora of ways.

Unfortunately, Mr. Runyon did not agree and rejected any attempts to provide a fresh solution to the issue. He wanted the red ribbon. Period. Howard Paine, the art director assigned to the project, worked with his production assistant, Tom Mann, to develop the red ribbon design. I must admit it worked as a stamp design, but by that time, it was overused. So much for fresh thinking.

When the design was shown to Mr. Runyon, it had been mounted on a black board with a thin edge of black showing around the all-white design. The red ribbon was centered vertically on the stamp. The design was rushed to the PMG's office for review and approval because it needed to get into production if it were to be issued in 1993.

When Azeez returned with the good news that Mr. Runyon had approved the design, I was relieved—at least until I was told that Runyon especially liked the inclusion of the black border on the stamp. Initially stunned and mystified, I soon realized he was referring to the black mounting board. Azeez had been reluctant to tell Runyon that the mounting board was not part of the design. I pushed back, saying that the black board would signify death, unlike the red ribbon, which symbolized hope. But Azeez said he would not go back to Runyon and that we had to do it that way. Under protestations, I had Howard and Tom incorporate a thinner black line around the ribbon, which we hoped would be seen more as a box to hold the ribbon design inside the totally white background. It must have worked because Runyon never noticed that the line was much thinner, and the black line never drew criticism from the public.

Another stamp of personal interest to Runyon was the Tennessee Statehood stamp of 1996. Runyon's ultra-contemporary home was built on the hillside of the Smoky Mountains in Tennessee. He had spent many years there when he headed up the Tennessee Valley Authority. So, when he was informed that, as standard policy, CSAC planned to issue a stamp commemorating the two-hundredth anniversary of Tennessee statehood, Runyon perked up.

Our group was already in the design phase, but that didn't stop Runyon from recommending that we contact a group based in Tennessee to design the stamp. This group, as we would eventually find out, had no graphic design experience but had done architecture-related work for Runyon. While those in the firm were very nice and cooperative, the designs never gelled. It was going to be my responsibility to craft an explanation to the PMG as to why this firm wasn't suitable for the job. That proved to be the easy part. My written justification seemed to satisfy him. But he still wanted to be involved in the design as it was developed. His recommendation for a design solution was to feature the State Capitol building. Usually, State Capitols can range from magnificent to god-awful ugly. Fortunately, the Tennessee State Capitol is attractive, though it is similar in design to numerous other State Capitols. We were reluctant to pursue the concept because we wanted to show the diversity of the state, from the mountains to the country music and other unique characteristics that would resonate with customers in other states. But the State Capitol was to be.

Phil Jordan found a night photo of the Capitol and mocked it up for review by the Committee, which they approved. But, as with all stamp designs, the Postmaster General had to give final approval.

I remember it being a quiet afternoon in the office, primarily because many of the bosses were either on leave or traveling. One of Azeez's managers, Valoree Vargo, was left in charge of the department. She received a call from the PMG's office requesting someone to come immediately to the PMG suite as Mr. Runyon wished to discuss the Tennessee stamp. Not knowing anything about the stamp, Valerie called me and told me I had to get up there ASAP. She was very apprehensive about what Runyon wanted as he rarely summoned us to his office.

With great fear and trepidation, I went to the tenth-floor offices. I was ushered into his suite where again the lights were very low. Perched behind his huge desk with that lone desk lamp glowing sat Runyon, huddling over a pile of papers, scissors, pens, and a bottle of glue. As I approached the desk, he looked up and motioned for me to approach the desk.

Once there, under the glow of the lamp, I could see what he was doing. He had made multiple copies of the stamp and was in the process of "redesigning" the stamp. He had cut out the type from one and was rearranging it on another. He had developed a number of alternative typographic arrangements by the time I arrived.

Incredulously and without thinking, I said, "*What* are you doing?" He slowly looked up and stared at me. My heart sank, and I thought I had gone too far again. But it didn't appear to faze him. He merely said that he didn't like the current typographic treatment and wanted to make it better. If it had been anyone other than the PMG, I probably would have delivered a stern lesson in how it was determined that this design was the best solution only after many options were considered. But being Runyon and knowing his temperament, I refrained.

He shared one of his design solutions with me and asked my opinion. In a very professional tone, I explained why it didn't work. He stared and then grunted. Then he pushed another design in front of me, which I summarily found fault with from a design perspective. After a third attempt, he sat back and said, "Convince me why your solution is better." Which I did. He stared, nodded in agreement, and scooped up all the paper cuttings and dumped them in the trash, saying, "I guess I should leave the designing to you guys." Another design hurdle successfully conquered.

I found, as did other managers who had encounters with Runyon, that over time, if you stood your ground, made your case, and presented yourself with confidence, he respected that and treated you accordingly. But if you showed nervousness, fear, or confusion, he enjoyed going for your jugular vein and reducing you to a puddle of quivering nerves. He was notorious for treating, or should I say mistreating, many of his managers during his tenure as PMG. I considered myself to be among the fortunate ones who he never mistreated. I will admit that internally, I was unnerved, but I managed to maintain my cool when dealing with him.

Upon Runyon's departure in 1998, Bill Henderson, a senior manager from North Carolina was appointed as Postmaster General. During his three-year tenure, he rarely got involved with the stamp program. He enjoyed attending some of the more high-profile first-day-of-issue ceremonies, usually at the request of Azeez, who had become a good friend of him and his girlfriend, Deborah Bowker, who, as Vice President of Communications, also happened to have been Azeez's boss in the 1990s.

Henderson's annual stamp reviews were the complete opposite of Runyon's. One year, I vividly remember attending a meeting with Azeez and Henderson, and the entire year's program was reviewed in five minutes. Henderson flipped through the pages of the book making almost no comments. He was stopped only once by Azeez, who asked him to consider attending the first-day-of-issue event for one of the stamps because "it will be a blast, and they'll throw a big party afterward." Henderson readily agreed to attend that one. Henderson would make occasional appearances at a CSAC meeting, usually during the Committee's opening statements on the first day of meetings. Azeez would coax him into attending, and his discussions were short and rarely pertained to stamps. He chose instead to give the members a quick update on the financial state and productivity of the Postal Service. The members showed little interest in those matters, wishing to discuss stamp-related issues instead.

Despite Henderson's lack of interest in stamps, he was savvy enough to realize the potential power stamps had as a bargaining tool. Azeez, the strong-willed manager that he was, saw this opportunity and seized on it while his friend Bill Henderson was in the top position.

The Stamps office was for many years an independent group reporting directly to the PMG. But in the late 1990s, it was moved under the Government Relations group. Then-Vice President Deborah Willhite convinced PMG Henderson that the move would provide better leverage with Congress as the Stamps group would report to her. But it was Azeez Jaffer who planted the seed for the move with Willhite. As Manager of Stamps, Henderson, though a good friend, would not have felt comfortable elevating Azeez to senior management. . Henderson instead gave him the title of Director, which Azeez accepted begrudgingly.

Eventually, Azeez was able to move the Stamps group under the direction of Government Relations, where he was soon appointed a Vice President position.

Surprisingly, few stamps saw the light of day due to Congressional pressure combined with internal Government Relations office pressure. In 1999, the previously mentioned Irish Immigration stamp promoted by Senator Ted Kennedy and the Prostate Cancer Awareness stamp produced to curry favor with Senator Ted Stevens were the only stamps to see issuance.

The last PMG that I had dealings with was Jack Potter, who, like Henderson, had risen through the ranks of the Postal Service. Potter assumed the mantle of PMG in 2001, and over the course of the next nine years, he inserted himself into the subject and design process more times than either Runyon or Henderson, which wasn't necessarily problematic. At least he showed more interest in the program than Henderson, who showed little interest, or Runyon, who showed the most interest only in subjects near and dear to him.

Potter's interaction with the Committee was much more positive and cordial than his predecessors. He regularly attended the opening sessions of each meeting held in D.C. and was well respected by the members. Additionally, his interest level when it came to the annual stamp program review was much higher than his predecessor. His review of stamp images frequently included questions, due to either his interest or his lack of knowledge about a subject, which was a good thing. We would rather have a PMG who asked questions than one who ignored the program.

Potter's very first annual review was in 2001 when the 2002 program assembled by CSAC was shown to him for approval. During the meeting, which I attended along with then-Director of Stamps Cathy Caggiano, Mr. Potter expressed interest in a specific image from the Masters of American Photography set of twenty stamps. He looked at the classic Edward Weston black-and-white photo of a seashell. Granted, it is a rather abstract depiction, so it was understandable that Potter was puzzled as to what it was. When he asked, I explained the photo to him. No comment from him was forthcoming, and we moved along. I assumed everything was fine.

It wasn't until we returned to the office that Cathy instructed me to find another photo by the same photographer to replace the seashell. I asked why, and she said, "Jack doesn't like it." We discussed our perceptions of the conversation, though argued would probably be a better term. When pressured to explain what Jack might have thought, Cathy said, "He's uncomfortable with it; it's too sexual." I was stunned by her interpretation of Jack's thoughts and pushed back. Not being able to convince Cathy that the seashell photo is iconic in the canon of Weston photos, I was instructed to find a replacement immediately. Cathy was nothing if not strong-willed and opinionated.

The three or four replacement photos I shared with her upset her even more. I had deliberately found even more "provocative" or "sexy" seashell photos to present. She pushed back again and said to keep looking. I waited a few days and then went back to her with a fabricated story. I related to her that we had contacted the Weston family to help us find a replacement even though they had signed the rights contract allowing us to use the current image. I told Cathy that the family was adamant that the original photo be used as it was iconic. It was only then that Cathy relented, but she warned me that if Jack asked about why it was still in the mix, I would have to be the one to explain it to him. I had no problem with that because I felt confident that Jack wouldn't be asking, which he didn't.

Potter did have a habit of occasionally making quick decisions, which were always hard to undo. One of his most rash decisions was to appoint a fellow Postmaster General to the Committee. Appointments to the CSAC were usually based on current needs for specific career disciplines—experts who could help us choose appropriate subjects. Not unlike the Larry King appointment, Jack Potter chose to ask someone to serve and then told us to work up the paperwork. Don't get me wrong, it was his Committee, and each PMG had the prerogative to add or remove members, but fortunately, that rarely happened.

One of the better choices of this sort was PMG Anthony Frank's selection of the actor Karl Malden. They shared a stage at the first-day-of-issue ceremony for the Comedians stamps at Grauman's Chinese Theatre on Hollywood Boulevard. Malden was representing the Motion Picture Academy as its president. Frank was so taken with Malden that he asked him on the spot whether he would consider being appointed to the Committee. Malden agreed, which resulted in a wonderful eight-year relationship.

But back to Potter. He attended the 2006 World Stamp Expo in Washington, D.C., sponsored by the U.S. Postal Service, for two weeks. Delegations from every postal organization attended this huge stamp exhibition. One of the exhibitors happened to be Benjamin F. Bailer, who had served as Postmaster General from 1975 to 1978. He was at the Expo to display his collection of Benjamin Franklin stamp-related items. He had a special interest in Franklin as his full name was Benjamin Franklin Bailer. Potter stopped by his display and was impressed by the range of items Bailer was displaying. Potter returned to the office and told us to ask Bailer to join the Committee.

The Committee is traditionally made up of individuals outside the Postal Service who provide expertise in their respective fields. We were reluctant to have Bailer appointed. Though he was a retired PMG, he was nonetheless not of our choosing. Bailer's subsequent tenure would be filled with numerous comments behind his back along the lines of "when I was PMG, we wouldn't have allowed that." But, in the long run, Mr. Bailer settled in and made limited contributions.

Jack Potter was the last of ten Postmaster's General I served under. My time in Stamps saw direct interactions with four of them. Each brought their own style to the table when we discussed stamps. To say the least, it proved to be an interesting and challenging twenty years with those four gentlemen.

The Board of Governors Weigh In

Under Postal reorganization in 1971, the newly-named U.S. Postal Service (replacing "Post Office Department") created a governing body to which the Postmaster General reported. The creation of this august body, the Board of Governors (BOG), was a new concept for a quasi-independent federal agency. As we soon found out, the members, who were appointed by the President of the United States, were usually political appointments—posts awarded as political payback for services they rendered to the current administration. The rule was, as still is, that the majority (five) can be of the same political party as the sitting president, and the minority (four) would be from the opposing party. Regardless of their political persuasion, many choices over the years had many people scratching their heads as to what their expertise and experience were in running a major government agency.

These members soon discovered that they wielded much power, and one area in which they felt most comfortable making demands, or "requests" as they termed it, was in the stamp realm. It was an easy realm with seemingly little controversy surrounding it, so it became a tool for pleasing constituents and friends alike.

One such member was Dr. Tirso Del Junco, a California surgeon, who rose to become Chair of the BOG for a number of years. Del Junco sent a "request" to our offices in 1996 for a stamp honoring Padre Felix Varela. Occasionally, we found ourselves a bit perplexed when an unknown name was submitted that required research to determine their importance and worth. In the case of Varela, we learned that he was a Cuban immigrant to Florida, where he did mission work. While his work was commendable, he was one of numerous religious figures we could have chosen to commemorate. That is, if we ever wanted to, which we didn't. Knowing that such a commemorative stamp would only open the floodgates to other religious organizations seeking commemoration of their own favored missionaries, we would not choose to develop such a stamp. But Chairman Del Junco would not accept no for an answer.

We created the portrait as a one-color, small definitive-sized stamp. It was felt that it would be more dignified in a single color rather than a full-color portrait that "glamorized" the good padre. To add interest to the design, the entire image was made up of microscopic type that repeated the initials "USPS" to create the lines in the artwork. That feature alone generated interest within the philatelic world. Certainly, without that unique production aspect, the stamp would have generated little or no interest, even in the Hispanic community. It appeared in 1997 and disappeared shortly thereafter.

Aside from that stamp, Del Junco's use of his power in the stamp program was more centered on the first-day-of-issue ceremonies. These dedications were (and still are) held nationwide, and in many instances involve celebrities. Del Junco, as with many other members, relished being listed as a dedicating official at these events. Over the years, it became standard practice that once the stamps were selected and the first-day locations chosen, the locations were forwarded to each member of the BOG. This was done not because they were interested in weighing in on the merits of the stamps; it was because they wanted to choose which ceremony they could attend as an active participant on behalf of the Postal Service.

One board member, Massachusetts Governor John Walsh, had strongly supported Senator Ted Kennedy's Irish Immigration stamp of 1999 and sought another stamp honoring the Special Olympics in 2003. In our response, we noted that we had already issued three stamps honoring the same organization in 1979, 1985, and 2000, which in itself had been a violation of CSAC's rule not to issue a stamp honoring the same subject more than once within a fifty-year period. Not to be dissuaded, Mr. Walsh arranged a meeting between me and Patrick Shriver, the head of Special Olympics and part of the Kennedy clan. Once again, the pressure was on us, and for political reasons alone, the organization received a fourth stamp in 2003. What made these situations so difficult is that the majority of the subjects we received requests from deserved stamps, but there was a limited number of stamps produced each year. To commemorate the same subjects repeatedly only kept other worthy subjects from receiving this honor.

One BOG Chair who wielded a big stick and made demands on the stamp program was James C. Miller. He had previously served as Director of the Office of Management and Budget under President Ronald Reagan, which empowered him to make demands for two Reagan stamps within a six-year period.

Insider Suggestions

Not to be outdone by the requests of senior management, the Stamps staff made numerous innovative contributions to the program over my twenty years with the program. Our group was responsible for providing guidance to the CSAC regarding public interest in the program. Based on sales data and letters from the public, our group would make recommendations to the Committee. Some were very specific subjects while others were much broader in nature. Discussions regarding subjects transpired within the confines of private, closed-door meetings, where certain subjects proved to be controversial and generated heated debates. But the CSAC members were, for the most part, very cooperative and agreed to develop many of the proposed subjects.

During the 1990s, I collaborated closely with Carl Burcham, the marketing and promotions manager. His title changed periodically over the years as was typical of government agencies when reorganizations occur. Regardless of his title, Carl wanted to bring new life to the program and subsequently made many recommendations for stamps, many of which were issued and met with great success.

Carl's list of ideas included The Civil War and Comic Strip Classics (1995), Endangered Species (1996), The World of Dinosaurs (1997), Classic Movie Monsters (1997), and the Nature of America series (1999-2010). Each of these issues was extremely well received and ranked among the most collected stamps of their respective issuance years, and they continually ranked among the most collected of all time.

Collaborating with Carl was one of the most exciting times in my Stamps career. Carl always exuded excitement and inspired other members of Stamps to be more creative. A prime example of his creativity was his promotional ideas for the Elvis Presley stamp. Everyone was confident that the Elvis stamp would be a bestseller because of Elvis' continued popularity. But Carl wanted to take it a step further. Even though I did not report to him, he and I worked closely together on projects such as this. In early 1992, he hosted a meeting between John Burke, a staff member, and me where we brainstormed innovative ideas to garner more attention for the issuance. The result was a concept to hold a public vote between the "young" Elvis from the early days of 1950s Rock and Roll and the "older" Elvis from his 1970s Las Vegas lounge act era. We had never had the public pick a design before, and to be quite honest, our concept was initially met with great skepticism. But as we discussed it more, others began to accept the idea. It was agreed that the public could choose the design so long as we controlled the designs to be voted on.

Howard Paine, art director for the entire Legends of American Music series, and I spent time discussing how to handle the series, but most importantly, the Elvis stamp. Would we use existing photography or paintings, or create something new, something that, in itself, would hopefully become iconic? We chose the latter but didn't want to have to rely on the visual interpretation of a single illustrator as we had done with other stamps. We tasked, instead, nine illustrators, each with a unique style, to develop concepts. The result was twenty-six images, some more finished than others. No restrictions had been placed on the illustrators as to what era Elvis should be depicted. We merely asked that they give us their interpretation of Elvis. Interestingly enough, the majority of the pieces received were of the "young" Elvis.

It was from this novel approach of multiple designs that the idea for the "young" and 'old" Elvis stamps came. An entire promotional campaign was prepared by staff and members of the Communications group that assisted the Stamps group in stamp promotion. Who else but Azeez Jaffer, the future Director of Stamps, headed the Communications group at the time. Azeez would make his move to Stamps from Communications a number of years later. By the time the wildly successful campaign was completed, its success was attributed to the Communications group and the one and only Azeez. He did play a role in its success, but, as he was prone to do, he took all the credit for an idea that wasn't his. Over the years, we learned to accept these boasts and to move on to the next idea.

The promotion garnered national publicity that resulted in the "young" Elvis receiving three-quarters of the 1.5 million votes cast by the public. It went on to become (and still is) the most popular commemorative stamp of all time with five hundred million stamps sold.

The World of Dinosaurs was another of Carl's brainchildren. Initially, he had suggested a scene of dinosaurs with four randomly-placed, different-sized, stamps perforated out of the scene. This technique had been used once before on U.S. stamps in 1976, when the set of four Bicentennial souvenir sheets depicting famous paintings of the Revolutionary War was issued. Carl suggested that this time, as a creative approach, we should develop our own illustrations and arrange the stamp shapes as a unit. As the designs progressed, the enthusiasm grew and so did the number of stamps, resulting in a total of fifteen stamps depicting two prehistoric scenes.

Carl's last big project proposal was for a series of souvenir sheets depicting various biomes of nature. It would be called The Nature of America. Like the successful World of Dinosaurs, he proposed that scenes depicting these biomes include ten stamps depicting either flora or fauna. What started out as a set of four, to be issued one a year, turned into an extremely popular set of twelve issues spanning 1999 to 2010. Art director Ethel Kessler was assigned to this massive project and John Dawson, a leading nature illustrator based in Hilo, Hawaii, accepted the challenge of developing this complex series. Over that twelve-year period, the annual issuance usually ranked among the most popular stamp issuances of the year based on polling of serious collectors by *Linn's Stamp News,* the leading philatelic publication.

Unfortunately, we lost Carl and his creative ideas and inspirations in the early part of the new century. He chose to move on to other career paths. It was definitely a loss to the Postal Service and the stamp program.

Selling Some Suggestions

Carl was hardly the only person on staff to recommend subjects to the CSAC. Our marketing group made several proposals, most of which saw the light of day.

The Postal Service would periodically sponsor a major international stamp exhibition. It was traditional for the host country to issue numerous stamps during the exhibition. In 2000, we hosted such an expo in Anaheim, California. The sale of the stamps would help underwrite the cost of the show. With that in mind, Rick Arvonio, Manager of Stamp Printing and Distribution and the show organizer, recommended the creation of a series of stamps and souvenir sheets commemorating Space and Space Achievements. Numerous stamps had been issued since the early 1960s commemorating this subject, but Rick's proposal was to make the stamps more distinctive. He encouraged the design team to work with the stamp printers to develop technologically innovative designs. Richard Sheaff functioned as art director, and the collaboration resulted in holograms and circular and other unique shapes never before produced by the USPS.

In addition to the glossy, photographic, innovative designs developed for the expo, the marketing group wanted to encourage children to collect stamps. The recommendation to the CSAC was that a set of four stamps entitled Stampin' the Future be created. The catch was that they wanted to host a nationwide children's stamp art contest. Audible groans were heard from a number of members. They had experienced and lived to tell about a set of Kids Care Earth Day stamps issued in 1995. That too was a nationwide children's stamp art contest. The massive process of receiving submissions, sorting through them, and selecting choices proved to be too much for the staff, forcing us to contract a firm in New Jersey to assist us. Many thousands of entries were received. It was my task to go to the firm's warehouse in New Jersey to brief the staff on how to weed out submissions that did not meet our established criteria for workable stamp designs. Upon issuance, the Earth Day stamps were met with little interest from the general public. Well, except for the families of the winners, who I'm sure bought lots of stamps.

So, when presented with the concept of yet another set of children's art stamps, the Committee expressed reluctance. But our marketing group assured them it would be a smoother operation this time around, which proved to be correct. The Stampin' the Future stamps were developed, produced, and issued at the World Stamp Expo 2000. Much like the first set of kid's art stamps, they were enjoyed by a small, select group of purchasers.

Coincidentally, one of the four Stampin' the Future stamps was illustrated by an eight-year-old, Zachary Canter, who turned out to be the grandson of a prominent New York illustrator, Saul Mandel, a fact we were unaware of at the time of the CSAC judging. Saul had illustrated one of the earliest Love stamps in 1986, which featured a cartoon of a small dog, and it proved to be one of the more popular Love stamps to date. Over the ensuing years, Saul would call me asking for new assignments. His request was not uncommon. I routinely received calls from illustrators, photographers, and designers from around the country looking for work. But Saul was unusually persistent in a New York kind of way. He would beg me for work, saying in his overly affected Jewish accent, "Terry. Give me a stamp. I need the work. I'm gonna die before you give me a project!" I was unable to find the right project for him. But when his grandson won the competition, I got yet another call from Saul. This time, though, the pitch was different. It went something like this: "Terry. What? I can't get a job, but you give my grandson a job? What?" All I can say is "Oy."

In 2006, the U.S. Postal Service again hosted an international stamp exhibition. Every postal administration worldwide was represented at the two-week exhibition. Dave Failor, the Director of Stamp Services at that time, requested a pane of fifty stamps to help offset the expo costs: The Wonders of America. Dave made the request for this pane of fifty based on the popularity of another set of fifty stamps issued just four years earlier called Greetings from America. The second set of fifty designs proved to be successful as well.

The Creative Drive

One of the best kept "secrets" of the stamp program is just how many stamps were suggested by the art directors under contract with us. Many of the most beautiful, and in many instances, most popular stamps were conceived and created by these very talented individuals whom I had the honor of working with, learning from, and calling friends.

When I made the move to the Stamps department in October 1990, three art directors were under contract to the Postal Service to assist in the development of stamp images: Howard Paine, Derry Noyes, and Richard Sheaff. As previously mentioned, both Howard and Derry served as CSAC members prior to stepping down to personally oversee the art direction of stamps. A few years later, Richard "Dick" Sheaff, a Boston graphic designer, was hired to become the third art director as the stamp program continued to grow.

Over the next twenty-five years or so, these three talented art directors made numerous recommendations of stamp subjects. The suggestions were usually based on the intrinsic visual beauty of a subject, which would make for an appealing stamp. It was a standing CSAC request that all of the art directors explore visual concepts for ongoing series such as the Love and Christmas series. The vast majority of stamps issued in these series came from the art directors. In addition to regular series stamps, they brought to the table subjects that reflected their personal outside interests.

A number of Dick Sheaff's personal collection of antique paper material made their way into Love stamps and even the Celebrate the Century series. Aside from personal interests, other recommendations of his resulting in beautiful historic stamps included The Stars and Stripes pane of twenty stamps depicting various designs of the U.S. flag over the past 200 years (2000), a specially designed stamp booklet on the history of Old Glory (2003), and the two fifty-stamp panes, Greetings from America (2002) and Wonders of America (2006).

Howard Paine's many contributions, aside from many small rate-change scenic designs and Christmas stamps, included the Cloudscape stamps of 2004. He proposed the concept of using photography to illustrate the different cloud formations. The original reaction, mine included, was "ho-hum." But eventually, he wore me down, and I agreed to let him develop a concept for presentation to the CSAC. The end result was fifteen stamps in three rows of five each. It was stunning and educational. I guess it was the *National Geographic* background coming out in Howard. Regardless, it proved to be a major success, much to the surprise of all of us. One of the reasons for its success was that television meteorologists nationwide featured the stamps on their evening broadcasts, prompting a run on them at the local post offices. Howard followed up with yet another set using the same format, this time with the subject of Earthscapes. Those fifteen photos depicted aerial views of earth. The scenes initially appear to be abstracts until you realize you were looking at a freeway interchange, a housing development, or a logjam on a river. Those 2012 stamps never received the recognition that Cloudscapes enjoyed.

Derry Noyes, the third art director, comes from a very artistic background. Her father is Eliot Noyes, the famed industrial designer who received postal recognition in 2011 as one of *Pioneers of American Industrial Design* honorees. Derry had studied at art at Yale under Bradbury Thompson, the dean of American typographic designers and CSAC design consultant.

Like Howard, Derry had her own unique style of presenting work to the art directors at our pre-CSAC meetings as well as the CSAC Design Subcommittee. Derry always had a very unassuming, quiet quality about her. Her appearance is that of a petite, very attractive, slender woman with an engaging smile and warm personality. You sense, when speaking with her, that she was truly listening and cared, a rare quality in this day and age. What lies inside that charming person's head was a wealth of knowledge combined with good taste and a great sense of design.

The Committee was always looking for beautiful, attractive images. One solution was to use existing masterpieces of American art. Derry excelled in making recommendations in this area. The one stamp that really started it all was the Georgia O'Keeffe Poppy stamp of 1996. Then-CSAC Chair Virginia Noelke had suggested to the Committee that we find a "pretty" stamp subject to issue if only because it would be an attractive addition to the corner of envelopes. Derry responded by mocking up the O'Keeffe image, which became an instant success. Its popularity spawned an entire series of Artist stamps. Interestingly enough, in some instances, such as the Alexander Calder (1998), Isamu Noguchi (2004), and Charles and Ray Eames (2008) stamps, they were not only favorite artists of Derry's but were all past or present personal friends of Derry and her family.

Derry's other exquisite designs commemorating the arts include Masters of American Photography (2002), Masterworks of Modern American Architecture (2005), and Pioneers of American Industrial Design (2011). Her incredible body of work included designs for Love, Christmas, and the ever-popular social awareness stamps promoting Animal Rescue (2010) and Spay & Neuter (2002).

In 1992, a few years after joining Stamps, I felt that we needed to add one or two art directors to our stable of creative talent as the stamp program was rapidly increasing in size. I queried the three art directors for suggestions for new candidates while also doing research on my own.

The art director selected to become the fourth member of the group was Phil Jordan, a Washington, D.C.-based art director of note. Phil had to his credit the honor of being the very first art director chosen for the Washington Art Director's Club Hall of Fame. I had worked with Phil a number of years earlier on the redesign of the Communications department's bimonthly *Postal Life* magazine, of which I was art director. My boss at the time, Vince Hoffman, had wanted outside input on redesigning the magazine, and Phil got the job.

Having served as art director of the Smithsonian Institution's *Air and Space* magazine for many years, coupled with being a licensed pilot and seasoned soaring pilot, Phil made wonderful contributions to the stamp program whenever we needed air and space-related stamps. He spent an inordinate amount of time on the beautiful set of twenty Classic American Aircraft stamps (1997) and the follow-up set of ten Advances in Aviation stamps (2005). When the one-hundredth anniversary of the Wright Brothers' First Flight was selected to be commemorated in 2003, the logical choice was Phil, who once again produced a beautiful design.

Phil didn't restrict himself to aircraft. He proposed to the Committee a set of stamps featuring photographs taken from the Space Hubble Telescope. The Committee loved the imagery so much that five stamps were issued in 2000. Again in 2007, his proposal to depict Aurora Borealis and Aurora Australis images wowed the members.

Shortly after Phil was hired, I hired Carl Herrman. To be honest, at the time, I had just heard his name but was unfamiliar with his body of work. The other art directors had suggested him as a possible candidate. I'm glad that I took their advice. Carl turned out to be a creative and colorful art director.

Carl brought with him a passion for graphic design and an eclectic taste in subject matter. One of Carl's earliest contributions, from a subject standpoint, was the Insects & Spiders pane of twenty stamps issued in 1999. It was in 1997 that Carl first suggested that we consider issuing stamps showing bugs. The immediate reaction from Committee members: "No way!" The public didn't want weird bugs on their envelopes. Fortunately, the other members were intrigued by the spider idea, especially after seeing a sample of Steve Buchanan's work. Carl had taken the time to mock up the existing spider illustration as a stamp to prove that it could work. And it did! The members voted to continue development of the stamp.

But Carl saw an even greater opportunity. He suggested a full pane of twenty insects and spiders. Surprisingly, Committee members agreed, and the stamps were among the top twenty collected stamp sets for years.

Carl's numerous other contributions included the DC Comics Superheroes (2006), Marvel Comics Super Heroes (2007), and Early TV Memories (2009) stamps.

As the stamp program continued to grow, I felt the need for yet another art director. So, the last art director I hired was an old friend, Ethel Kessler. Ethel had been a prominent figure in the Washington, D.C. graphic design community for a number of years, working at the U.S. Information Agency (USIA) before opening her own studio.

She served as president of the prestigious Art Directors of Metropolitan Washington and as a board member of the American Institute of Graphic Arts (AIGA) Washington chapter.

Ethel rarely influenced the Committee on subject matter. Her forte was coming up with unique illustrations and design solutions. After her initial difficulties with the Frederick Law Olmstead design, a far more challenging project was assigned to her which proved to be one of the most difficult subjects: breast cancer research. Her eventual solution was brilliant and stands, to this day, as one of the most unique designs ever produced by the USPS. Her collaboration with Baltimore illustrator Whitney Sherman produced an image that resonated throughout the country. It is still on sale, thanks to renewed Congressional bills and continued sales. Ethel has probably been most proud of this design of all the design work she has done over the years and rightly so.

Shortly after completing the semipostal, Ethel asked to be involved in designing a newly approved social awareness stamp honoring Adoption, scheduled for issuance in 2000. Her pitch to me was that Greg Berger, a designer on Ethel's staff, was adopted and that the two of them wanted to collaborate on a design. She and Greg came back with a solution that eventually was chosen by the CSAC. The most touching aspect of the design process was that on the day that the CSAC formally approved the final design, Greg was meeting with his birth mother for the very first time.

Aside from the influence of the art directors on the stamp program, I have to confess that I have influenced the Committee occasionally on stamp subjects of personal interest to me, apart from my role as facilitator of the program where I helped guide the Committee on stamp subjects.

The first time I inserted personal influence was in 1991 when the American Music series was in its initial development stage. We were working with a list of music subjects compiled by the Smithsonian Institution's music division. I couldn't help but notice that the entire list was people rather than genres of music. Realizing that genres such as jazz, classical, rock and roll, etc., were all being represented by specific musicians, I felt there was one genre that wasn't represented, and that was Broadway musicals. I recommended adding it to the list, and the Committee agreed. I personally did the research and recommended four stamps, one from each decade from the 1930s through the 1950s. I art directed the four subjects: Showboat (1920s), Porgy & Bess (1930s), Oklahoma (1940s), and My Fair Lady (1950s). It was a tough decision when it came to the 1950s selection. To my way of thinking, there were two great musicals during that decade: My Fair Lady and West Side Story. I chose one of my favorite illustrators, Wilson McLean, to create original designs. I had him develop a design for West Side Story as a possible fifth stamp in the set. Story was his favorite choice over Lady. But when the Committee decided that four rather than five stamps would make up the set, My Fair Lady was selected.

Aside from my personal interest in the theatrical arts dating back to my high school days, I also stand accused of promoting subjects my family members recommended. I know, I know. We're supposed to be unbiased in our selections, but as has been noted, everyone from the PMG down to the art directors and everyone else involved with the stamp program have at some time or another managed to get one of their pet subjects selected.

I influenced one of the fifty Greetings from America stamps issued in 2002. No, not the entire pane, but merely one little element of the Virginia stamp. Having lived in that beautiful, historical state for the past twenty-seven years, I felt I knew something about the state that might be useful when designing that particular stamp.

One of the important considerations when designing the series was to utilize scenes and sites that best typified the state—but avoiding sites that would require intense rights negotiations that could ultimately impact the sales and marketing of the stamps and ancillary products. Many of the historic sites in Virginia fell into that category. Also, many of those same sites had already been featured on postage stamps over the years.

Over dinner one evening with my wife Ann, I shared our dilemma about choosing an appropriate subject for the Virginia stamp. She stared at me and slowly said, "What about Oatlands?" Oatlands Plantation is an historic home seven miles south of our home in Leesburg, where Ann just happened to work as a paid guide. It's a beautiful 1803 property, very typical of classic Virginia homes of the period, and had not yet appeared on a postage stamp. Some critics have since questioned the inclusion of Oatlands over Jefferson's Monticello and other great homes. They felt that the home was not "significant enough." But those critics all hailed from central

Virginia where Monticello and other homes are located. Jealousy was a factor, I believe.

The Director of Oatlands had already approached me about a possible stamp in 2003 for the home's two-hundredth anniversary, but I assured him it probably wouldn't happen. The Committee received far too many such requests from similar homes, and very few, if any, were selected. But the idea of including it on the Greetings from Virginia stamp, I thought, might just work. I gave imagery to Dick Sheaff, the art director on the project, and he worked with the illustrator, Lon Busch, to incorporate the building into the design. The resulting stamp turned out quite nice despite critics' complaints.

On numerous occasions, I was responsible for adding stamps to an existing subject series, as were the art directors. As designers, we often saw the opportunity to expand on a subject to produce a more attractive set of stamps. The Jim Henson and the Muppets stamps issued in 2005 is a good example. The original request was for a single Jim Henson stamp.

I was an avid Henson (and Muppets) fan as I remembered seeing Kermit in the early coffee commercials in the 1960s and then curling up on the sofa in the mid-1970s with our two children every Saturday evening to watch the classic *Muppets Show.* This gave me the impetus to pursue this project with great interest. I immediately requested that the Committee broaden the scope by including Muppets characters on multiple stamps instead of just one. I suggested that we would be missing a golden opportunity to appeal to not only adults but children as well. The Committee saw the wisdom of the suggestion and allowed me to pursue "multiple" stamps for the issuance. Given latitude on the number of stamps, I ran with it. Working with Derry Noyes, who asked to be assigned to the project as art director and designer, we developed eleven stamps, one showing Henson and ten showing the Muppets.

Derry created a brilliant solution for the Muppets stamps. Each character would be depicted bursting through white paper as if they were bursting out of the envelope the stamp was affixed to. The Henson group loved the concept and set up a time for the photo shoot. Bill Gicker and I had the great pleasure of attending the shoot at a rented sound stage in Hollywood. I got to "meet" Kermit, Miss Piggy, the Swedish Chef, and all the other Muppets. I felt like I was a kid again.

Expanding the original single Henson stamp to include ten of his brilliant creations made for a much more exciting and fun issuance.

I would employ that same tactic of increasing the number of stamps numerous times. The Art of Disney series started out as one set of four stamps but led to a total of twenty stamps issued between 2004 and 2008. The popularity of the Disney stamps prompted my suggestion, in collusion with the Disney team, to produce *Pixar* stamps. That venture produced two sets of five stamps each in 2011 and 2012.

Based on the popularity of the 1995 Comic Strip Classics stamps, I recommended to the Committee in 2008 that we explore another set of comics stamps. This time we would include more recent comics. The 1995 set stopped at comics that began in 1945. The Snoopy stamp from the Peanuts comic strip in 2001 broke down the barrier of not featuring commercially produced strips. My initial suggestion was for ten stamps, but a certain member of the Committee fought vehemently to hold down the number. He had certain subjects he wanted included that year, so he fought diligently to convince the members to hold down the number. He won, unfortunately, and to this day, my favorite strip of all time, Pogo, has never been seen on a stamp. Instead, we issued five stamps in 2010. I guess I can't win them all!

The last subject I was influential in commandeering through the Committee was the joint issue with France in 2012 honoring musical greats Edith Piaf and Miles Davis. The French Post (France's postal service) had contacted us a few years prior to the issuance seeking a joint issue. As we continued to suggest various subjects back and forth, we met with strong resistance from our French counterparts.

Their goal was to honor Jacqueline Kennedy. We certainly liked the idea, but we had already attempted to make that stamp happen on our own a year earlier. Even after meeting with the Director of the Kennedy Library in Boston and having art director Derry Noyes intervene with her personal friend, Caroline Kennedy, we were left empty-handed. It seemed that Caroline did not want to have a stamp honoring her mother as a Renaissance woman. She insisted that her mother would never have approved of such a commemoration. She said that if it were an issue honoring her as First Lady, she might consider it. We weren't ready to issue a set of First Lady stamps, which is what would have happened if we issued one for Mrs. Kennedy. So, despite continued pushback from the French, we were left without a common subject.

Dave Failor, the Stamp Services Director at the time, proposed a face-to-face meeting to resolve our issues. Due to budget constraints, Dave felt we were not in a position to travel to Paris, so we invited the French officials to New York City. They agreed, indicating they had other business to conduct while in the city.

I had the PhotoAssist team do a lot of research to identify potential common threads in our history and culture. Out of this mix, I found both Edith Piaf and Miles Davis. Davis was, and is, much loved by the French. So much so that they had issued a stamp in his honor a number of years before. "The Little Sparrow," as Piaf was known, was not only loved by her countrymen but had made numerous appearances with great success in the U.S. Additionally, her name was still known in the U.S. because of the critically acclaimed 2007 film, *La Vie en Rose,* which garnered a Best Actress Academy Award for Marion Cotillard. By pairing these two great musicians, I felt we might have a workable solution.

Dave, Bill Gicker, and I flew to New York to meet with two French Post representatives. I arranged a meeting at the American Institute of Graphic Arts offices in lower Manhattan. After the usual pleasantries were exchanged, we got down to the business of identifying a subject both administrations could accept. I led off with my suggestion for the two music legends, which was met with initial silence from the French, but within moments, they warmed to the idea even though they admitted they had issued individual stamps for both performers in the past. They called back to their offices in Paris to share the idea with their stamps director and received approval the same day. The resulting stamps were beautifully designed by Greg Breeding, one of the new art directors assigned to stamps after my retirement and were subsequently issued in 2012.

Aside from the subjects mentioned, I was diligent in revisiting the stamps vault to re-review art that was put on hold for one reason or another but never saw the light of day. From those searches, I resurrected such stamps as Garden Flowers in 2004 and Holiday Evergreens in 2010. I was ever reluctant to let perfectly good illustrations go unused. The stamps archives held many such unissued little gems of art. After my retirement, the entire archives were turned over to the National Postal Museum.

Given the complexity of the stamp design process, it's easy to see that it requires numerous people and organizations to achieve a successful program. As I've described, everyone, starting with the American public's thousands of ideas and maneuvering through myriad political influences, not to mention the internal pressure of striving to provide the best subject choices and designs, are all part of the unique, complex process of creating stamps.

Chapter 4

Let's Make a Deal

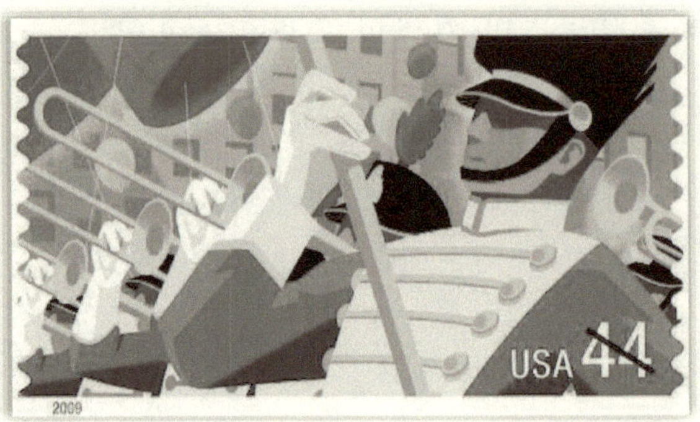

Influences, whether generated by the public, Congress, USPS staff, or CSAC members, play an important role in stamp development. Still another critical component to this ever-evolving puzzle is the partnership with leading organizations, retailers, and businesses.

As the stamp program grew and became more business-oriented, it was only natural for the Postal Service to seek out partners to assist in promoting its more contemporary subjects. For better or worse, these partnerships helped to generate millions of dollars in additional revenue from the sale of stamps. But the journey wasn't without some very interesting, productive, and yes, sometimes very frustrating collaborations along the way.

The Greeting Card Industry

One partnership, which seemed to be a natural fit, was with the Kansas City-based Hallmark company. Their need for mailing services to deliver the millions of greeting cards they created had produced an ongoing business relationship between us. It wasn't until the one-hundredth anniversary of Hallmark in 2010 that a relationship with the creative teams of Hallmark and Stamps was formed.

As is the case with many stamp proponents, the Hallmark folks had their own ideas about what the stamp would look like. Unfortunately, because of the CSAC Guidelines, honoring the organization on their anniversary was forbidden. Hallmark was not to be dissuaded. Postal management, which also maintained other business connections with Hallmark, approached us in an attempt to persuade us to bend the rules for one of the Postal Service's best customers. In an effort to comply, we went back to Hallmark and suggested that they search their archives to find greeting card imagery that might translate to stamps.

Following that suggestion, we received a layout utilizing what Hallmark said was the most popular greeting card they had ever issued, still produced to this day. It was an attractive, quaint illustration of a small cart with two wheels filled with a bouquet of pansies. I asked Derry Noyes to use the image to develop a stamp. Flowers are always good sellers when it comes to stamps. But in this case, we met some resistance—not from the public but from a CSAC member.

Jessica Helfand, the Design Subcommittee chair, simply detested the imagery. Jessica's background was as a Design Professor at Yale University. She found the image dated and not well executed, and she strongly resisted our attempts to gain approval from the Subcommittee. I had to intervene on a few occasions during the Subcommittee deliberations to encourage the acceptance of the design. While we all knew that Jessica's assessment was fairly accurate, the public would not see the design in the same light. We expected the stamp to be popular as part of the ongoing Love stamp series. It took three CSAC meetings over a nine-month period to convince Jessica to approve the image. Derry worked diligently to rework the design to downplay the "offensive" parts of the original illustration. Once the cropped image was shown, Jessica reluctantly accepted it. It went on to become one of the bestselling stamps of 2010, much to Jessica's chagrin.

At the same time, the Love Pansies stamp was being developed, another division of Hallmark held meetings with our staff to explore the feasibility of creating a special stamp for their square-formatted greeting cards. These envelopes, by postal regulations, required additional postage. They petitioned the Postal Service to create a stamp specifically for that rate. Until then, customers had to affix two stamps to meet the then-current rate of sixty-five cents. As to be expected from a retail organization, they approached the solution from a very different perspective than the Stamps group. After much trial and error, we settled on a square stamp, to emulate the square envelope, and Derry Noyes suggested a butterfly, which would work well on any greeting card. As the rates increased, a new square stamp with a different butterfly would be issued. The Hallmark group was thrilled to get the stamp series. But our group was rather perplexed and frustrated to see the latest Hallmark initiative released the following year. Hallmark worked with another USPS group to develop a preprinted stamp image directly on the envelope and offered the card and envelope, complete with postage, as one package deal. While we felt it was a good idea, we were not amused that we had gone to all the trouble to create a special series only to see them work with another group to develop a stamp on their own.

The Fast-Food Industry

As I've mentioned, developing social awareness designs is very complex and requires a lot of time and effort to find the appropriate solution to best convey the message. Adoption, while not the hardest subject in the series, was nonetheless difficult. After working through the internal issues between two art directors and their competing personal interests in the project, Greg Berger, a designer working for art director Ethel Kessler, developed a unique, beautiful design. At that point, our marketing people asked that we identify a partner for the issuance. Their suggestion: Wendy's, the fast-food chain. Why Wendy's? Because Dave Thomas, the founder of Wendy's, an adopted child himself, was a strong advocate for adoption.

Fortunately, Wendy's did not insert itself into the design process as it was already approved and ready for printing. But they did wish to partner on the first-day-of-issuance event, held in Los Angeles in 2000. Stamp Director Azeez Jaffer, set up a lavish dinner in a private dining room, complete with a menu personally selected by him was held on the evening before the first-day event at the Hyatt Regency Hotel, Azeez's regular residence when he traveled to California.

Dave Thomas did attend the dinner, but it was soon noticed that he was not in the best of health. He had an aide sitting with him periodically feeding him pills. I sat across from Mr. Thomas and was only able to engage him in intermittent conversation. He seemed to be a little out of it but was a very pleasant man. I later learned that he had been living with a tumor for years and died twenty months after that dinner at age 69.

The Retail Industry

Another major retailer, Macy's, approached us for a stamp, not for their stores but for their ever-popular Thanksgiving Day Parade. They had taken the liberty, as Hallmark had done, to develop designs to submit to us. While their designs were interesting, their illustrations were not what we were looking for. Once the CSAC approved the subject, I assigned art director Howard Paine to work with illustrator Paul Rogers. We knew that we could never capture the scope of that gigantic parade in one single stamp, so Howard and Paul expanded it to four horizontal stamps showing many elements of the annual parade, from the giant balloons to the marching bands. Needless to say, Macy's was thrilled not only with our design solution but that they got four stamps instead of one. The Macy's team was very cooperative throughout the entire process, something that was not always the case.

The Film Industry

The partnership with Warner Bros., on the other hand, proved to be more difficult than expected.

In 1995, James Tolbert, the manager of Stamp Development, and Kelly Spinks, our Rights and Permissions legal person, and I visited Warner Bros. Studios in Burbank to explore the possibility of putting Bugs Bunny on a stamp. Specifically, we wanted to make Bugs a mascot for the Youth Stamp Program we were about to develop. We had a very productive meeting with Warner Bros. officials and, after lunch in their studio commissary, we returned to their offices to finalize the next steps. It was at that point that they excused themselves only to return a few minutes later with a package for us to bring back to Azeez and Loren Smith, our chief marketing officer.

We took the sealed package, unaware of its contents, thanked them for their hospitality, and left.

Upon arrival back in D.C., we delivered the package to Azeez. It wasn't until a few days later that James, Kelly, and I were brought into the loop. It seems that Azeez and Loren had flown to L.A. weeks before our visit and negotiated an entire contract with Warner without sharing this information with us. The three of us felt like idiots and were very upset to be played in that manner. To this day, I have no idea why Azeez did this to us. But there were many things that Azeez did that I will never understand.

One would think that developing stamp images incorporating the classic Looney Tunes characters would be easy and fun. Neither was the case.

It took us more than eighteen months to agree on Bugs Bunny, the first in a series of five stamps issued annually between 1997 and 2001. Countless trips were made to the West Coast to work with Brenda Guttman, the Warner Bros. creative director assigned to the program, along with her team. It was exciting to watch them sketch out these classic characters. But their concept of what should appear on the stamp differed wildly from what we were looking for. Hundreds of rough sketches were submitted, none of which worked for us.

Part of the problem was Warner's intention to create imagery to be reproduced on licensed product indicating little interest in how the design worked as a stamp. In fact, we soon discovered they would submit all of their sketches to their entire chain of command, all the way up to Mr. Semel and Mr. Daly, the two heads of Warner Bros. Once they approved it, it would be sent to us for "final approval." After numerous rejections by both parties, tension began to build between the two groups. I was then sent back to L.A. numerous times to work on new concepts.

Once there was a mutual agreement on the final Bugs Bunny stamp, the remaining four images came a little easier.

One of the bonuses of working on this complex, drawn-out project came during the evening before the first-day ceremony for the Bugs Bunny stamp. A lavish reception was hosted by Warner Bros. officials at their newly designed Animation Museum and Gallery on the Warner lot.

After the usual speeches, I mingled in the crowded reception room when a Warner official approached asking me to accompany him to meet Chuck Jones, the legendary animator and creator of many Looney Tunes characters, who had been looking for me.

To my surprise, Jones was seeking me out to plead with me to allow him to create and illustrate the remaining stamps slated for the series. I was dumbstruck by his request. I would have assumed that he'd have taken his request to Warner officials, not me. When I shared that thought with him, he scoffed and said that his request had fallen on deaf ears. For whatever reason, Warner Bros. brass was reluctant to allow him to create the art, instead assigning it to staff artists. Detecting that I was being pulled into an internal struggle, I politely told him that I would intercede on his behalf to attempt to make it happen. He said he appreciated my help but remained skeptical that it would happen. His perception was correct. I was summarily dismissed with a sly smirk when I broached the subject on my next visit to the studio. It would have been a golden opportunity, lost to the ages.

It was still a very complex project, not the fun project I had envisioned. What I walked away with was a lot of heartburn. Brenda, on the other hand, was awarded a vice-presidential position at Warner Bros. Sometimes, there is just no justice!

If the Warner Bros. experience was difficult, to say the least, collaboration with another film studio proved to be just the opposite.

As the licensing representative for Stamp Services, Kelly Spinks received many calls from corporations wishing to have their properties appear on postage stamps. In 2001, the Disney Corporation was no exception. A division within the corporation, Disney Consumer Products, contacted Kelly to explore the possibility of Disney-related stamps. Our initial reaction was surprise and then dismissal. After all, we had been told not to approach them about stamps after they had reluctantly given us the rights to reproduce Snow White as part of our Celebrate the Century series. And now, here they were again, asking us to develop stamps for them. Much discussion ensued about how to respond to their request. In the end, we agreed to meet with them on our next trip to California.

A few weeks later, Kelly and I flew to California and met one afternoon with John Gong, the V.P. of Disney Consumer Products, along with three select members of his staff. It was obvious from the start that not only was this a different staff, but there would be a different tone to the proceedings. We were greeted warmly despite underlying skepticism on Kelly's and my part.

For the next hour, we were treated to one of the most enjoyable and creative meetings either of us had ever participated in. John's team had prepared a special presentation that included a handmade book describing the stamps they were proposing. They had gone so far as to create color concepts for the stamps, complete with warm, inspiring text, read aloud to us by Barbara Bazaldua, a staff writer.

The concept was brilliant. The presentation booklet was entitled "How is a Mouse like a Post Office?" They likened Mickey Mouse to the Postal Service as two entities that connected to the American public. Mickey's ability to connect people through optimism, integrity, humor, laughter, and friendliness was not unlike the Postal Service's ability to allow people to communicate and share important emotional moments in their lives through letters.

Their stamp proposal wanted to communicate Mickey's classic appeal in visual stories that connected with the reasons people wrote to one another. Four themes were chosen to convey the concept: friends, love, celebration, and Mickey's simple, cherry "Hello!" Using a "Rockwellian," American small-town approach, the team developed four-color illustrations by artist Peter Emmerich.

At the end of the presentation, John asked for our thoughts. Not wanting to tip our hand, both Kelly and I expressed gratitude for the work put into the presentation. Maintaining a reserved demeanor, we said we would take the proposal back to the Committee and get back to them. Years later, we were told by John that after Kelly and I left the meeting, they were perplexed over whether they had succeeded in winning us over. They said they could not "read" us.

If only they had seen Kelly and me as the elevator doors closed, they would have had their answer. We pumped our fists in the air and let out a whoop! We were ecstatic with the entire concept. It was exactly the type of partnership we were always looking for, and we couldn't wait to return to D.C. with the news. In the interim, John and his staff had to sit back patiently, not knowing whether they had succeeded.

At the following CSAC meeting, I presented the concept to the members. A number of them were very reluctant to embark on such a "commercial" venture, as they described it. They thought it was going too far down the commercial road. But the postal staff conveyed their strong wishes to make such a collaboration happen. It was at that point that the members turned to both Karl Malden and Jean Firstenberg, the two film industry representatives, for their opinions.

Karl thought it was a wonderful idea and strongly supported it. Jean asked to borrow the presentation book Disney had made for us. She wanted to study it overnight. Upon returning to the meeting the following morning, she gave her assessment, saying that she thought it was one of the most brilliant presentations she had ever seen. A more emphatic endorsement wasn't possible. But she did strongly caution that "Disney is notorious for being the most difficult studio to negotiate with." She wished me luck, laced with a note of skepticism about our chances of pulling off such a project.

To say that I was elated would be an understatement. But Jean's warning gave me cause for concern. Would I be able to pull it off? Or would I be "used and abused" in their efforts to promote their properties and products on stamps? I was still bearing the scars of my five-year relationship with Warner Bros. Only time would tell.

I waited until the week after the CSAC meeting before I called John to give him the results of the Committee deliberations. But I didn't give him the good news right away. I merely said that we needed to discuss it further. The ensuing weeks before our return to the Disney Studios were filled with anticipation and apprehension for Disney as we didn't know whether the project was a go or no-go.

Much to John's relief, our next meeting in L.A. was a good one. We informed them of the CSAC's interest, but the Committee wanted reassurances about the scope of the project. John agreed to provide more information. Three months later, I shared that information with the CSAC, which made them more comfortable. They did have additional questions, which I then shared with John, and all concerns were addressed to everyone's satisfaction. We received a green light to begin the project.

But I had forgotten one equation in the project: Azeez.

While Azeez was a creative thinker, if someone came up with an idea and he wasn't in a position to take immediate credit for it, he resisted the idea. The Disney project is a case in point. He was preoccupied with other matters and never intervened in the first set of meetings with Disney, unlike his involvement with Warner Bros.

So, when the Disney project was presented and accepted by the CSAC, Azeez felt that he had lost control. But, being Azeez, he found a way to derail the project, even though it was only temporary.

He expressed shock and concern that we were negotiating with Disney, "the same group that was so difficult to work with on the Snow White stamp," to use his words. Despite being assured that this was a new era and staff, he expressed strong reservations as to whether we should be pursuing this project.

I believe that one of the underlying reasons for Azeez's reluctance was that he was still riding a high from his five-year collaboration with Warner Bros. on the Looney Tunes stamps. He saw that we were now collaborating with a rival studio on another animation project. And, because he had not been involved in the initial meetings, he couldn't take the credit for it. So, he had to find a way to stop it or change it to make it "his" project.

He met privately with the new Postmaster General, Jack Potter, and shared his concerns about the project. He convinced Potter that the project wasn't adequately thought through and that we needed to pull it—even though all four illustrations had been completed and approved by the CSAC and were being prepared for production and issuance the following year. He planted the seed in Potter's mind that Mickey Mouse was passé, and the only reason Disney wanted to do the stamps was to get Mickey back in front of the public. For whatever reason, Potter agreed and added that his children were Disney fans, and maybe we should do some of his kids' favorites like Dumbo and Peter Pan. With that endorsement, Azeez derailed the entire project overnight.

John Gong was as stunned as I was when I shared the news with him. I asked that we get together to try to salvage the project. I flew to California the following week with other staff members for a brainstorming session with John and his staff.

Thanks to the creativity of the Disney staff, we were able to reshape the entire project and expand on it at the same time. So, in reality, Azeez did us a favor by derailing the project. Disney had said from the outset that they were only interested in the one set of four stamps, nothing more. So this change in direction opened the door to a much bigger selection of Disney characters, creating a win-win situation for both parties. But it meant a delay in the first stamp issuance. The Disney and Postal staffs worked hard to develop the first set, entitled Friendship. Mickey still played a prominent role in each set of stamps, and the basic thematic approach to the subsequent stamp sets maintained the same message. The other three designs in each set utilized other classic Disney characters.

What began as a one-time issuance of four stamps eventually developed into a five-year run of twenty stamps commemorating the top ten Disney films, just as I had hoped for back in 1997 when we were limited to the lone Snow White image. It's amazing how things sometimes work out in the end.

And, oh, as for that very difficult corporation to work with, they turned out to be the most delightful group I worked with in all my years in Stamp Services. To this day, I count John and his staff as good friends. I only wish our other partnerships were as productive, creative, and pleasant as the Disney connection.

Based on the successes of the five years of Disney stamps, our group returned to Disney again as the final set of stamps called Imagination was being prepared for print. Over the years, we had discussed developing a set of Disney Villains, but that subject only came to pass seven years after my retirement. In the interim, discussions led to pursuing films from Pixar, one of the properties that Disney controlled.

After discussing the feasibility of such a series with John Gong, I returned to D.C. and proposed it to the CSAC. Considering the age of some of the members, it wasn't surprising to hear one of them say they had never heard of Pixar. But Jean Firstenberg again came to the rescue and strongly supported it, offering to also enlist the support of John Lasseter, the creative genius at Pixar. She placed a call to Lasseter and gained his support. It was off to Hollywood again for our first meeting with John's group on the project.

As with the Art of Disney stamps, the Pixar stamps were a delight to develop. Because the artwork was CGI, or digital, in nature, we didn't have the luxury of creating all-new imagery as we had on the previous project. Nonetheless, the resulting two stamp sets were equally delightful and a success.

The subject matter for the second set of Pixar stamps, called Send a Smile, had been selected and the art was in initial design development when I retired. Bill Gicker oversaw the completion of the stamps from the Postal Service side. All in all, the nine years of collaboration with the Disney group was the highlight of my career in Stamps.

Two other Hollywood-based partnerships bear mentioning. The first occurred in 2001 when we attempted to collaborate with the Jim Henson group on a set of stamps featuring the Muppets. I say "attempt" because we were eventually unable to find a solution on how to feature the Muppets on stamps.

We had both been looking at stamps promoting the environment as a teaching tool for children, but despite a number of hilarious and creative think-tank sessions with the Henson group at their studios, we couldn't make it work. We agreed to abandon the project after almost a year of searching for a good solution.

It was very frustrating, but at the same time, an absolute delight working with the Henson group, who would ultimately be acquired by Disney. The Henson group was, and is, housed in the old original Charlie Chaplin studio on La Brea Avenue in Los Angeles. As if the ornate Tudor-style buildings weren't distinctive enough, we couldn't miss it because the Henson group had affixed to the peak of the main building a large sculpture of the bright-green Kermit. Being the film buff that I am, it was an additional treat to be given a tour of the lot where Chaplin created many of his masterpieces, including his offices, which served as his home on the lot.

The other Hollywood connection was with the Academy of Motion Pictures. Since the very first telecast of the Academy Awards in 1954, I had never missed watching the show. As a film buff, meeting and collaborating with members of the Academy was a unique and special experience for me.

At the time of this collaboration, which began in the late 1990s, Karl Malden was an active member of the CSAC and a past president of the Academy, not to mention an Oscar-winning actor. Karl was obviously a big supporter of the Legends of Hollywood series, but he felt the rest of the film community needed recognition as much as the actors. He suggested to the Committee that they consider another set of stamps to alternate annually with the Legends series. His initial proposal was to honor a specific film, such as *Gone with the Wind*, by honoring the director, cinematographer, producer, composer, etc. While the members thought it was a worthy subject, they felt it might be too many Hollywood-based stamps every year. Karl was asked to rethink his suggestion. Over the next two or three years, he and Ethel Kessler, the art director assigned to the project, attempted to find a workable solution to the problem. Would it work to highlight the top ten films of all time? By whose choice? Or the top ten musicals? Again, whose decision? After much discussion, it was decided to issue one set of stamps honoring the chief disciplines involved in filmmaking. The result was The Art of Filmmaking: Behind the Scenes, issued in 2003.

Karl facilitated a number of meetings at the Academy headquarters with Executive Director Bruce Davis, Academy President Rick Robertson, and other staff members. Academy executives eagerly endorsed the concept and offered whatever support we required to make the stamps happen. Their only request was that it be issued on the Academy's seventy-fifth anniversary in 2003. As expected, they asked that we somehow reference their anniversary on the stamp pane. CSAC guidelines forbid commemoration of events other than in fifty-year increments, preventing us from honoring the request. But we did agree to issue the stamps during that year.

The Academy opened the doors of their archives at the Margaret Herrick Library, a beautifully restored, abandoned waterworks building on La Cienega Boulevard which Karl Malden had been instrumental in developing. Over the next year or so, Ethel worked with Kyle Cooper and his design team at Imaginary Forces to develop the designs. Kyle was selected because of his involvement with the film industry as the leading film title designer, following in the footsteps of the genius (and my idol and mentor) Saul Bass. At the time of the stamp project, Kyle was just completing work on the design and look of the annual Oscar telecast, so he and his work were familiar to the Academy.

The Postal Service pays designers, illustrators, and photographers a flat fee of $5,000 per stamp design. Kyle would be no exception. The final set of ten stamps netted him a whopping $50,000. Unfortunately, for Kyle, which was a drop in the bucket given what he put into the project, having delivered numerous elaborate presentations over the year, each of which would cost any other client $50,000 each. But Kyle never said a word. He merely proceeded to produce ten unique, innovative designs honoring directors, producers, makeup artists, composers, and six other roles in the film industry. To this day, these are among my favorite designs—not just for their design excellence but for the subject matter as well. The working relationship with the Academy was another of the great partnerships I enjoyed during my years in Stamps.

The Television Industry

As the fifth and final set of The Art of Disney stamps was being readied for release, our marketing division encouraged us to pursue a partnership with Fox Studios on *The Simpsons* TV show. There was much heated discussion at a few CSAC meetings about the proposal. Many members were against it initially, but after further discussion with the marketing group, they agreed to pursue it.

Having enjoyed seven wonderfully creative years working with the Disney team, I wasn't ready for what awaited me with the Fox partnership. It was obvious from the start that, unlike Disney, we were not dealing with a creative team but instead a team of aggressive marketing specialists who weren't afraid to throw their weight around, confident of the fact that their property (*The Simpsons*) gave them a strong position from which to control things.

Jean Firstenberg had offered to facilitate a conversation with the TV series' creative director, James Brooks, the Oscar-winning director. Jean gave me his phone number and encouraged us to talk about the direction of the stamp project. After numerous voicemail messages, I finally received a message from him to call him in the morning, which I did.

Unfortunately, at the time of our call, Hollywood was in turmoil because of a writers' strike in the offing. Brooks was, at the time of my call, in his car on his way to the picket site, so our conversation was occasionally interrupted by driving distractions. Nonetheless, Mr. Brooks expressed great enthusiasm for the project and offered to lend his total support to it. To him, in his words, it was a great honor to receive recognition on stamps.

But that was not to be the case. The Fox marketing group let us know that they were in charge and that "creatives" such as Mr. Brooks would be consulted, but that was for them to do, not us. At our first meeting at Fox Studios, the Postal staff was heavily outnumbered by about three to one. And, rather than negotiating terms, they laid down the rules and said, in effect, that they were in charge. They presented their ideas on how the stamps should look, though we did push back, saying we would explore a number of options. We asked if Matt Groening, creator of *The Simpsons*, would be drawing the stamps. We were assured that would not be happening. It became apparent that Mr. Groening was treated like a mogul who the staff groveled in front of. As for "consulting the creatives," no further contact was made with Jim Brooks.

The stamp development process was long and slow, not to mention frustrating. It would take months to get anything out of the Fox group, and when we did, it was unsatisfactory. Derry Noyes, who had accompanied us to the initial meeting, was very frustrated as well. She had expressed interest in being the designer, but as the process became increasingly exasperating, she wished she hadn't gotten involved.

Eventually, an agreement was reached on the stamp designs, comprised of simple portraits of the five main characters from the show with solid color backgrounds behind them. It was a great deal of effort and frustration for what eventually led to a simple, straightforward solution. The only good thing to come out of the entire process, from my standpoint, was my meeting with Matt Groening.

It was after the stamps were completed but prior to the first-day event on the Fox Studios lot that I was asked by Fox to participate in a joint, short PR film interview with Matt Groening about the stamps. I readily accepted the invitation and flew to L.A. for the filming.

The day of filming came, and I arrived at the Fox marketing offices waiting to be escorted to the sound stage for the shoot. If I hadn't known better, I would have thought the Fox staff was awaiting the arrival of the President of the United States or even Jesus Christ. Everyone was anxious, overdressed in fancy suits, and nervous. Certainly not because of me. Matt Groening was coming! I was simply amazed (and amused) at how much sway Matt held over these people. Yes, he was the creator of the most successful animated TV series in history and the creator of a number of other hits shows, but you would have thought he was the Queen of Hearts from *Alice in Wonderland*, walking around yelling, "Off with their heads!"

Nothing could be further from the truth. In walks Matt in casual clothes and the most casual demeanor. He knew that he had control, and everyone was at his disposal, and he loved it. He spent a lot of time making casual digs at the staff, putting them down for their nervous attitudes. He was not into the pomp and ceremony they wanted to lavish on him. He loved having a good time, and as a result, I had a good time as well. We spent the entire time joking around. While perched on two tall directors' folding chairs for the interview, we kibitzed our way through the interview.

After shooting was over, Matt sat down to draw a few of the Simpson's characters as a small gift for me and Bill Gicker, who accompanied me on the trip. Matt professed that he had not drawn Homer, Bart, and the rest of the cast for years. He was out of practice and said that if he were to do a blind audition to draw the characters for the show, he would have failed. But he made the effort and produced a couple of drawings for us, which he signed. Bill received a special one wishing him a happy birthday for his upcoming birthday. Interestingly, when Matt would start a drawing and make a mistake, he would push the sheet aside and start another drawing. Immediately, one of the Fox marketing minions would grab the art and tear it up, fearful that a Matt Groening "original" might fall into the wrong hands. Ah, the price of fame!

The stamps were eventually released in 2009 with a lot of fanfare at the Fox Studios lot complete with cast members who voiced the characters among other celebrities.

Among the great experiences I had during my twenty years in developing stamps were the opportunities afforded me to experience firsthand the world of entertainment in its many forms. Thinking back on my weekly visits as a child to my hometown movie theaters, I now realize how fortunate I was to have the opportunity to be a part of such a creative world.

Chapter 5
Design Challenges

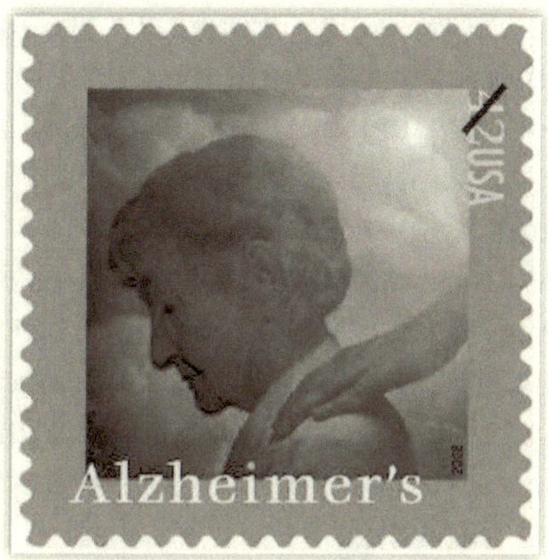

Once the numerous challenges of having to deal with powerful influences, concerns, and wishes from assorted parties such as Congress, the Board of Governors, and the Postmaster General are addressed, the design process can begin. But designing a stamp can present its own set of challenges. I enjoyed the design challenges far more than the politically charged challenges. I think that is one of the most unique and creatively satisfying aspects of being a graphic designer. There is an old "insider" joke often cited by graphic designers that "even our mothers don't understand what we do." Graphic design is, simply put, problem-solving utilizing visuals. The challenge of any graphic designer is to convey a message in the simplest, most effective, and most attractive manner. This applies to stamp design as well. But some challenges presented to stamp designers are unique to that very small rectangular product, which can have a very large impact.

Making the Right Choice

Once a stamp subject is approved, the target audience identified, and the art director assigned to the project, a critical design decision must be made. Which illustrator, photographer, or designer should be asked to create this miniature work of art? This decision initially rests with the art director, who must formulate a concept of what they want to convey on the stamp. Once the AD identifies the potential artist for the project, their name was shared with me for my concurrence.

Unlike some foreign postal administrations, such as Royal Mail in London, which develop design concepts from multiple sources, rarely did we use more than one artist to develop a concept, due in part to budget constraints and the number of annual issuances. But in a few instances, specifically Elvis Presley and Marilyn Monroe, we broke that rule and commissioned numerous artists to develop concepts for our review. Howard Paine was assigned to create the Elvis stamp. Knowing that Elvis would be a blockbuster stamp, we wanted to make sure that we got just the right image. We could have taken the easy road and purchased any of thousands of existing images of the King of Rock and Roll, but we wanted to create our own iconic image of the King.

Howard and I had numerous conversations regarding our choices of artists. Elvis wasn't the only music icon Howard was assigned to commemorate I had put him in charge of developing the look and feel of the entire Legends of American Music series. Kicking off with the issuance of Elvis, this series would continue for seven years totaling seventy-eight stamps representing fourteen genres of music. We agreed that each music category should have its own illustrator. Selecting an illustrator whose style was best suited to the music genre was challenging, but Howard and I enjoyed reviewing portfolios in our search.

In the case of Elvis, however, we took it a step further and asked nine different illustrators and designers to develop concepts. We gave them the freedom of interpreting Elvis in their own way, whether it be the young, hip-shaking rocker of the 1950s or the sequined, white jumpsuit-wearing Las Vegas crooner of the 1970s.

The results were unique and varied, as we expected. A number of the illustrators developed multiple concepts, which resulted in the Committee reviewing twenty-six pieces of art. Some were more polished and finished than others, but all generated much conversation in the CSAC meetings.

As the excitement began to wind down after the release of Elvis, the Committee decided to inaugurate a new series of Legends of Hollywood stamps, the first being Marilyn Monroe. It would appear two years after Elvis in 1995. Once again, because of the iconic stature of Marilyn, the decision was made to ask multiple artists to submit concepts. Carl Herrman was the AD assigned to the stamp and we again had nine artists sending us concepts. The results were equally interesting, but everyone was drawn immediately to the work of Michael Deas. Michael would go on to create several dozen miniature masterpieces for the Postal Service in the years to come.

Sometimes, the selection of the artist is a natural and obvious choice. No question about it. He (or she) is the one!

The obvious choice for the 1997 Star Wars set of fifteen stamps? Drew Struzan. Drew, who had previously illustrated a number of Legends of Hollywood stamps for us, was well known in both the design and film communities for his iconic posters for such series as the Star Wars, Indiana Jones, and Harry Potter films. Though the Star Wars project proved to be more difficult than expected, the end result was unique. Unfortunately, Drew's vision for the stamp set differed from the Postal Service's and Lucasfilms. His concept was to produce the fifteen subjects in a more traditional stamp format, not as a montage as we had proposed. Reluctantly Drew created the set as requested but was never satisfied with the outcome.

Another obvious artist choice, which at the time wasn't quite as obvious to us, was Nick Gaetano, the illustrator of the Ayn Rand stamp commemorated as part of the Literary Art series in 1999. Phil Jordan was assigned as AD on the project, and he began a search for potential illustrators. He and I were on a trip to Madison, Wisconsin to visit the governor about the upcoming Statehood stamp. While in flight, we picked up a copy of the in-flight magazine. Featured in the magazine was an article about Gaetano and how he had created the covers for recent reprints to Rand's classic novels, *Atlas Shrugged* and *The Fountainhead.* Both Phil and I were very impressed with his style and thought that Nick would be an obvious choice for the stamp portrait. He readily agreed to accept the assignment and went on to create one of the most unique illustrations in the entire series. We were also very fortunate in our selection. As standard practice, upon completion of the art, we share the illustration with the families or estate representatives for approval. In the case of Rand, the estate was elated with it and told us that we had made the right decision to hire Nick. In their words, he was "the only illustrator we would have approved."

Sometimes, though, the apparent best choice doesn't work out the way we thought. Case in point: the Family Unity stamp of 1984. I was not part of the Stamps group at the time, but working in the Communications department gave me inside access to what was happening in the stamp world.

Postmaster General William Bolger had requested that the Postal Service show children's art on stamps. I was never clear on his reasoning. My only guess is that he thought it would be appealing to the public. That has since proven not to be the case. Children's art, while "cute," does little to increase sales or appeal to the general public. Nonetheless, Bolger made the request, and the Stamps group complied.

Two stamps resulted from a nationwide request for submissions of children's art. The first was the Family Unity stamp, and the second was a Christmas stamp depicting Santa Claus. Both were issued in October 1984 with separate ceremonies, the latter for the annual Holiday stamp issuance and the former extolling the virtues of family unity. The Family Unity theme was agreed upon after the art was chosen by Mr. Bolger. He liked the black-and-white stick figures of Mom and Dad, so characteristic of a small child's innocent interpretation of family. Unfortunately, the real age of the artist was to present a problem.

Bolger had asked that the two winning designers be brought to Washington for the unveiling of the stamps. Danny La Boccotta, an eight-year-old New Yorker who submitted a crayon drawing of Santa Claus, was delighted to receive national recognition at the media event. But Mr. Bolger was stunned when he was introduced prior to the press conference to Molly LaRue, the illustrator of the Family Unity image. As we had all assumed (incorrectly, as we would find out), the art was not created by a small child. Instead, it was cunningly created by this seventeen-year-old high school student who knew she had a better chance of winning with a simplified drawing. Bolger was very upset, feeling he was misled as he was not informed of the situation. None of the staff had ever thought to question Molly as to her age. Lesson learned!

Tackling Difficult Subjects

Choosing the appropriate illustrator or designer for a stamp project is, in many instances, one of the easiest parts of the process. Finding a solution to the design problem is a more daunting task. This is especially true with what we termed the "social awareness" stamps. How do you depict in such a small space the complexities of breast cancer, family violence, prostate cancer, hospice care, or diabetes? To make it even more difficult, the solution must be attractive and appealing so the purchaser will want to buy it and affix it to an envelope. The task of the stamp illustrator is to find a new and unique way of conveying the message.

The earliest of the social awareness stamps was the 1957 Religious Freedom in America stamp. It was soon followed by a set of three environmentally-centered subjects urging Forest, Soil, and Water Conservation in 1958, 1959, and 1960, respectively. Over the next two decades, an additional eighteen stamps were issued commemorating such worthy causes as Employ the Handicapped (1960), Register to Vote (1964 and 1968), Humane Treatment of Animals (1966), Giving Blood Saves Lives (1971), Prevent Drug Abuse (1971), and Family Planning (1972), a controversial subject that some religious groups protested.

In 1981, a watershed low point in social awareness stamps was achieved with the issuance of a typographic-designed stamp proclaiming: "Alcoholism. You can beat it!" While the subject was indeed worthy, the message was misconstrued, resulting in it being forever labeled as one of the worst designs ever issued. It seems that when the stamp was affixed, innocently, to an envelope by the sender, the receiver often felt it implied they were an alcoholic. Needless to say, the stamp went largely unused. As one can imagine, even the wording on stamps is critical to their success.

Dealing with the incredibly small canvas of 1" x 1.5," that all stamp designers are faced with can prove to be a detriment, but one that never seems to be insurmountable. This challenge is especially great with a subject such as the classic, mammoth Thanksgiving Day Parade, a subject that began development in 2009. How do you convey the scope of this enormously long, multifaceted parade, complete with floats, marching bands, and giant hot air balloons, on a postage stamp? You don't. You instead spread it over four horizontal stamps.

Returning for a moment to the typographic pitfalls of stamp design as noted in the Alcoholism stamp, even a stamp's denomination can prove to be a problem. It is a continual challenge for the designer to locate the obligatory denomination somewhere in the design, making it easily recognizable without dominating the design.

But, despite the pressures of solving the placement and size of the denomination, in one instance, even the very number became a problem.

In 1992, the USPS began a twelve-year series of Lunar New Year stamps in an effort to be more culturally inclusive. It had been noted that very few stamps had been issued before then honoring Asian-Americans or their cultural contributions to America. Ironically, the fastest-growing segment of the international stamp community was in Asia. With that in mind, a very successful series was developed. Dick Sheaff art directed the original concept working in tandem with Clarence Lee, a prominent Asian-American designer from Honolulu. In the subsequent years, I assumed the role of art director for the series.

As the series was drawing to a close, management wanted to explore how to keep it alive due to the success it had achieved. Collectively, it was decided that we would reissue all twelve designs as a set on a decorative pane of stamps in 2005. Because stamp prices had increased incrementally between 1992 and 2004 from twenty-nine to thirty-seven cents, we decided we would issue the complete set with the current denomination of thirty-seven cents each. The full pane of twelve stamps would thus be sold for $4.44.

During discussions in internal planning meetings, PhotoAssist, in their role as fact-checkers and verifiers, brought to our attention a "slight" problem. It seems that in the Asian culture, the number four is considered bad luck and signifies death. So, with a denomination of $4.44, we were, in effect, saying, "Die! Die! Die!" Hardly the statement we wanted to convey to our Asian customers. Back to the drawing board! We explored charging a rate other than first-class, but we didn't want to be perceived as gouging the purchaser. After much discussion with management and the printer, the suggestion was made to try something new and innovative: a double-sided pane. Printing the same stamps on both sides of a pane of stamps would double not only the number of stamps but the total cost as well. Now the pane would sell for $8.88—and eight just happens to be a good luck number. Problem solved; disastrous PR nightmare avoided.

Changing the Art

Virtually every piece of stamp art undergoes revisions of one sort or another. But occasionally, a particular stamp is subjected to major revisions if not a total redo of the art. This occurs more often in portraiture. The families or estates of the honoree have rights of approval on the design. One thing I discovered in my many years of stamp design is that families bring to the table their own personal ideas of what the stamp should look like. This mindset made my job harder because we approached the art from a different perspective than the family. The resulting clash of concepts could only complicate rights negotiations.

Over the years, we had to do several revisions of portraits for the likes of pioneering nurse Mary Breckinridge (1998), novelist Edna Ferber (2002), and film legends Edward G. Robinson (2000), Judy Garland (2006), and Gregory Peck (2011) to mention only a few. Many of these I will discuss in more detail in another chapter while addressing the one-on-one negotiations with family members, all of which proved simultaneously fascinating, rewarding, and frustrating.

National events play a role in the revamping of art. I previously mentioned the World War II stamp commemorating the dropping of the atomic bomb on Hiroshima and the resulting protests, necessitating a completely different design. But the horrific events of September 11, 2001, also necessitated a change in design. At the time of the attack on the World Trade Center in NYC, we were finalizing a set of fifty stamps entitled Greetings from America. Each of the fifty designs represented the states in the style of the 1930s linen postal cards commonly known as the "Greetings from…" series. The design for the state of New York featured as one of its elements the skyline of New York City. Unfortunately, displayed prominently in the design were the Twin Towers that were destroyed in the 9/11 attack. Again, the ever-alert PhotoAssist team brought this to my attention, prompting a reworking of the art. Because this set of stamps was so complex and had taken so long to develop, a small element such as this could easily have been overlooked until the last minute, or even printed, which would have been disastrous.

Living People on Stamps

For many years, there has been an ongoing discussion about living people on stamps. According to a federal regulation (U.S. Code

5114), the depiction of living people on U.S. securities, meaning money and postage stamps, is forbidden. One past member of the CSAC (also a leading philatelist), John Hotchner, made it his mission to continually point out to the public that the Postal Service continues to violate this regulation. Internally, the Postal Service always figuratively nodded its head, acknowledging John's protestations, but we chose not to do anything about it. We had clarified the position with our legal team and felt we were not violating any regulations.

The key word in the regulation is that no living person shall be "honored" on U.S. securities. The Postal Service has taken great pains to adhere to the "honoring" aspect. In fact, for many years, there was a rule instituted by the CSAC that an individual had to be deceased ten years before being considered for commemoration on a stamp. In 2007, the Committee altered the rule to change the length of time to five years in an attempt to make the program more contemporary.

A few years after I retired from Stamps, the new management decided to drop the five-year rule, allowing living people to be commemorated on stamps. It was publicly announced with the approval of PMG Patrick Donahue. They even solicited online ideas for stamp subjects of current figures from the public. The person receiving the most votes was Lady Gaga, the outrageously costumed popular singer. But before any living person could find their way into print, the Postal Board of Governors got wind of the idea and nixed the entire concept, reinstating the five-year rule. Then management quietly allowed the five-year rule to lapse. Now individuals can, and are, honored as early as one year after their passing.

Regardless, John has continued his mission to keep the public abreast of the most recent violations of the regulation. For example, John's position is that even if the subject matter, such as Alzheimer's Awareness, depicts a woman lost in her past, the woman who modeled for the illustrator is still alive, and hence, constituted another violation of the regs. I have always found that almost laughable, but I must credit John for being persistent if nothing else.

But I have a confession to make. There have been a few times when the illustrator has pulled one over on us. That has occurred when it's been discovered, after the fact, that the illustrator had painted himself into the picture, much like Norman Rockwell used to do. Two such stamps come to mind.

In 1986, Stamps commissioned Thomas Blackshear to illustrate a portrait of Jean Baptiste Point du Sable, an African-American pioneer credited with establishing what was to become the city of Chicago. The stamp would become the next in the very popular Black Heritage series. It was Thomas' very first stamp commission and, once completed, we realized we had a very talented young man whose talent we wanted to utilize again, which we did.

Because stamp commissions were handled through mail and phone discussions, no one knew what Thomas looked like. This was in the early days of computers, so there were few websites promoting artists, let alone Facebook and the likes of what we are used to today. It wasn't until 1991, after I had joined the Stamps team, that we first saw a photo of Thomas. I had been tasked with developing a book to house the Black Heritage stamps issued to date, and I commissioned Thomas to create all-new portraits of past stamp subjects in the series. I asked him to send a personal photo for inclusion in the credits, which he did. When I received it, it struck me that he looked familiar. It took a few weeks until I happened across the Du Sable stamp image, and it hit me. Thomas, who was African-American, had painted a self-portrait of himself as Du Sable. When asked if this was indeed the case, he confessed that it was true. His explanation was that there were no images of likenesses of Du Sable, so he used himself as a model. He admitted he was unaware of this continuing controversy about living people on stamps. We both agreed to keep that little secret just among ourselves, which we did for many years.

A mere two years after the Du Sable stamp, another artist did the same thing. In this case, it was the Letter Carriers: We Deliver! issuance of 1989. Jack Williams and Joe Brockert of the Stamp Design group at the time had commissioned the famed *Mad Magazine* cartoonist Jack Davis to develop an illustration depicting three U.S. Postal Service letter carriers. After the stamp was printed and I had access to the image to create the lobby poster promoting its issuance, I couldn't help but notice the striking resemblance between Jack Davis and the middle-aged letter carrier on the left. I pointed this out to Jack and Joe. When Jack Davis was asked, he "fessed up," saying he thought it was a neat idea and didn't think anyone would object. It was too late to change the design, but in retrospect, I don't think it really mattered. Very few people noticed the resemblance.

Fast-forward seven years and our solutions to these visual problems had changed dramatically. In 2007, we issued a pane of fifteen stamps honoring *Star Wars*, still the most popular science-fiction movie series ever. Once again, we faced the dilemma of how to depict these great characters, so beloved by the public, without specifically identifying the actors. We chose to take the stance that we were honoring the characters of the film, not the actors. Of course, there was vehement dissent from John Hotchner, who was serving on the CSAC at the time. Cooler heads prevailed, though, and the series proceeded. The set met with good success.

The Russians had Nothing on Us

When the USSR wanted to remove someone from their ranks, they did it ever so discreetly. And then, almost comically, they sought to erase any trace of their existence. Previously published photos depicting an array of officials at major events were commonly altered. In a very crude retouching style, the poor soul who was now an "unmentionable" was sliced from the photo and the other individuals were moved to fill in the blank space. To the Western world, it was laughable, but to the Soviets, it was serious business.

In the same way, the USPS was occasionally accused of using the same method. In their case, though, no "unmentionable" individuals were removed—only offending objects, primarily cigarettes. Not wanting to be seen as endorsing this habit, the Postal Service had an unwritten policy of not depicting smoking on stamps. Gone were the days of the suave Paul Henreid lighting two cigarettes at the same time and smoothly handing one to Bette Davis. So cool in the 1940s, but no longer.

When we were honoring the great blues legend Robert Johnson in 1994 in the Jazz Singers/Blues Singers category of the Legends of American Music series, we were caught in a dilemma. It seems that there were few photographs of Johnson. The most famous and best images depicted him with a cigarette dangling from his lips, almost as if it were about to fall into his lap. We instructed the illustrator, Julian Allen, to eliminate the cigarette.

Upon the image's release, many Johnson fans noticed the missing cigarette and made their displeasure known. The media got wind of the controversy and, before we knew it, the Postal Service was accused of altering images. Yes, we did alter them, but for a good reason. But that didn't matter to the purists. They felt it was heresy.

Not only were we vilified in the media; we received numerous letters of complaint, not to mention phone calls. One such call I vividly remember was from a woman who wanted to vehemently complain about the omission. It wasn't that she was necessarily a Robert Johnson fan or even a blues fan. It seemed she was a fan of cigarette smoking. This became obvious as she lit into me about how awful it was to not show him smoking. As she grew more indignant, her voice grew louder, only to be interlaced with distinct hacking. Having grown up in a house of smokers, I recognized that cough immediately. She sounded just like my mother, who always insisted that her cough was due to allergies. I guess both my mother and this irate complainer suffered from the same allergies! No explanation was going to change her mind. She insisted that we needed to reprint the stamp with the cigarette. I reassured her that wouldn't happen, and I closed by saying that she might want to take care of that cough. With great indignation, she replied, "I have allergies." With that, she slammed down the phone. Case closed!

The curious case of the missing cigarette resurfaced five years later as part of the Celebrate the Century series. The 1940s set included the commemoration of the radical change in the art world courtesy of Jackson Pollock. As with Robert Johnson, we chose a seminal image of Pollock. It depicted him crouched on the floor on top of his canvas, drizzling paint with a cigarette dangling from his mouth. Again, we deleted the cigarette when Julian created the illustration. The newspapers were more outspoken than the public that time around.

Nine years passed before the cigarette issue again became a topic of controversy. This time it was over the Bette Davis stamp, the fourteenth honoree in the ever-popular Legends of Hollywood series. Michael Deas created yet another masterful portrait of the great actress. He chose to depict her clutching her gloved right hand while wearing a fur coat. Internally, we questioned whether we should depict her in fur. The last thing we needed was protests from PETA, the animal rights group. But cooler heads prevailed, and we asked Michael to complete the art as shown in the original source photograph.

When the image was unveiled, we received inquiries from *Linn's Stamp News* and other media sources regarding the missing cigarette. This time we were prepared. There was no cigarette in the photo. Yes, the positioning of her hand gave the appearance that we had removed a cigarette from it. Ms. Davis was known to be a smoker, so it was only natural to assume that the Postal Service had done it again. We were very pleased to correct the misconception to anyone who asked. The questions and doubt subsided.

I had the privilege of representing the Postal Service at the Bette Davis first-day-of-issue ceremony in Boston later that year. While waiting for the ceremony to begin, Davis family members and friends, who included another great actress, Lauren Bacall, all gathered for photos and refreshments. While conversing with family members, I mentioned the cigarette issue and lightly laughed off the notion of us removing the cigarette. One of the family members then dropped the bombshell. It seems that the original photo did include a cigarette, but at some point, years after the photo was taken, someone chose to airbrush the cigarette out. It was a reproduction print of the retouched photo that was in general circulation and the one we chose to work from. We chose not to mention this or try to correct it in the media. But at least this time it wasn't the Postal Service pulling the old Soviet elimination trick.

Hiding in Plain Sight

As if the diminutive size of a postage stamp isn't difficult enough for a stamp designer or illustrator to work within, adding elements to the design can be problematic, especially when they are not supposed to be there. Two such instances come to mind immediately.

In 1986, three years before my move to the Stamps department, a controversy arose surrounding the definitive stamp honoring Bernard Revel, a noted rabbi. The stamp was a single-color engraved image to be issued as part of the Distinguished American series that ran from 1986 to 2009. Normally, stamps such as this one was issued with little or no fanfare. While the subjects in this series were certainly worthy of commemorative treatment, the stamps were all issued in rates other than the first-class letter rate.

What caused the controversy was not the fact that we were

commemorating a religious figure (which normally brings out the atheists and "separation of church and state" proponents), but a little something hidden in the beard in the engraved design. It seems that a Bureau of Engraving engraver took the liberty of hiding within Mr. Revel's beard the Jewish Star of David. The engraver, who was Jewish, felt compelled to add it on a whim and in jest, not intending any harm. The philatelic community was fascinated with this hidden image, but Postal management was less than amused. The engraver was chastised for his actions but not fired.

A 1991 Summer Olympics issuance never received the media attention that it could have due in part to our not knowing what was hidden in the five-stamps until a few years later.

The Postal marketing group came to the CSAC with a promotional tie-in proposal following the announcement that the USPS was selected as an official sponsor of the 1992 Summer Games. They proposed issuing five stamps in 1991 as advance promotion of the Games. They recommended utilizing the talents of the official Olympic artist, recently hired by NBC, which won the contract to air the Summer Games.

CSAC members, postal staff, and the art directors were all shown the work of the illustrator, Joni Carter of Los Angeles, and no one was very impressed with the quality of her work. The Committee members accepted the idea of producing the stamps but were reluctant to commission Carter. The marketing group applied pressure, and the Committee reluctantly agreed. In retrospect, the Committee was correct in their reluctance to accept her work.

Computer illustration was a relatively new medium in the early 1990s. Joni Carter, an admittedly self-taught illustrator, saw the opportunity to promote herself, somehow convincing NBC officials they should hire her and, as a bonus, promote this new artistic medium. They fell for her proposal hook, line, and sinker. Maybe it was the "cheesecake" photo of her perched atop her computer table next to the monitor with her cowl-neck sweater revealingly pulled down, exposing her right shoulder. I believe her real talent was in promoting herself, not her limited illustration abilities.

As one can imagine, the final designs were poorly executed. They were garish in color, but even more evident was the lack of ability to render the human figure. They were all awkward and stilted. We sent the artwork back numerous times for revisions, hoping they would be closer to our standards. Eventually, we ran out of time. Because of the time crunch and regardless of the inherent illustration flaws, the marketing group pushed the CSAC to approve the designs to meet their promotional timetable, which the CSAC felt compelled to do. While the stamps proved to be popular with collectors, it was primarily due to the Olympic connection, not the designs. The CSAC was less than enthusiastic with the finished product.

Ironically, it wasn't until a few years later that we discovered the hidden images in the stamps. I received a letter from Carter asking for another stamp commission because, in her words, "the first set was so wildly popular." She encouraged me to check out her updated website to see her latest work. I did in deference to her request but mainly out of curiosity—certainly not because I wanted to work with her again. Developing the first set of stamps proved to be very difficult and frustrating. She had balked at making any changes and expressed indignation that we would even question her judgment.

Whether it was out of naivety or simply that she forgot what she had posted on her website, it was there that I discovered the trick she had played on the Postal Service. She blatantly stated that the Postal Service was very difficult to work with, and out of her frustration, she decided to show those bureaucrats a thing or two. She was very proud of the fact that she pulled one over on us, which she certainly did. She hid her name in a few of the stamps, writing it very small, backward, and upside down in the figures. I will admit that she did hide them very well. We certainly never saw them. She even showed the hidden signatures in close-up on her site.

Unfortunately, it is a U.S. federal regulation that designers of currency and postage stamps are prohibited from signing their work. Clearly, Ms. Joni Carter had violated that regulation. To make matters worse, she was displaying the stamps carrying her own copyright. Her contract explicitly stated that the images became the property of the USPS with all rights assigned to them.

It was with great delight that we had the final word. I shared the hidden image and copyright information with our Law department who wrote a stern letter to Carter demanding that she pull those images from her website and stop attributing the copyright to her name. They eventually received word from her agent that they would comply. I think it is safe to say that we never considered using the "talents" of Ms. Carter again.

At the very same time, Carter was hiding her name in the Olympic stamps, the Postal Service was discussing another "hidden" name in stamps. The Postal Service had contracted with famed caricaturist Al Hirschfeld to create a series of portraits of famous entertainers. A total of two dozen images were developed by Hirschfeld under the art direction of Howard Paine. From those numerous images, five were selected to be issued as Comedians stamps, slated for release in 1991, the same year as the infamous Olympic stamps.

Anyone familiar with Hirschfeld's work knows of his clever insertion of his daughter's name, Nina, in the caricature. Initially, the Postal Service had instructed Hirschfeld he would not be allowed to incorporate the "Ninas" into his designs because of the federal regulation. But cooler heads prevailed. Or should I say a cooler Postmaster General's head prevailed? PMG Anthony Frank reviewed the five Comedians designs before their release to the printer and immediately questioned where the "Nina" was. When informed that it wasn't there, his response was, "Well, it should be!" Following a discussion regarding the regulation, Frank said that the "Nina" would not constitute an artist's signature. It didn't say Hirschfeld, so it was OK with him.

Howard Paine rushed to New York and sat with Hirschfeld to attempt to incorporate the name into as many of the twenty-four finished illustrations as possible. A few of them Hirschfeld just could not hide. He normally incorporates the name as part of the image as he creates the caricatures. Doing so after the fact would be more difficult, or in a few cases, impossible. The Comedians stamps were issued with the hidden name in four of the five designs and subsequently, in 1994, a second set of Hirschfeld caricatures were issued on the ten Silent Screen Stars stamps. Unlike the Olympic stamps, the Postal Service seized the opportunity to encourage the public to find the hidden Nina's.

Aside from these few instances, both wanted and unwanted, the Postal Service has routinely used a hidden image to help deter counterfeiters. The printers incorporated microprinting in many stamps, primarily in single-design images, which were more prone to being counterfeited. "USPS" or other wording pertaining to the subject matter were routinely hidden by the printer working in conjunction with my staff and me. Despite our efforts to downplay these security features, *Linn's Stamp News* made a regular habit of locating the image, enlarging it, and reproducing it in their magazine. So much for security!

In 1997 and for the next eight years, the Postal Service added a hidden image to a total of forty-two designs, which we labeled Scrambled Indicia. In an effort to make counterfeiting even more difficult, we partnered with a Florida-based firm called Graphic Security Systems to produce these images based on the process they developed. The first designs issued were part of the Classic Movie Monsters stamps of 1997. We included hidden images of bats, howling wolves, lightning bolts, etc., all based on five monsters.

The process required a special decoder (which the Postal Service was most happy to sell you for $4.95), which, when placed over the stamp and turned to a certain angle, the image would "magically" reveal the image. It could not be seen with the naked eye.

Eventually, the gimmick wore thin, and it was dropped. The art directors and I were not disappointed to see it go. It had proved very difficult to achieve the exact colors we wanted because the imagery was hidden within one or more of the color plates, altering the amount of color required to obtain a faithful reproduction.

Getting it right

How difficult can it be to design a stamp? You just make a picture of something and then print it on the stamps, right?

Wrong!

I have repeatedly heard that misconception about the stamp design process from unknowing members of the public. But nothing could be further from the truth. As I've mentioned, when the entire process, complete with its myriad complexities, is described to them, their universal amazed response is: "I had no idea!"

One of the critical elements of that process is, to put it simply, getting it right. After all, stamps are considered to be a U.S. security, just like the currency you carry in your wallet. We're not allowed to make mistakes. We're the government. We should know better. If only that were true! The next chapter will reveal in detail some of the unfortunate mistakes that have been made. But for now, I want to share some of the complexities involved in trying to avoid such mistakes.

The majority of stamps depict historic events and individuals. It is imperative that whatever or whomever we depict, it must be accurate. Unfortunately, in the case of historic events of the eighteenth and nineteenth centuries, it's hard to find two scholars who readily agree on all aspects of events or individuals. Our goal was to reach a consensus on what the majority of experts believe to be the case. Thinking back on those twenty years of stamp development, numerous stamp issuances come to mind.

The Civil War

Is there any subject that elicits, as it has for the past 150 years, as much controversy and subjective analysis as our own Civil War? Yet, in 1993, the Postal Service chose to wade into the complexities of the war.

Twenty stamps honoring the people and battles of the Civil War were to comprise the second issuance of a newly created series of stamps, aimed squarely at stamp collectors, called Classic Collections. Rather than waiting for the 150th anniversary to commemorate this ever-popular war subject, Carl Burcham, the manager of stamp marketing, asked the CSAC to issue this set on the 135th anniversary in 1995.

Making the subject choices would prove difficult, a task that even CSAC members were reluctant to undertake. The Committee was reluctant to face the wrath of hardened, fanatical Civil War buffs. No matter which individuals we chose, we were bound to receive letters complaining and demanding that their favorite general, whether from the North or South, be included.

While the Committee members were willing to share their opinions on which subjects should be honored, they felt it necessary that Civil War historians and experts weigh in initially. Our office contacted three prominent historians: Edwin C. Bearss, former chief historian of the National Park Service, Dr. William J. Cooper, Jr., Professor of History at Louisiana State University, and Dr. James M. McPherson, Professor of American History at Princeton. They were asked to recommend twenty subjects worthy of commemoration. Our only stipulation was that the individuals chosen had to consist of eight Northerners and eight Southerners. We also wanted women and African-Americans included. The remaining four subjects would be important battles.

Upon receiving the three lists, a master list was compiled. At that point, we had more than twenty possible subjects, and none of us, neither the Committee members nor staff, were about to go out on a limb and make the final decision. We all knew that no matter which subjects we chose, we would be subjected to criticism as to why we left out other individuals. It was a thankless task, for which we wisely chose not to be responsible.

After much deliberation, the decision was made to contact yet another expert in the field, Shelby Foote, the very knowledgeable and entertaining historian whose name was very prominent at the time due to Ken Burns' immensely popular PBS documentary series, *The Civil War*. We shared with Mr. Foote and his agent our dilemma and inquired whether he would assume the task of making the final selection. His choices would help defend and deflect any criticism from the legions of Civil War buffs. Shelby knew and understood our dilemma and agreed to take on the task.

Within a month, we received his choices. Most of them were obvious: Lincoln, Grant, Lee, Frederick Douglass, etc. But among his choices were a few that stunned everyone in the office. Who, in God's name, was Stand Watie? And why was the most famous of all battles, Gettysburg, eliminated? I drew the short straw and had the unenviable task of calling Shelby to question his judgment.

Speaking with him was an exciting experience as I've enjoyed listening to his languid Southern drawl on *The Civil War* series. With as much diplomacy as I could muster, I nervously asked him to explain his choices— "just so we can better understand" is how I put it, as I recall. He walked me through all the choices, which made sense once you heard his rationale. But he had included four more individuals than we could feature. After discussing which ones to eliminate, Foote said, "There'll be tears on my pillow tonight if we remove him [Confederate General James Longstreet]." But in the end, he agreed to drop one of his personal favorites.

When we got to Stand Watie, he explained that he was a Native American and the last Confederate officer to surrender. I guess I missed that in the TV series if it was in there at all. But regardless, it was a brilliant addition to the set.

This then brought me to the question of the omission of the Battle of Gettysburg. His thinking was that it was so "overdone" that it didn't need inclusion. Putting on my marketing hat, I countered that its omission would cause much controversy, which is exactly what we were trying to avoid. After much discussion, he agreed to allow Gettysburg to be included.

While the Committee had abdicated their subject selection to outside experts, none felt guilty about it. In fact, they were quite comfortable standing behind the towering judgment of Shelby Foote on this one.

After making changes to the list advised by Foote, we were ready to begin the painstaking process of research and painting, which consumed eighteen months of our time. In retrospect, the subject choices proved to be one of the easier tasks.

Hundreds, if not thousands, of documents and images were collected by our research team at PhotoAssist. Armed with this data, Dick Sheaff was named as art director, and he again recommended using Mark Hess, the talented illustrator from Connecticut who had just completed what was to be the first of the Classic Collection series, the Legends of the West, slated for issuance in 1994.

Keeping in mind that whatever we created in this series was bound to be closely scrutinized by Civil War experts, both professional and amateur, the task of reviewing each piece of art for its accuracy fell to the PhotoAssist research team. Collaborating with leading experts, the team addressed such questions and concerns as: Is this the right amount of buttons on uniforms? Is the smoke blowing in the right direction off the USS Monitor? What were the weather conditions on the day of the battle between the Monitor and Virginia? Were there clouds in the sky that day? If so, how cloudy was it? Why is General Lee's horse, Traveler, rearing up in the background? One expert insisted that Traveler was always very calm and would never have reared up. My initial thought was, *Can anyone verify that a horse 135 years earlier had never reared up in fear or surprise?* No one was going to commit to such a statement, so Traveler was painted rearing up as we originally planned.

Hundreds of such comments, suggestions, and concerns were addressed. It was at this point that my patience was wearing thin, as were my nerves. I soon realized that no two experts would agree on anything. It fell to my office to make the final decision, based on input from all parties, as to what we would do in response to concerns from outside experts. Biting the proverbial bullet (how appropriate in this instance), we collectively made internal decisions to keep the process moving. A final review by the experts passed muster, albeit with a few grumblings, and the art was shipped off to the printers. A collective sigh of relief by all parties was heard throughout the office, not to mention the offices of PhotoAssist, Dick Sheaff, and Mark Hess's studio.

In the end, when the stamps were issued, we received numerous letters and phone calls from "experts" of all kinds, both pro-North and pro-South, who thought we made the wrong decisions and recommended we issue another set to include their choices. But it would be another fifteen years before the Postal Service again recognized the war. But that time, they confined the subjects solely to battles. A souvenir sheet depicting two strategic battles in each of the five years of the war has been issued annually.

In reflection, I believe this one project involved more complex problems than just about any other project before it or since.

Coming off the Legends of the West and Civil War projects, one would have thought we would have balked at the opportunity to tackle yet another massive project. Nope. Between 1995 and 1997, we set out, once again, to create a large series of stamps that entailed a vast amount of research, verification, and differences of opinions from experts, artists, and staff. One underlying question repeatedly surfaced: Is there room for artistic license? Subject experts—not to mention our legal team, who usually cringed at the mere mention of the term "artistic license"—thought so. But others saw it differently. The illustrator assigned to the project, the art director, and I all tried to find a better balance to make a better product.

In 1995, the third Classic Collection, Comic Strip Classics (1995), proved to be much easier to develop. We turned to Mort Walker, the creator of "Beetle Bailey," and the Cartoon Museum to provide a list of subjects. Walker polled all the leading cartoonists, who provided the final twenty choices. They also provided existing artwork.

The fourth Classic Collection issuance was to be the Summer Olympic Games, slated for Atlanta in 1996. The twenty Summer Games subjects were selected based on their popularity and TV demographics. The art, created by Richard Waldrep, was beautiful in its simplicity. But its simplicity belied the amount of research required to create this series.

The fifth Classic Collection issuance in 1997 returned with full force to the complex, mind-numbing, exhausting research and verification of the Civil War stamps. The new set was entitled Classic American Aircraft. Subjects ranging from the Wright Brothers' first flight in the early days of aviation through the two World Wars and commercial aircraft of the recent past.

Again, the CSAC asked that aviation experts be asked to recommend aircraft subjects, which was done. The final list, unlike the Shelby Foote Civil War set, was compiled internally based on input from the various experts. Bill Phillips, one of the most accomplished aviation artists working at the time, was selected by Phil Jordan, the art director, to assume the arduous task of developing twenty paintings. Assigning Phil to the project was an easy and obvious decision. Phil had been the designer and art director of the Smithsonian Institution's monthly *Air & Space* magazine for years. Additionally, Phil was an avid soaring pilot. What Phil brought to this project was invaluable. His knowledge and passion for the subject drove the project and kept it, and all of us, on track. He routinely questioned the comments of the experts as they reviewed the designs in progress—so much so that he actually took the time to build scale-model versions of a few of the planes in question. A few of the experts had insisted that from the angle depicted, a certain element of the plane was not in proper proportion, or an element could not be seen. Phil proved them all wrong with great delight, not to mention a great deal of passionate dialogue complete with rising blood pressure and a reddened face. But it all proved to be for the best. The resulting series still stands as a magnificent set of images.

Not having learned our lesson about large, complex issuances, we once again began development of an even bigger set of stamps. This time, we weren't going to settle for a "little" set of twenty stamps. Our goal was fifty stamps this time, one for every state in the Union. It was to be issued in 2002, aimed not just at the collecting community but the general public as well.

Dick Sheaff proposed the concept of the Greetings from America series to the CSAC. His proposal was based on the 1930s and 1940s old linen postcards that carried "Greetings from" each state and, in many cases, different cities nationwide. An ephemera collector of note, Dick realized the potential of developing stamps that would capitalize on the nostalgia surrounding these postal cards. The Committee eagerly endorsed the idea, and work began.

PhotoAssist again was tasked with locating images that reflected the cultural diversity of each state. One goal was to avoid the use of popular tourist destinations that might have previously been featured on stamps as well as subjects requiring special licensing agreements that might prohibit reproduction of the stamp images on licensed products, whether by the Postal Service or vendors purchasing a license from us. This made PhotoAssist's task especially complex. But, as always, the team rose to the occasion, and the resulting set of stamps proved to be extremely popular. So much so that upon exhausting the initial run of two-hundred million stamps, they were reprinted, something that was rarely done at that time. The second printing proved equally popular.

Despite their popularity, they were not without their detractors. We had anticipated how the public was going to react initially. Upon announcing the impending issuance, post offices, collectors, and the general public all questioned how they could get a sheet honoring their particular state. They said they weren't interested in the other forty-nine states, only their state. The philatelic media in particular was very harsh in criticizing our decision to release it only as a set of fifty different states. They intimated that we were "foolish" to release them in that manner.

What these Monday-morning quarterbacks didn't realize is that we had thought it out in great detail. We had tried to justify releasing the stamps in individual panes of twenty for each state, but collectors routinely and loudly complained that all stamps must be available in all post offices nationwide for their collecting convenience. This request was (and is) not feasible for both financial and logistical reasons. The cost of producing individual state stamps would have meant canceling the issuance of most, if not all, of the remaining stamps slotted in the 2002 program. Despite the hue and cry, primarily from collectors, the stamps, as I said, proved to be a sellout.

Correcting Christopher Columbus

Aside from the large projects I've just described, we had to contend with selecting, researching, designing, and printing an average of eighty to one hundred additional stamps annually. These issues included single-design subjects, blocks of four subjects, and other small multiples. The issues of twenty and fifty designs were time-consuming and exhausting for all concerned. Whether it was a single design or multiple designs, we were tasked with maintaining the same level of thoroughness that we applied to large issuances. Despite our best efforts, questionable aspects of a design sometimes surfaced during development. Fortunately, with the checks and balances system we were using, potential errors were avoided.

In 1991, prior to the existence of the research firm PhotoAssist, we had employed numerous freelance researchers. One was Mrs. Sara Day. A British subject by birth, Sara soon became one of my favorites. Her droll British wit, combined with her acute sense of knowing what I was looking for, forged a solid working relationship for a number of years.

One of Sara's projects was to review the artwork submitted by Richard Schlecht, an artist who had illustrated numerous stamps in the past and was one of the favorite "go-to" artists by other members of the Stamps staff. He always produced quality illustrations on time. Unfortunately, he also had a large ego and didn't care for criticism. Well, he hadn't met Sara yet.

I asked Sara to verify all four of the illustrations he created for the 1992 Voyages of Columbus stamps slated to commemorate the 500th anniversary of the discovery of America. In Schlecht's defense, the way that most stamp designs were created up to that point was that artists did their own research and created images for final approval. This approach could, and almost did in this instance, prove to be disastrous if the images were not factual.

The four Columbus images were less than factual. In fact, after Sara reviewed the art and submitted her report, I knew instantly that there would be a clash between artist and researcher. It seems that Richard used as his reference nineteenth-century engravings of the same subject matter. As one might imagine, nineteenth-century book illustrators were not subject to the scrutiny and potential litigation that twentieth- and twenty-first-century stamp designers were (and are). The 19th nineteenth-century art featured props and backgrounds that did not exist in Columbus' day. As Sara rightly pointed out, the art would have to be redone.

When this was diplomatically explained to Richard, he exploded. No one had ever dared question his illustrations in this manner, and when he produced his references, we explained the dilemma once again to him. His temper tantrum continued for weeks, but we held firm and eventually repainted the images, much to his dismay, and he expressed his reluctance to work with us on future projects.

The vast majority of stamp images submitted for review do not require the extensive redo the Columbus images required. But many changes on a much smaller scale were made.

Oops!

Philatelists (stamp collectors) live for the day they will find an error on a stamp that can not only potentially make them rich but give them prestige in their little world of philately. I, on the other hand, lived in fear of those same errors. Those mistakes never meant fame or fortune to me or to the Postal Service. They meant headaches, frustration, embarrassment, and eternal kidding by friends and colleagues. So, while every attempt was made to avoid these dreaded mistakes, they happened and will probably happen again to whoever works in Stamp Services. It's almost impossible to try to stay ahead of all the pitfalls that can befall the program.

Undoubtedly the most famous error on a U.S. postage stamp is the classic Inverted Jenny of 1918. It wasn't an error in the original design, though. It occurred in the printing when a full pane of one hundred stamps passed through the press a second time to add the black-ink illustration of the Curtis Jenny airplane. Inadvertently, one pane got turned around, and the pane printed the airplane flying upside down. Entire books have been written about this mistake, and millions have been made on the sale of these stamps. It is one of the rarest and most collectible of all U.S. stamps. Fortunately, mistakes made during my years in Stamps were not of that magnitude. One comes close, but it never matched the monetary worth of the Jenny.

Family Matters

Let me preface the issue of "mistakes on stamps" by saying that despite our best efforts to ensure the accuracy of every image and associated text on all stamps, sometimes families get in the way. The 1994 Nat King Cole stamp in the Legends of American Music series is a good example. While not a "major" stamp error, it was nevertheless an error.

The Cole family readily approved the image and signed the agreement giving us permission to reproduce it. It was his two daughters who gave the approval. It wasn't until the actual day of issue of the stamp— September 1, 1994—that the error was noticed. There, bigger than life on the stage, was an enlargement of the stamp, something we have done for years for stamp dedications. Also on stage, along with dignitaries, postal officials, and the Cole family, was Cole's widow. She brought the error to the attention of one of the officials on stage that the birthdate attributed to her husband was the wrong year. It should have read 1918, not 1917. Fortunately, the type was small and written vertically up the left side of the stamp, and most people were not even aware of it. It seems that the two daughters neglected to share the final stamp image with their mother.

Picking the Right Pickett

In the early 1990s, the CSAC discussed developing a set of stamps honoring "Western Americana." The original concept was to produce four poster-like images showing Wild West shows. But it didn't take long for the members to see the potential for a much more interesting and larger series. The resulting stamps would be the first set of "Classic Collection" stamps. Two Committee members were from the Western part of the U.S., and their suggestions resulted in a set of twenty designs entitled Legends of the West. It would include such legendary characters as "Wild Bill" Hickok, Kit Carson, Geronimo, Annie Oakley, "Buffalo Bill" Cody, Wyatt Earp, and Chief Joseph, in addition to eight other individuals and four scenic corner stamps depicting Home on the Range, Native American Culture, Overland Mail, and Western Wildlife. Such controversial individuals as Butch Cassidy and General Custer were vetoed.

Because of the size and scope of this project, work began immediately. Visual research was amassed and passed along to Mark Hess, the illustrator recommended by Dick Sheaff, the project art director. Mark worked for months on end creating these colorful images. Colors were chosen by Mark because the supplied reference material was in black and white.

Researchers were assigned to check the art against the photo references and cross-check them with other photos and information regarding the individuals. A separate genealogical research firm was contracted to identify any descendants of the sixteen individuals. It was expected that a number of the individuals might not have any living relatives to sign a rights agreement. Little did we know!

Over the next two years, Mark diligently created the twenty illustrations. At the quarterly CSAC meetings, progress reports were given and the finished illustrations were shared with Design Subcommittee members. Everything seemed to be moving along nicely.

The research reports came in, and as expected, a number of the individuals had no estates or heirs with whom we would have to sign legal agreements. The CSAC gave the entire pane a "go," and it was sent to the printers. A few months later, the first shipments of stamps were sent out to post offices nationwide.

Standard procedure on all stamp shipments required that labeling instructions be provided to the Postmaster and staff regarding the official release date. The labels instructed the staff to not begin sales of a particular stamp until the day following the official first day of issue, which usually occurs in only one city. But, as Headquarters came to realize over the years, individual post offices often disregard these instructions. In fact, virtually every stamp issuance finds its way into the hands of customers before the official first day of sale. When questioned, the staff uses the excuse that they were running low on stamps, so rather than requesting additional stamps in the current inventory, they broke open the boxes of new shipments and sold them. Under normal circumstances, this would not be an issue. Unfortunately, in this case, it proved to be disastrous.

During the first few months of 1994, prior to the first-day ceremony scheduled for later that spring, 183 Legend of the West panes of stamps were sold nationwide in randomly scattered post offices.

At the same time, those 183 stamp panes were making their way into customers' hands, questions were being raised about one of the stamp images. In an effort to be diverse in the selection of subjects, one of the individuals chosen for commemoration was Bill Pickett. While Pickett's claim to fame was not of the scope or prominence of "Wild Bill" Hickok, Sitting Bull, or some of the others, Pickett deserved his own stamp.

The text printed on the reverse side of the stamp best summarized who Bill Pickett was: "Fearless black cowboy, rodeo showman and rancher said to have invented bulldogging. Both Will Rogers and Tom Mix served as his assistants." Pickett's career extended from the later days of the Wild West until his death in 1932. His later years were spent making Western movies.

When given numerous images from which to create the portrait of Pickett, Hess chose an oft-produced black-and-white image of him in his younger years. The majority of images depicted him in his later years. Hess, Dick Sheaff, and I all agreed that the younger image portrayed a more "glamorous" cowboy image. The photo Mark used as his reference carried a unique label. Written on the negative of the original photo in crude hand lettering was the following identification: "Bill Pickett, famous Negro cowboy. First man buldogger [sic]. Also used his teeth bull dogging instead of hands on horn method used by cowboys today."

This image was probably the most well-known and reproduced image of Pickett. It was accepted as the image of Bill Pickett by leading authorities, including the Professional Rodeo Hall of Fame in Colorado. Numerous publications such as *The Black West*, *The American Cowboy in Life and Legend*, *Bill Pickett, Bulldogger: The Biography of a Black Cowboy*, *Smithsonian* magazine, the Time-Life book *The End of the Myth*, and the Library of Congress' exhibition catalog *The American Cowboy* all reproduced the image. So what could go wrong given all this validation?

It wasn't Bill Pickett. It turned out to be his brother Ben.

The genealogical research firm hired to locate heirs stated in their report that "no known relatives exist for Mr. Pickett."

Wrong.

In actuality, there were 215 living descendants who held annual reunions; they were incorporated in Michigan as the Bill Pickett Family Foundation. Needless to say, that genealogical firm no longer has a contract with the Postal Service!

Questions began to arise when the full pane of Legends of the West stamp images was unveiled on December 7, 1993. A few Western historical firms called us to alert us that we might have depicted the wrong person. Based on our reference material and the handwritten inscription on the original photo, we thanked them for their concern but stood by the image. Over the next few weeks, the identity question continued to surface in different areas of the country from other individuals. Eventually, the Associated Press ran a story about it, prompting calls from the *Washington Post* and *The New York Times*. The individuals who made the claim about the wrong Pickett image suggested to the media that they contact Pickett's great-grandson, Frank Phillips, who just happened to live in Silver Spring, Maryland, just miles from Postal headquarters.

Phillips was totally unaware of the stamp and proposed issuance. In fact, he claimed that he had written numerous letters to the CSAC requesting a stamp for his great-grandfather but had never heard anything. Considering the some 40,000 letters received annually from the public, it certainly would be easy to lose track of an individual request. I suspect that the suggestion for a Bill Pickett never found favor with the Committee as an individual issuance. No record indicates that his name was retained for future consideration. It only resurfaced when the concept of the Legends pane was developed.

When Phillips was contacted by the media, he, in turn, contacted Postal Headquarters in early January 1994. He met with James Tolbert, the Manager of Stamp Development. Listening to his plea, Tolbert promised to get back to him with an answer or a solution to the issue by January 19.

But, on January 18, Azeez Jaffer, who had been appointed Director of Stamp Services only two weeks before, told Phillips that all of the stamps would be destroyed, and a new set printed with a correct image of Bill Pickett. Rather than work through the process with his staff, he "took charge" and made the decision. More than five million panes—more than 104 million stamps—were recalled from the post offices and destroyed, a task easier said than done. While I have no doubt the decision was the appropriate one, it could have been handled in a less grandiose manner.

I had yet to be apprised of the meeting with Mr. Phillips because I was, at the time, meeting with China Post officials in Hawaii regarding an upcoming joint issue between the two countries. I was awakened one morning, at six a.m. Honolulu time, by the phone. Concerned that something was amiss back at home, both my wife Ann and I were jolted awake. When I answered, I was greeted by the sound of Azeez yelling into the phone: "Wake up, McCaffrey. You're on a %$#@$% conference call." If the sound of the ringing phone hadn't jolted me awake, being cussed at, did. Sitting upright in bed, Azeez then bellowed, "You put the wrong %$#&$% person on a stamp!" Stunned, I tried to think, but no specific individual came to mind, so Azeez explained, using very colorful language, what had happened. I agreed to get on it as soon as I returned to D.C. a few days later.

Upon returning to my D.C. office, I found it in a bit of disarray. One of my file draws was standing open. It didn't take long to realize that someone had gone through my files to locate the one printed pane of Legends stamps I had retained from the press inspection months earlier. Azeez had instructed the staff to turn the offices upside down to locate any sheets such as the one I had in my files. He wanted to ensure that every single pane was accounted for. What none of us knew at the time was that 183 of those stamp panes were already in the hands of customers.

While the stamp "roundup" (how appropriate) was taking place, I went into high gear to get a new painting done, this time showing the real Bill. Discussing the issue with both Dick Sheaff and Mark Hess, we agreed that we should repaint only the face on the existing painting so we wouldn't have to spend time starting over from scratch. I agreed, but I would later regret that decision.

Mark painted over the younger Ben's face with the older Bill's face, and we rushed the art to the printers. Immediately, they began production on the new, "correct" pane as it came to be known. Meanwhile, I was given five days by Azeez to reverify the identity of every single person on all twenty stamps. In reality, it took a few weeks due to the complexity of this task. Comments from experts during this second review brought up subtle suggestions for changes but nothing substantive. The decision from the PMG was to only change the Pickett stamp and get it printed.

When word got out about the change and that 183 panes of the wrong Pickett were sold to customers, the collecting community was thrilled. The very idea that these rare stamps were out there and that collectors might have the opportunity to find and purchase them had many a serious philatelist breathing a heavy fog of mist on their trusty magnifying glasses. Serious philatelists rarely trust the Postal Service. Many were convinced there must be more panes out there, and they had to find them. Unfortunately for them, that was not to be the case.

Those 183 panes immediately increased from a face value of $5.80 to between $5,000 and $6,000 each, with one auctioned for $12,500 on the collecting market. Many owners of the panes were approached by collectors nationwide to sell them. I didn't know who had them or whether they sold them to other dealers. I was too busy creating the new stamps to worry about that. The philatelic community was abuzz about one of the greatest rarities in the U.S. program.

The new stamps were rescheduled for issuance in October 1994. The news media kept the story alive for months prior to the issuance, even putting it on the front page.

Despite protestations from the philatelic community and even members of Congress, Azeez stood firm on his decision that all of the original stamps would be destroyed. But in June, an announcement came from J. Sam Winters, the Chairman of the Postal Board of Governors, detailing the plan to sell 150,000 incorrect panes to offset the cost of printing the first set of stamps, which Congressional members had demanded. There would be a "lottery" in which collectors would be able to submit mail orders for the panes for a one-month period beginning on October 1. If more than 150,000 requests were received, a random selection would be used to select the orders to be filled. This arrangement was agreed upon by the Congressmen, Postmaster General Runyon, BOG Chair Winters, and Frank Phillips, representing the Pickett family. Long before the end of the one-month period, the Postal Service had received well in excess of 150,000 requests. The lottery began, and shortly thereafter, the Postal Service proceeded to start shipping out the 150,000 panes to the lucky customers.

Not wanting to see their initial "Ben" Pickett stamp pane devalued from $5,000-6,000, those unlucky collectors cried "foul." Together, they brought a $10 million suit against the Postal Service. A protracted court battle kept the now-infamous cowboy in the spotlight for the next few years. The Postal Service eventually emerged as the victor in the case. Despite the costs, man-hours, frustrations, and office-wide tensions, one good thing came out of this controversy: a revamped and more complex vetting process when new subjects were recommended for future issuance

Searching the Canyon

A mere five years after the Pickett incident, we were faced with another "error" on a stamp. This time, it was not a case of mistaken identity but a case of misplacing a famous landmark.

In 1998, the CSAC began developing what was to become a very popular series of international rate stamps known as the Scenic American Landscapes. The concept was to promote beautiful and diverse landscapes throughout the U.S., much like miniature travel posters, which would be seen by recipients around the world. In 1999, the first two subjects, Niagara Falls and the Rio Grande, were released.

A third image depicting the Grand Canyon was slated to be released in early 2000. The Postal Service Media Release group distributed the standard four-by-five-inch color transparency to the usual news media outlets, both philatelic and national. A week or so after the mailing, I received a call at home from a member of the USPS media team who had relocated from our headquarters in D.C. to Denver. Having worked closely with Jim over the years prior to his move to Colorado, he had my home number. But I was still surprised to hear from him after office hours.

In an agitated and excited state, Jim shouted into the phone that we had another $%#@ mistake on a stamp. My heart sank, but I couldn't figure out which stamp he was referring to. I finally got him to calm down long enough to identify it as the Grand Canyon. My immediate reaction was, "How could we make a mistake on that stamp? It's a photograph!" But the photo wasn't the issue. It was what was printed underneath the photo in the small white selvage area.

Days before releasing the art to the printers, the CSAC had recommended that we add a small line of type identifying the site and its location so that foreign recipients would know what it was. Not that most people wouldn't know the Grand Canyon when they saw it, but the Committee was trying to address the issue as future stamps in the series might not be as readily identifiable. The rationale sounded great, but the eventual execution proved to be more than problematic.

Ethel Kessler, the art director, and designer for the entire series, went back to the original four-by-five-inch color transparency she received from the stock photo house to get the pertinent data off the protective transparency sleeve. In her haste, she copied the following text as written on the sleeve label: "Grand Canyon, Colorado." Without stopping to think about what she had just copied, she added that line, verbatim, to the print file. What she failed to notice was that the credit line continued to a second line, which read: "River, Arizona." So, with the click of the "Save" and "Send" computer keys, she had moved the Grand Canyon to Colorado from Arizona!

The line of type displayed at the bottom of the stamp was so small (four- to five-point) that it was almost illegible to the naked eye. So, throughout the entire print prep process, no one questioned or even noticed the geographical mistake. It wasn't until Jim noticed it on the transparency, he received that it was discovered. Thus, the frantic phone call that evening.

The following morning, I reported what I had been told the previous evening. Once again, the air was blue, and chaos ensued. But, unlike the Bill (or should I say Ben) Pickett stamp, the Grand Canyon stamps had not yet been released to post offices. Oh, to be sure, they had been printed, but they were all still at the printing plant. A lockdown was ordered to prevent any of those stamps from getting out and into the hands of the public. All stamps were immediately shredded just to be sure. For years after that, the philatelic media still questioned and suspected that some panes were kept under lock and key. I hate to disappoint anyone, but I can assure you that was not the case. In fact, after the shredding took place, then-Director of Stamp Services Cathy Caggiano presented me with a single shred of spaghetti-like paper on which I could still read that infamous title, "Grand Canyon, Colorado." Regretfully, over the years, I lost that small treasure.

The reprint of the stamps with the correct verbiage did not receive the same Congressional scrutiny as the Pickett stamp. The print run for these international stamps was so small in comparison to the Legends of the Wild West that there was no serious debate about costs. So, no lottery and no lawsuits, though there was some media attention.

When media outlets got wind of the mistake, they displayed the incorrect image which had been originally provided by the postal communications group. It even made national television news. Tom Brokaw had a field day with the story, as did numerous other news sources.

When the stamp with the correct identification was issued, we expected a few comments from the news media that we had "finally found the Grand Canyon," but we weren't ready for what we heard.

The day after the first day of issuance, I received a call from one of the National Park Service officials at the Canyon. The thirty-by-forty-inch enlargement of the stamp unveiled at the dedication ceremony that allowed attendees a close-up look and a good photo-op was left behind for use by the subject's supporters—in this case, the National Park Service.

My conversation with the Park Service official went something like this:

"Mr. McCaffrey, I believe we have a mistake on the stamp."

My first thought was that whoever sent out the enlargement made it from the old, incorrect image. But I was mistaken.

"No, sir. The text at the bottom of the stamp is correct," he said when I raised that possibility. "It's the photo that is wrong."

"How could the photo be wrong?" I said in an incredulous tone.

The Park official calmly said, "Well, I looked at the stamp image and then stepped to the right to view the same scene across the actual Canyon. Then I stepped back and looked at the stamp again. Then back to look at the Canyon again. It appears that the photo has been flopped."

At that point, I about flopped to the floor. It had happened again. Another screw-up on a stamp! I thought my days as a stamp designer were numbered. Begging off the phone conversation, I assured the Park official we would get back to them.

Scrambling to make sense of this, I contacted Ethel, my bosses, and anyone else who could possibly lend assistance in putting out this little fire. After a thorough investigation by all, it was determined that the photo had indeed been flopped. But by whom, we would never know. Was it flopped when the photographer made a duplicate transparency (which is not uncommon)? Or did Ethel flop it while scanning? Or did the printers flop it during file prep? It was never fully determined where the fault lay. All we knew was that the Grand Canyon was flopped.

The next big question was whether we should pull the stamps, reprint them, and then face intense criticism not only from the media but from Congress. Because the print run was small with sales mostly limited to international mail, we chose to allow the stamps to be sold as-is.

Of course, the news media got wind of it and once again, Tom Brokaw did an interesting, humorous piece at the expense of the Postal Service. Despite such embarrassment, it was still easier to take media criticism than Congressional oversight and lawsuits.

Orientation and verification of "right-reading" photographs became yet another aspect of the stamp verification process. After the Bill Pickett incident, which some have termed the biggest mistake on U.S. stamps since the Inverted Jenny of 1918, the flopped Grand Canyon was much easier to deal with. We just hoped and prayed each day that there wouldn't be any more such mistakes.

It's All in How You Look at It

Well, at least there was a ten-year period between "mistakes." Considering that there were more than 1,100 individual stamp designs issued during that period, it was a pretty good record. But all it took was one little photo to ruin the streak of good luck. That streak ended because of a certain Las Vegas lady.

In the 2007-2008 period, we were, as always, exploring new patriotic images The Liberty Bell had appeared on the first Forever stamp issued in the spring of 2007. It was an unwritten rule that the Postal Service must always have a U.S. Flag stamp for sale. Where this tradition came from is a mystery to me. But we found that if customers did not have access to a flag stamp for their envelopes, we got letters and phone calls, some of which were less than friendly.

That being said, it was an ongoing design challenge to create fresh new approaches to the U.S. flag. We would occasionally add a patriotic icon to the mix, such as the Statue of Liberty, which met with approval from our patriotic customers.

The group under my direction was tasked with developing hundreds of designs at any given time, so many of the art directors preferred to devote their time and creative energies toward the development of more interesting subjects than the standard flag/patriotic icon imagery. So, in an effort to assist them, I did double duty and took on the task of developing multiple flag and icon images for future use. Among them was the Statue of Liberty.

Lady Liberty had appeared on almost two dozen previous stamps, either in full-body, three-quarter view, closeups of the torch, or in only a few images, the head only. I wanted to find an extreme close-up photograph of her face, which had only been featured two or three times but always in an illustrative engraving.

Typing in "Statue of Liberty" as a search item on three national stock-photo-house websites, I spent an entire afternoon searching through thousands of photos of Lady Liberty. Many began to look alike as there are only so many ways that icon can be photographed. My search did yield three images that I felt I could work with. After sharing the stock file numbers for those photos with our research team, PhotoAssist acquired working files from which designs could be developed.

I worked closely with Greg Breeding of the Journey Group to develop concepts based on the photos I had selected. My first choice of photos came from the Getty Images group, and it was exactly what I was looking for. It was a very tight closeup of her face and part of her crown. With little cropping, the design was developed as a forty-four-cent stamp and eventually as a possible Forever stamp replacement for the overused Liberty Bell image. Research had shown that the American public was constantly looking for new images, and the Liberty Bell was fast wearing out its welcome.

Much back-and-forth discussion with CSAC members led to the Lady Liberty image being paired with another U.S. Flag design I was preparing at the same time. The decision was made to initially use them on coil stamps, to be followed with ATM and Booklet versions.

The Lady Liberty and U.S. Flag stamps were officially issued with little or no fanfare on December 1, 2010, one month before my retirement after forty years at the Postal Service. It wasn't until three months later that I would once again have to deal with a "mistake" on a stamp.

Now comfortably retired, my wife and I went to San Antonio to visit our son Chris and his family to celebrate his birthday. On March 11, the day after his birthday, I received a call on my cell phone. I vividly remember walking through the local H-E-B grocery store in New Braunfels, Texas, where I would eventually retire, when the call came in from Sidney Brown of PhotoAssist.

"Well, we've done it again" was the first thing Sidney said. Having been out of the loop for three months, I was perplexed. "The Lady Liberty stamp isn't of the New York statue. It's the one from Las Vegas that stands in front of the New York, New York Hotel." With the immediate pressure of the work environment no longer weighing on me, I burst into laughter. Incredulous as it would seem, we had chosen the wrong statue.

It had been brought to the attention of the Postal Service in March

2011, in an email from SunPix, a small Arizona stock photo firm. It didn't take too long to reach the conclusion that they were right. Upon very close inspection, very subtle differences between the New York Harbor original and the Las Vegas replica became evident. Of course, this information found its way to *Linn's Stamp News*, which would eventually call it "one of the biggest blunders in U.S. stamp history." A bit exaggerated, I would say. But then, what with the ever-waning popularity of stamps and stamp collecting, whatever excitement that can be generated is a plus for the philatelic media.

As usual, the national news media picked up on it and had a good time chiding the Postal Service yet again. But because the initial print run of coil stamps was more than two billion, the Postal Service buckled down and said they would not reprint. They acknowledged the error but would continue to sell the stamps. In fact, the following month, the ATM version was issued, and, in September, the Booklet version was issued, all with the Las Vegas Lady Liberty. The majority of the American public did not hear about the snafu, nor did they much care if they did.

It wasn't until two years later that the issue arose again. But this time, it was of a more serious nature. The sculptor of the Las Vegas statue decided to sue the Postal Service for copyright infringement. The Postal Service had not obtained his permission to reproduce his sculpture's image on postage stamps, so he was seeking payment for damages. After several years of legal discourse between the two parties, it went to trial in New York City in 2017. Eight days of hearings and testimony later, the judge announced a ruling would be forthcoming in a few months.

It wasn't until many months later, in 2018, that the judge finally announced his ruling. He found in favor of the sculptor. Needless to say, I was very disappointed with the decision, and felt, quite frankly, that the judge had distorted some of the testimony I gave during an eight-hour video deposition in 2015.

Despite the Postal Service's wish to file an appeal, a decision I roundly applauded, the Justice Department, in early 2019, chose to accept the court's decision and closed the case, awarding $3.5 million to the man whose "creativity" had been maligned. This stamp has now been added to the annals of "stamp mistakes," which the philatelic community loves to find, collect, and potentially get rich from.

Chapter 6
The Rights Stuff

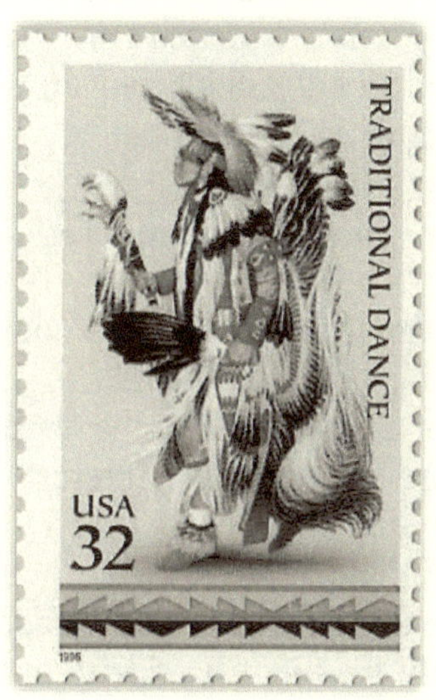

One aspect of the stamp design process that many people rarely take into consideration when viewing stamps is the legal aspect. In talks with numerous people over the years regarding the process, virtually everyone admits to never contemplating that we (the Postal Service) would have to purchase the intellectual property rights for famous people, buildings, works of art, and just about anything else appearing on postage stamps.

Over the years, the rights process has played a larger role as subjects are reproduced, not only on postage stamps but in almost every form of communication in our media-conscious culture. Before my move to Stamp Services in late 1990, rights became an issue for the Postal Service in three instances.

Having the Last Laugh

W.C. Fields, the great comedian, was the first stamp subject to a rights challenge. Upon the stamp's 1980 release, the Postal Service was contacted by Roger Richman, a prominent Los Angeles talent representative representing the Fields estate. Postal Service staff expressed surprise that they needed to obtain and pay for permission to reproduce Fields likeness on a postage stamp. After much discussion, Richman accepted their apology for their ignorance of the process and accepted a check from the Postal Service for exactly one dollar. Years later, when I visited Mr. Richman to obtain rights for another stamp, he proudly displayed an enlarged photocopy of the $1.00 check. We both had a good laugh.

Sing the Same Song

In early 1985, illustrator Jim Sharpe was commissioned to create a portrait of Duke Ellington, the legendary jazz composer and big band leader. Jim's portrait captured the essence of the genius of Duke. But his art also captured the interest of a certain Japanese photographer. It seems that Jim based his portrait on this photographer's copyrighted photo.

It appears that obtaining rights for images in the creation of stamps was not exactly the highest priority of the development team in the early years. In fact, rights were rarely ever obtained unless the rights holder brought up the subject.

The photographer contacted the Postal Service regarding his copyrighted photo and wished to discuss the situation. To the credit of the development team, they were able to convince the photographer to accept, as an apology for their oversight, one hundred panes of the stamps, which meant that at fifty stamps per pane and the going first-class rate at that time of 22 cents, they paid him off to the tune of $1,100. A bit more costly than the W.C. Fields stamp, but a rather fair price by today's standards.

Strike!

In 1991, the Postal Service was immersed in its official sponsorship of the Olympic Games. As part of the program, USPS upper management decided that we should host a design competition for an Olympic Baseball stamp to be issued in 1992. Baseball was being recognized as a first-time Olympic sport that year at the Atlanta

Games. In the past, such stamp design competitions have proven to be complex, difficult, and with mixed results. But, because of the Postmaster General's interest, we were mandated to do it.

In an effort to avoid receiving thousands of unacceptable, amateurish designs, it was suggested that there be a $100 fee to enter the competition, effectively limiting the entries to professionals. The end result was only eighty entries, which certainly made the selection by the CSAC much easier.

At their next quarterly meeting, the members discussed and recommended to the Postmaster General their choice. For whatever reason, the newly appointed PMG, Marvin Runyon, was not sold on their choice, and after reviewing all eighty entries, made his own selection. Mr. Runyon would go on for the remaining six years of his tenure to influence the stamp program, for good or bad, numerous times. Initially, we thought his choice of baseball images was a good one, an acceptable alternative to what the members had recommended. That would prove to be a wrong assumption.

The stamp was issued in April 1992. Shortly after its release, we were notified by *Sports Illustrated* that we were in violation of a copyright. They noted that the original photo, which the stamp illustrator had used as a reference, had appeared in their magazine as an enormous two-page photo spread five years earlier. The Stamps group was devastated.

As part of the signed agreement when the illustrators paid their entry fee in the competition, they had to attest their art was original and not derivative from other work. In reviewing the image *Sports Illustrated* forwarded to us, it was obvious the illustrator had copied the black-and-white photo in question. When we contacted the Boston-based illustrator, Anthony De Luz, he initially denied the accusation but later admitted that he had used it. But, to his way of thinking, he had altered the image in numerous ways, making it an original work of art. Bad assumption!

The entire situation became very contentious with both *Sports Illustrated* and the illustrator. Lawsuits were threatened, and during discussions with the illustrator, he said in a very cavalier manner, "So, sue me. I don't have any money." We were informed that he was just beginning his career in illustration and, indeed, had little financial resources.

The stamp was eventually withdrawn from sale nine months after its issuance. All of those stamps were pulled from post offices and destroyed. *Sports Illustrated* was paid a fee for the copyright, and Stamps learned yet another lesson in the world of copyright law.

Shining the Light

The same year as the Marilyn stamp, we were embroiled in another copyright infringement issue. This time it wasn't with a celebrity but an iconic historic lighthouse. Following the popular issuance of a set of five Lighthouse stamps in 1990, St. Joseph's Lighthouse on Lake Michigan was included in the set of five Great Lakes Lighthouses stamps slated for 1995. The illustrator, Howard Koslow, was once again commissioned to create the five images. Working from a reference photo, Howard painted a beautiful image of the famed lighthouse. But when the photographer was offered an art reference payment, a normal procedure in this business, the photographer threatened to sue us.

Howard had a friend who lived near the lighthouse go out and take his own photo from the same vantage point, and Howard reworked the painting to match the new photo. But the original photographer claimed that we had already violated her rights and planned to sue. Eventually, an agreement was reached after some very heated and protracted negotiations.

Dance with Me

It seems that our office couldn't get a break from all the legal issues surrounding stamps. Mere months after the Lighthouse issue, yet another legal issue arose.

In an effort to be all-inclusive in the stamp program, the Committee recommended we find a subject reflecting the cultural contributions of Native Americans. The result was five stamps depicting Native American Dancers to be issued in 1996. Five beautifully detailed illustrations were created by Keith Birdsong. Initially, we guessed that with a name like Birdsong, Keith might well have Native American blood in him. Unfortunately, that wasn't the case. Birdsong was of German origin. Well, we tried.

Our research team, PhotoAssist, did extensive visual research for Keith, and when the five tribal dance illustrations were completed, they contacted the owners of each of the unique costumes used for reference. Each costume owner was very honored and readily signed permission to use the costume. I learned soon after that no two dance costumes are alike. We were to be forcefully reminded of that after the designs were unveiled.

It appeared that one costume depicted in a Traditional Dance stamp was not created by the individual we had been told it was. The expert PhotoAssist used to verify the various costumes said that the image actually depicted his son's costume. We dutifully had his son sign the agreement, assuming it was a done deal.

Not so fast. In fact, it was not the son's work but the creation of a different dancer who immediately protested the issuance of the stamps. When the expert was confronted with this information, he admitted that he might not have looked as closely at the costume as he should have, and yes, there were differences, and the other dancer was right.

The offended dancer demanded all profits from the use of his image—in his estimation, $10 million—for his inconvenience. The USPS was reluctant to pay him, not having paid the other dancers. Phone conversations became very heated. Birdsong received a phone call from the dancer, who threatened to "punch him out" if he dared to attend the first-day ceremony at a huge tribal dance show in Oklahoma later that year.

On the day of the stamp ceremony, we provided security protection for Keith despite the fact Keith was a physically fit man who could have probably stood his own in a brawl. Fortunately, no confrontation took place. Instead, the dancer brought his mother to the ceremony and confronted members of the news media about how he had been maligned by the Postal Service. He even had his mother cry on cue for the cameras. His version of the story got little media play, and the stamps went on to become very good sellers.

The Elusive Princess

As part of the massive Celebrate the Century project developed in the final years of the last millennium, one subject recommended by the CSAC for inclusion in the 1930s decade was the first full-length animated Disney film, *Snow White and the Seven Dwarfs.*

In order to begin work on the design, we had to obtain an image from the Disney Corporation. When my colleague Kelly Spinks contacted them, she received a short rebuff stating that Disney would not be able to provide any such images. Period. End of discussion. Their response surprised and disturbed us. A follow-up call to ascertain why they refused our request provided us with more information but not enough to dissuade us from pursuing it further.

Their justification for refusal? They had been instructed by then-CEO Michael Eisner not to license any Disney images for use on postage stamps. We found this puzzling as we had seen numerous stamps of various Disney characters featured on foreign stamps from around the world. That was the problem. It seems that some of those tiny nations had been obtaining licenses from Disney for X amount of stamps but then produced more stamps than agreed upon. That precipitated a memo from Eisner mandating no sales of any stamp licensees.

We took that information back to the CSAC. As luck would have it, Karl Malden, a Committee member happened to be a personal friend of Roy Disney. When Karl heard the news, he placed a call to Roy that evening. The following day, we received an email from Disney saying that they had been instructed to provide us with whatever image we could agree upon. It's amazing what things can be fixed when you have friends in the right places.

Our face-to-face meeting with Disney a few weeks later, however, was less than friendly. They were very professional but cool. We received the desired image, but as we were leaving, they made sure we understood that there would be no Disney stamps in the future for the USPS. How wrong they were. Five years later, it was Disney that called on the Postal Service to produce Disney stamps. Those stamps, all twenty, would be among the most popular issuances the Postal Service has seen to date.

The Memorial War

In 2001, John Hotchner, a member of the CSAC, former president of the American Philatelic Society, and leading CSAC advocate for more historic stamps, proposed that the Postal Service issue a stamp honoring the fiftieth anniversary of the end of the Korean War. His proposal was unanimously approved, and I assigned Dick Sheaff as art director.

There had been two previous stamps issued honoring the Korean War and its veterans, in 1985 and as part of the Celebrate the Century: 1950s pane. Dick's approach this time around was to use photography rather than illustration. John had suggested we consider the Korean War Memorial, a recent addition to the National Mall in D.C. Both Committee and staff agreed it was a good idea—but maybe not so much after what unfolded in the next few years.

The stamp was dedicated on July 27, 2003, with a large event at the Memorial. But it wasn't until much later, three years to be exact, that the controversy arose. No, we hadn't misplaced the Memorial in another state. Nor had we misidentified the memorial, nor had we reversed the image. It seems that we never obtained a license from the sculptor of the platoon of soldiers featured so prominently in the Memorial and the focus of the stamp.

The standard practice when there was a matter affecting two federal agencies was to send a common courtesy letter, so we sent one to the National Park Service notifying them of our intended use of a Memorial image. But somewhere in the quagmire of bureaucracy, our letter never fell into the right hands. It did go to the proper office, but the individuals with knowledge about the rights associated with the sculpture never saw the letter. If they had, it might have averted the legal hassles that would follow for the next eight years.

It wasn't until 2006 that Mr. Gaylord, the sculptor of the platoon of soldiers at the Memorial, filed a lawsuit. Unlike other National Park Service sculptures, Mr. Gaylord had retained the rights to the sculpture. Everyone, including us, assumed that they had been turned over to the Park Service. Over the next few years, we were to learn more details concerning why Gaylord had retained the rights.

I was told that Gaylord expressed frustration over additional changes that the Park Service had demanded of his sculpture, and eventually threw up his hands and walked away from the project, informing the Park Service that they could make whatever changes they wanted. He was finished and wanted nothing more to do with it. Subsequently, the Park Service did make changes and completed the art and installed it on the Mall. Gaylord and the Park Service continued to tussle with one another over the rights, but Gaylord never gave in, thus retaining the rights.

Next to enter the picture was John Alli, a Catonsville, Maryland, photographer who took numerous photos of the Memorial as a way of paying tribute to his father, who had served in Korea. Alli's photos had been posted on a stock photo house website where Dick Sheaff came upon them. Liking what he saw, Dick ordered a variety of images depicting the Memorial during various seasons of the year. Upon review, everyone felt the winter image, complete with snow, were the most appropriate choice. Alli was paid the rights for his photo and Dick completed the art, which received unanimous approval from the CSAC and subsequently by the Postmaster General.

Now we advance three years later to when Gaylord first came forward to sue for damages.

After much legal maneuvering by both parties, the lawsuit was brought to trial. Along with Dave Failor and Chuck Delaney, I was called to testify about our involvement with the design. The judge ruled in favor of the Postal Service because, as he stated, the art on the stamp was derivative and therefore a new creation. It was shown that John Alli's photograph depicted the sculptured soldiers blanketed in snow and that, as I testified, Dick Sheaff and I determined that the color of the original photo was too bright, and we were attempting to show the cold bleak atmosphere of the Korean winter so we darkened the colors. Those two elements were key to the "derivative" nature of the art.

As expected, Gaylord appealed the ruling and eventually won the case. The USPS appealed that ruling and lost again. The final judgment was in Gaylord's favor. He received $540,000. The amount was based on ten percent of the revenue generated from unused stamps by collectors and product produced by the Postal Service and its licensees. If we had known in advance that Gaylord owned the statues, we would have negotiated a price of $1,500, which was the standard rate. Gaylord had stated that he would not have accepted that amount had he been offered it. My point is that if he did refuse such payment, we would have dropped the image and gone in a different direction to portray the Korean War.

If we had only known.

That phrase has been uttered more than once over the years at the Postal Service. It just shows how complex the entire design process is. If only we had known it was Ben, not Bill, Pickett. If only we had known the Grand Canyon was backward. If only we had known it was a replica of Lady Liberty from a Las Vegas gambling casino.

If only.

Chapter 7

It's All in the Family

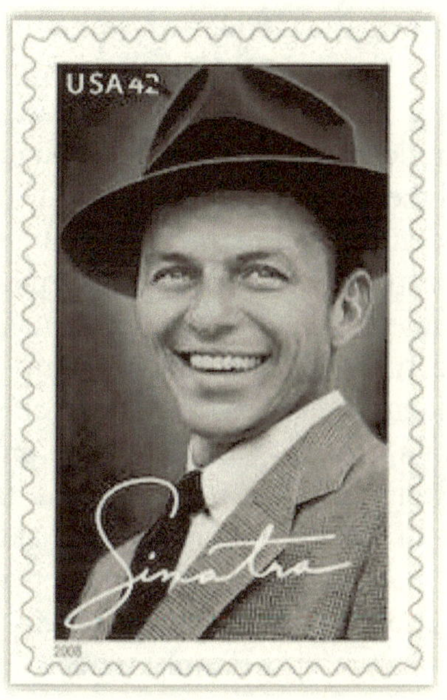

One of the most interesting, fun, perplexing, and yes, even sometimes frustrating aspects of my job was dealing with the families of individuals recommended for commemoration on a postage stamp, whether they be politicians, movie stars, or other individuals whose life's work had an impact on our nation's history. The following stories reflect just some of those situations.

One criterion in the Postal Service's stamp program, as developed by the CSAC with the approval of the Postmaster General, is that U.S. presidents could be honored with a postage stamp on their first birthday after their passing. Depending on when the President passed, it meant we could be faced with issuing a stamp in a very short timeframe. To avoid such situations, we developed portrait stamps prior to their passing. I know it sounds a big ghoulish, but it had to be done.

Presidential Approvals

The Richard Nixon stamp was the first Presidential stamp with which I was involved. He was not a very popular president, having put the country through the Watergate scandal and eventual resignation, but we were mandated to prepare a stamp. Daniel Schwartz was commissioned to develop the portrait. When Mr. Nixon passed on April 22, 1994, we waited an appropriate time before contacting the family to share the painting and obtain their approval. The family initially liked the portrait, but they requested we include the American flag in the background. We balked at the suggestion and told them we were unable to do so. Our rationale was that previous Presidential stamps had not featured the flag, and we didn't want to set a precedent. We were surprised (and delighted) that they accepted our rationale and withdrew their suggestion.

Our major concern with the Nixon stamp was the issuance. Traditionally, Presidential stamps are issued on the birthday of the honoree. Mr. Nixon's birthday was less than nine months later, on January 9, 1995, leaving us little time to obtain family approval, not to mention print and distribute millions of stamps to more than 30,000 post offices nationwide. After speaking with the family, we agreed to hold the issuance until a time after his birthday, following an impending rate change. The family agreed to at a later date for issuance rather than having the stamp become obsolete a month later.

Following the stamp's release, our offices were inundated with irate calls from citizens demanding the withdrawal of the stamp, which caused our HQ phone system to break down due to the number of calls. My staff and I fielded many loud, passionate, "vocal" comments such as:

"That so-and-so was a crook and doesn't deserve a stamp."

"I want my money back. I'm not supporting that crook."

"What in the $#%% were you %$## thinking?"

"I'll spit on the back of this stamp in protest." (We still had "lick-and-stick" stamps at the time, so he needed to affix moisture of one sort or another anyway.)

Our standard response to such complaints, regardless of the situation, was that he was still a (former) U.S. president and deserved commemoration. Others took to creative measures and affixed the vertical stamp horizontally on the envelope. By doing so, the four straight-line cancellation marks that cancel the stamp image made it appear that Mr. Nixon was behind bars. Never underestimate the creativity of the public!

Learning a lesson from the Nixon stamp, we decided to be more proactive and developed presidential art before their passing to avoid a last-minute rush. Upon reading the news that President Reagan had developed Alzheimer's and that his health was beginning to deteriorate, I assigned Howard Paine as art director and instructed him to begin design development. Howard chose two illustrators with decidedly different styles to develop art.

One portrait was felt to be too "soft-focus," which the Committee rejected. The second, a more casual portrait style, depicted a broadly smiling president. But that work came across as more of a caricature than a dignified portrait, though many of us involved with the development process liked it and thought it was a good solution.

Coincidentally, Larry Speakes, former Reagan Press Secretary, and Mark Weinberg, an assistant to Speakes, had landed positions in the Postal Service's Public Affairs and Communications Department after Mr. Reagan left office. To expedite and hopefully influence the decision, we asked them to comment on the art, knowing of their intimate knowledge of the likes and dislikes of the Reagans. Both gentlemen agreed upon reviewing it that the Reagans would reject the illustration as being too "cartoony." Howard was asked to develop a third, more serious and dignified concept using yet another illustrator.

When PhotoAssist provided the initial visual reference material, one was an existing painting, originally commissioned by TV Guide, painted by Daniel Schwartz, who had previously illustrated the Nixon stamp. Both Howard and I liked the portrait and agreed to contact Schwartz to ascertain whether he still owned the illustration and if we could negotiate reproduction rights to use it. By doing so, we could potentially save some money in our ever-tightening budget to avoid paying the full rate of $5,000 for an original work. Schwartz did, indeed, have the portrait and was willing to give us reproduction rights.

Once the portrait was mocked up in the stamp format, we prepared to share the design with the Reagan family and staff. Again, we asked Speakes and Weinberg to intercede on our behalf and get feedback from the Reagans. A few weeks later, we received a memo from them indicating the more serious portrait by Schwartz was selected, though with a few revisions to the art requested. Very reluctantly, Schwartz agreed to alter his art per the family's request, for which he was compensated. Upon completion of the revised art, we shared the family's choice with the CSAC and relegated the altered art to what we commonly referred to as our "bank" to await the issuance upon Mr. Reagan's passing.

Upon Mr. Reagan's passing on June 5, 2004, we waited a few weeks after the funeral before contacting the family and staff to discuss the stamp issuance. As a courtesy, we chose to share the approved portrait once more with the family to refresh their memories as it had been some time since the original selection was made.

Much to our surprise (and dismay), we received a call from Mr. Reagan's former Chief of Staff, Joanne Drake, who said that neither the staff nor Mrs. Reagan had ever seen the portrait and that "Mrs. Reagan hated it."

Shocked by this news, my manager, Dave Failor, and I immediately offered to work closely with the staff to develop a new design. Because Mr. Reagan's birthday was fast approaching and we were committed to issuing the stamp on that date, a solution was of the utmost importance.

Dave agreed that we should meet personally with the Reagan staff in Los Angeles as soon as possible. We caught a flight the following morning and immediately went to their offices. The meeting went well, and numerous images were considered. Many of the staff's suggestions, however, would not have translated well to stamp size. But looming over us from the back of the conference room was the solution: an enormous enlargement of Mr. Reagan, which in recent days had become one of the most iconic images. The photo depicted him in a white cowboy hat and an open-neck blue shirt. It had just been reproduced on the cover of the Time magazine commemorative issue a few weeks before our meeting.

The staff was very partial to the photo, but Dave and I expressed concern that it was not dignified enough for a memorial postage stamp. We shared images of the other presidential stamps we had done to make our point, and they reluctantly agreed. It was then that I offered a possible solution.

Going out on a limb, I said that we could have an illustrator use the photo as a reference, but he/she would remove the cowboy hat and put a suit on him. Everyone readily agreed that could work. Mrs. Reagan was not in attendance, but we knew that we couldn't proceed without her approval.

At this point in the meeting, an aide stepped into the meeting and spoke to Joanne:

"She wants you up at the house—now."

We all knew who "she" was as we were familiar with stories in the media about how demanding "she" could be. We witnessed her power firsthand when Joanne immediately stood up and said: "We'll have to end the meeting here. I have to go."

We encouraged Joanne to share this concept with "her" so we could proceed, which Joanne agreed to do. Leaving the offices, Dave and I were a little disgruntled that we had dropped everything and flown to L.A. on short notice to rectify the situation, only to be cut off in the middle of the meeting.

The following morning, Joanne called to say "she" liked the idea, and we were to proceed. Now came the challenge of telling the illustrator what he had to do and how fast. In the meeting the previous day, we had shared various illustration styles for the staff to review. Michael Deas's style was immediately chosen as the only way to go.

Michael had created numerous portraits over the years for the Postal Service that were acclaimed as some of the finest portraitures on stamps. Michael is also a perfectionist, not to mention slow and methodical in his work. We were always pushing Michael to finish a portrait, but his incredible talents were not to be driven by deadlines. So, it was going to be a difficult task to ask Michael to create this work within one month. His normal timeframe was four to six months.

To make matters even more difficult, Michael had a habit of not wanting to use reference photos, which the family and my staff had agreed upon. He frequently came back with his own choice. I have to admit that the majority of the time, Michael's solutions were better—in fact, brilliant. It just made my life more complicated when I was tasked with going back to the parties involved to convince them that his solution was a better one. Usually, when they saw Michael's version, they immediately agreed.

Knowing we would not have the luxury of months to create the art, coupled with the demand that a particular photo had to be used and oh, by the way, you have to remove a hat and put a suit on the man, I feared that Michael would turn down the job. But Michael, a consummate professional, after much stroking and cajoling, was convinced to accept the project and meet the one-month deadline.

The finished stamp is living proof that Michael pulled it off. Dave and I returned to Los Angeles within a month of our last meeting with the Reagan staff and shared the new portrait, which received an ecstatic response. But we all knew that the final decision rested with one and only one person: "her." Joanne took the art to Mrs. Reagan's home that night for approval. The following morning, I received the call that she had loved the art, and it was approved. Crisis averted.

But why had the original Schwartz portrait never been seen by the Reagan entourage? When Dave and I asked that question of the two former Reagan aides, we discovered that indeed neither Mrs. Reagan nor her staff had ever seen the art. It was never sent to them for approval. The two aides in D.C. had decided between themselves which image they preferred and felt it unnecessary to share their choice with the West Coast offices. Dave and I were most happy to share with them our displeasure with their actions.

The 37-cent stamp was issued on February 9, 2005, and was very well received by the public. The Chairman of the Postal Service Board of Governors was equally pleased. Chairman James C. Miller, armed with this allegiance and his admiration for his former boss, Miller insisted that the stamp be printed in larger quantities (170 million) than originally planned and be kept on sale indefinitely rather than the standard one-year period.

In June of the following year, Chairman Miller insisted that we reissue the Reagan stamp with the new first-class rate of thirty-nine cents, citing the public's continued interest in purchasing the stamp. Despite sales figures showing otherwise, there were still sufficient quantities of the first stamp available, so we were forced to reprint the stamp at the new rate. It, too, had to remain on sale indefinitely by edict of the chairman. The second stamp did not sell as well, as we had expected, but it was difficult to reason with someone so enamored with the president.

As if the first two stamps weren't enough, Chairman Miller mandated yet again that we issue a third stamp honoring Mr. Reagan. This time, it was to commemorate his one-hundredth birthday in 2011, a scant four years after the previous stamp. CSAC criteria usually prohibited stamps commemorating the same subject more than once every fifty years, but Chairman Miller was not to be ignored.

At least this time we were able to convince everyone that a new illustration should be created. A square-formatted stamp was chosen to help differentiate it from its two predecessors. Numerous visits were made to the stunningly beautiful Reagan Presidential Library in California to once again meet with Joanne Drake and her staff in an attempt to create a new, fresh image. It was a task made more difficult because Michael's original portrait was so perfect.

Bart Forbes, one of the most honored and respected illustrators of his day, created a pleasing, more relaxed portrait of Mr. Reagan, which Mrs. Reagan readily approved. In fact, it was Mrs. Reagan's suggestion that the new stamp depict her late husband in a more relaxed manner. The third stamp was released in February 2011, and as we (internally) expected, the stamp received little notice and sales were no better than any of the other issuances that year.

Based on this history of Reagan stamp(s) development, we decided to attempt once again to be more proactive in developing other Presidential stamps. Initially, we thought it might be a bit "ghoulish" to approach the living ex-Presidents to ask for recommendations on how they would like to be portrayed on a memorial stamp upon their passing. But it was brought to our attention that on assuming office, each President is given a book in which he is to record his last wishes regarding funeral arrangements, etc. Armed with that knowledge, over the next few years, we approached four of the remaining living ex-presidents (Gerald Ford, Jimmy Carter, George H.W. Bush, and Bill Clinton) for their initial input, an approach that usually proved problematic for design development. Family members often had a preset mental image of what the portrait should be, which often presented logistical and stylistic problems for the artist. Convincing the families to "turn the reins" over to us to develop what we felt would be a winning design was in some cases difficult.

Speaking of politics, presidents aren't the only politicos honored on stamps. Although in the first one hundred years of U.S. stamps, the vast majority honored nothing but politicians, that ratio in more recent times has reversed itself. Now it's the rare politician who makes the cut.

The Supreme Decision

The Supreme Court is supposed to be above politics, but we all know how that dynamic is changing in our society as we speak. Not many justices have been honored with stamps, but one that I was directly associated with was the Thurgood Marshall "Black Heritage" series stamp issued in 2003. Even though Justice Marshall had died in 1993, the members of the CSAC knew that he was certainly worthy of commemoration and took steps to begin development of the stamp a few years before a full decade had passed. A few years later, the CSAC revisited the "you have to be dead for ten years" rule and changed it to five years. One of the examples cited during the rule change deliberations was the Marshall stamp.

Art director Dick Sheaff developed numerous concepts utilizing photographs provided by PhotoAssist. Dick recommended using a black-and-white photo in lieu of a full-color portrait. His rationale was that when one thinks of the Supreme Court, the first image that comes to mind is the black robes. He felt a full-color portrait might be distracting. The Committee agreed with his direction and chose one of the black-and-white images. But they recommended that the family be in agreement with the choice. Kelly Spinks contacted Marshall's widow and arranged a meeting the following week.

Mrs. Marshall lived in the D.C. area, which made it easy for all of us to meet for lunch at the Loews Hotel across the street from Postal Headquarters. Having seen numerous photos of Justice Marshall, I knew that he was an unusually tall, imposing man. When I rose to greet Mrs. Marshall as she walked into the restaurant, I was struck by how small in stature she was. I immediately pictured her standing beside her late husband, dwarfed by his height. It brought a smile to my face. But I was soon to discover that, despite her small stature, she was a woman who commanded one's attention.

She brought with her one of her two sons, John W. Marshall, who had achieved prominence of his own as Director of the U.S. Marshals Service. The luncheon proved to be a pleasant one complete with reminiscences of "life with Father." Once the pleasantries were out of the way, Kelly and I shared the image that

Dick had mocked up in addition to backup images in case she didn't respond favorably to our proposal. She was immediately drawn to a full-color image that her son also liked. We discussed the pros and cons of the two competing images, and, to our surprise, Mrs. Marshall agreed with our choice of the black-and-white photo. Her son demurred and pressed for the color image, but his mother, as mothers are wont to do, turned to her son and gave him "the look." John immediately turned to Kelly and me and said, "Whatever Mama wants, Mama gets." At that point, he withdrew his recommendation. Just like a good court case!

In an apparent effort to save face, however, he offered this explanation, in the form of an anecdote, for his withdrawal. He said: "Around our house, it was understood that Father could leave the house each day and make important decisions which impacted every American citizen. But in the evening, when he returned home after removing his judicial robes, 'Mama is in charge,' as he put it."

I could only picture this small woman shaking her finger at her husband towering over her and telling Thurgood Marshall what to do. It was one of those special moments that made my job so much more interesting.

Picking the Right One

Four months after the January 2003 Thurgood Marshall dedication, another political figure was accorded the honor of a postage stamp. It was not a government official this time but someone whose life's work impacted millions of people trying to eke out a modest living: Cesar Chavez.

Carl Herrman, as art director and designer, developed what we felt was a brilliant solution to the design challenge. Using an existing portrait photo, he converted the photo to a high-contrast image, eliminating all the tonal quality, a process often used in posters for many decades. Placing the black image against a brilliant red background, he, in effect, mimicked the look of the grape pickers' union posters of Chavez's time. Not only was it an appropriate design solution; it was an incredibly striking stamp. We felt we had an immediate winner when the CSAC agreed and approved the stamp.

But not all brilliant solutions end up being acted on.

The design was sent with an accompanying letter to the Chavez Family Foundation, whose governing body included members of the Chavez family. Their immediate reaction was to reject the design. Shocked beyond words, we called to find out the reason for the strong, firm, rapid denial. No amount of persuading changed their minds. Eventually, the reason emerged.

As with other families, the Chavez's had pictured in their minds how Cesar should be depicted. Rejecting the very stylized poster effect of the original design, the family had been doing a little research of their own, looking at recent stamp issues to get a feel for how their beloved father, brother, uncle, and friend could best be depicted. They referenced the Marilyn Monroe stamp and others in the Legends of Hollywood series as more in line with what they had in mind. Stunned, I had to bite my tongue and refrain from commenting on the idea of comparing the glamorous blonde bombshell with the founder of the grape pickers' union, but I used my best diplomatic skills to discuss their concerns. Their request was for a full-color portrait of Mr. Chavez, not the stylized portrait we proposed. They insisted that the full-color image was necessary because, in their words, "This will be the most popular stamp of all time, even surpassing 'Elvis.'" I only wish I had a nickel for every time I heard that statement from a family member.

Carl went back to the drawing board and this time selected Robert Rodriguez, an illustrator we had commissioned for previous stamps, to create a more iconic portrait with the vineyards in the background. While it was a nice portrait, and we hoped the family would give their approval this time, we still yearned for the opportunity to issue the "poster" version. But we all knew that wasn't going to happen.

Armed with that knowledge, we scheduled a face-to-face meeting with Foundation members. They indicated that a board meeting at their compound would be the best time to discuss the new design with everyone present. Little did Kelly, Carl, and I know what lay ahead.

The compound, a few hours north of Los Angeles, was in a desolate, hilly region, very different from the sprawling city of L.A. Kelly and I drove together, and Carl drove up from his home in Carlsbad, a couple of hours south of L.A. Despite detailed directions, both Kelly and I were skeptical as we turned off the highway onto a small dirt road. As each mile passed, we grew increasingly concerned that we were lost. But eventually, the compound came into view.

Driving onto the grounds, we followed two well-worn wheel ruts. At one point, Kelly yelled out, “OMG, we almost ran over a grave.” It seems that some of the foundation’s members are buried on the property and buried a little too close to the “road.” It gave us a scare, and an eventual chuckle, when we considered that running over a grave would not be a good way to start our meeting.

Upon arriving, we met up with Carl and were informed that the board meeting was in progress, so we were asked to wait outside. After the arduous trip, we had a little time to relax and take in the beautiful countryside until a board member summoned us inside. The board meeting room was unlike any corporate meeting room I had entered. True to the character of Chavez and his foundation, it was a stark, plain, warehouse-like room complete with concrete floors, folding tables, and no portraits of pompous past board members adorning the walls. Instead, the walls were almost all glass. A very stark boardroom indeed.

Once settled, we soon discovered that the entire board was made up of members of the Chavez family. Our task was to convince not only his widow but twenty-five sons, daughters, nephews, nieces, uncles, aunts, etc. They reviewed the art, listened to our rationale for our image, and then asked us to wait outside while they conferred. To our surprise and pleasure, the design was approved by the entire board. It was the first and probably the only time I had to explain myself to a jury of twenty-five family members. Future meetings with families would be equally interesting, but not as crowded.

Open House Tour

One of the kitschy, touristy things to do while visiting Hollywood is to stop along one of the many streets in the area, pull up beside a young person sitting in the shade trying to stay cool, and buy a map showing the homes of the stars, both past and present. I had no need to resort to such measures when it came to meeting with the families of celebrities. Along with accompanying staff, I was invited to visit their homes. As a longtime film fan, this was beyond anything I could have imagined.

One of the “tours of the stars’ homes” happened when we

arranged an initial meeting to discuss the 2004 Legends of Hollywood subject, Henry Fonda. Our contact was his widow Shirley. Because Mr. Fonda's one-hundredth birthday was fast approaching, some of the staff assumed that we'd be meeting with an elderly widow. Such was not the case. In fact, Shirley, Henry's fourth wife, was much younger than her husband.

Shirley was very excited and insisted that we meet her for lunch. Assuming, and hoping, we would be meeting at one of the better restaurants in Hollywood, we were soon brought back down to earth by her suggestion of lunch at one of her favorite restaurants on Sunset Boulevard, Hamburger Hamlet. Stunned, I believe, would be the appropriate reaction to her suggestion, but of course, we readily agreed. For those of you who are not familiar with this chain, it's been around since the 1960s. While the burgers are good, the entire chain was rather tired and was in need of some rejuvenation.

Rejuvenation was exactly what the Hamlet on Sunset needed. Bill Gicker and I met Shirley for a 1:30 late lunch that day. It seemed by that time that most patrons had already departed, leaving almost the entire restaurant to Shirley, Bill, me, and the cleaning lady who vacuumed the carpets as we ate. Not exactly the idyllic image of a posh Hollywood lunch but interesting, nonetheless.

Shirley proved to be a real dynamo. She expressed great enthusiasm for the project and readily signed the initial agreement for us to do the stamp. She expressed eagerness to meet again to review the design.

Months passed, and after illustrator Drew Struzan completed the portrait and approval from the CSAC was given, Bill and I flew to L.A. for a second meeting. Fearing another late lunch at the Hamlet with Shirley, we were pleasantly surprised by her offer to meet us at her house.

Driving up into the Hollywood Hills, we turned off the road and made a sharp descent into the circular stone driveway of a white stucco Spanish-style home complete with orange tile roof and black wrought-iron ornate gate, which was standing open, awaiting our arrival.

Shirley greeted us warmly at the door and took us into a side study off the front entrance. Before we began discussions, she asked that we wait a moment as a friend would be joining us. A few moments later, Robert Wolders walked into the room. Shirley said she wished to have Robert weigh in on the image. I kept starring at him thinking that I should know that name. The face I didn't recognize, but it was the name that gnawed at my brain. Eventually, it came to mind. He was a Dutch-born actor and the widower of actress Merle Oberon and later the longtime companion of Audrey Hepburn. Upon Hepburn's passing, he became a friend and companion of Shirley Fonda. Hollywood is nothing if not interesting!

Shirley loved the image, as did Robert, despite a few comments that gave Bill and I pause, thinking he was about to sway Shirley's mind. But Shirley's enthusiasm was enough to sell the image. She had hoped that Jane Fonda, who was in town at that time, would have been able to attend the meeting, but previous engagements prevented her from attending, much to Bill's and my dismay. Also, Henry's son Peter was in town but also unavailable. Ironically, he was staying at the same hotel where Bill and I usually stayed. We hoped to maybe cross paths with him, but that, too, was not to be.

As we rose to leave, Shirley asked a silly question: "Would you like to see the rest of the house?" Of course, we'd love to see it. She had told us that Henry had owned it since the 1930s and that it was one of the prime locations in the Hollywood Hills. So off we went on the house tour, with Henry Fonda's widow as our personal guide.

It was a sprawling, beautiful, yet comfortable home filled with artifacts and memorabilia from Henry's six-decade career in films. Aside from being one of the best actors ever to grace the silver screen, Henry was an accomplished artist. His numerous oil paintings were scattered throughout the house. Shirley said that each year, she gave a painting to each of the children and grandchildren. Even though she had been doing that for years, there were still many more paintings to eventually pass along to their descendants. Not content to show us the main living area, she treated us to a tour of every room in the house, even the laundry room. Going out back, we were then shown the orange tree grove that Henry started back in the 1940s, which still produces fruit to this day. The view of Hollywood from that vantage point was one of the highlights of the tour.

Leaving her house that day, I felt as if I had stepped back in time to the glory days of old Hollywood, complete with sprawling Spanish-style homes with incredible views and filled with memories of those golden days. Shirley was a consummate hostess, and I will be forever in her debt for giving me such memories.

Henry Fonda rightly holds his place in the annals of Hollywood as one of the greatest actors of his time. His numerous legendary roles in classics such as The Grapes of Wrath, Mr. Roberts, 12 Angry Men, and Young Mr. Lincoln, to name only a few, left an indelible impression on moviegoers. Yet another performer who gave the definitive performance of a popular literary character was Gregory Peck as Atticus Finch in To Kill a Mockingbird. His performance, like those of Fonda, has resonated with audiences for decades. I was soon to discover, in dealing with Peck's family, just how far the stars' families would go to protect the image of their loved ones.

Picking the Right Peck

Over a span of four decades, Gregory Peck starred in numerous films, making him one of the most bankable stars of his time. It was a given that when the time came, he would be honored with a stamp in the Legends of Hollywood series. His recommendation and selection were aided by his personal friend, Jean Firstenberg, then-Chair of the CSAC. It helps to have friends in the right places. It wasn't that Peck would have been overlooked in the selection process, but having Jean there to help facilitate the process was an invaluable resource.

Jean called Peck's widow, Veronique, to facilitate the initial meeting between the USPS and the family. We were invited to visit her home in "old" Hollywood—Hollywood and Beverly Hills—not one of the gargantuan mansions along the coast in Malibu.

While not palatial by today's standards, it was a very large, beautiful Spanish-style white stucco home. We drove through the imposing iron entrance gate and around the large, Spanish-style courtyard fountain before parking under large shade trees. We then walked across the decorative brick patio to a massive, solid wooden door with a large, heavy wrought-iron door knocker.

Veronique greeted Bill Gicker, Derry Noyes, and me warmly and asked us in. From the entryway, we could see the home had been impeccably designed, complete with beautiful furniture and art. We were asked to join her in the den, where we met both her family and friends. Not a large study, but cozy. The built-in bookshelves were lined with photos of Gregory with numerous famous personalities. Prominently displayed on the back shelf was his Oscar for To Kill a

Mockingbird. Glancing around the room, it was as if we were in a museum dedicated to his memory.

I had asked Derry Noyes, the art director, to accompany Bill and I even though Phil Jordan had been assigned to do the Peck stamp. Derry happened to be on this trip to L.A. with us on another stamp project honoring the great design team of Ray and Charles Eames, who just happened to be family friends of Derry's. The highlight of that part of the trip was a personal tour of the iconic Eames house, which is rarely open to the public. Surprisingly, Derry had never been to the house as a child. We invited her to join us at the Peck residence thinking she might enjoy seeing the house and meeting the Peck family.

Bob Finkelstein, Peck's agent, was there along with the Peck family attorney, Monroe. Bob and I had had dealings before when we developed the Frank Sinatra stamp. We had hoped to meet the Peck children, Tony and Cecilia, but they were unable to attend this initial meeting (they did join us at subsequent meetings as the design was developed). Tea and small sandwiches were presented by the maid before we got down to business.

A range of photos of Gregory was spread out on the coffee table for discussion. It became evident early on that Veronique had strong opinions on what she wanted. She seemed lukewarm to most of the photos presented. Ensconced in a large, overstuffed armchair, Veronique shifted back and forth as she reviewed the photos. I had assumed the small white cloth draped across her right leg to be a shawl. To my surprise, the shawl moved suddenly. It turned out to be a very small dog, one of two we were to discover. Veronique immediately picked it up and cuddled with it. It was apparent that she was extremely fond of the dog. Fortunately, the dog did not interfere with the proceedings. In fact, she spent the remainder of the meeting in Veronique's arms.

After a rather long, protracted discussion regarding which decade and which image to depict him in, Veronique asked me to turn around and look behind me on the wall. There, prominently displayed, was a color painting based on one of the black-and-white photos we had submitted for review. Veronique said, quite confidently, "I believe I like that one best of all." At least we reached an agreement. Or so I thought.

We commissioned Kazuhiko Sano to create the portrait based on that photo. We invited Veronique to attend the unveiling of the Frank Sinatra stamp, which had also been created by Sano. We felt it would allow her to see how the stamp events are handled. But we stressed very strongly that she was not to mention to anyone, especially the media, that a stamp was in the planning stages for her late husband. She assured us that she would not say a word.

Fast-forward one month. At the end of the Sinatra media unveiling, a reporter asked Veronique about the Sinatra stamp and she concluded her comments with the news that her Gregory would be getting a stamp real soon. That news, when relayed back to us in D.C., did not go over very well.

A few months later, we returned to the Beverly Hills home for a review and hopefully an approval of the art. The same players—Veronique, Monroe, and Bob—were there in addition to Peck's son Tony. His sister Cecilia would arrive later during the meeting to offer her opinion as well. We mentioned the "slip-up" in speaking to the media about the Peck stamp, and Veronique's response was that she was so excited about the stamp, she couldn't contain herself. I strongly suspect that she had planned to share her good news all along. Jean Firstenberg, knowing Veronique, had warned us that she could be difficult and demanding, which proved to be very accurate.

At the meeting, the family members had trouble deciding whether they liked the art or not, eventually deciding it wasn't the right photo to work from. They recommended another photo, which we dutifully carried back to D.C. to begin work on a second portrait.

That second portrait met the same fate as the first one. Again, the family was indecisive and vacillated on what they liked and didn't like about the art. During those meetings, I began to regret not learning French when I was in school. Cecilia would hover over Veronique's armchair offering advice to her in French. French was Veronique's native language as she had been a French newspaper reporter when she first met and fell in love with Gregory. It irritated us that they would resort to such measures in an effort to collude against us. Again, the question arose as to which photo we would use to paint a third portrait. It was very rare that we were forced to create so many portraits to please the family. The only other subject that comes to mind is the Edward G. Robinson stamp ten years prior to Peck's inclusion in the Legends series.

During this third time through the process, it became apparent that

Veronique was interested in going in a totally different direction, one that I now believe she was leaning toward the entire time.

Since the Marilyn Monroe stamp in 1995, the first in the Legends of Hollywood series, each pane featured a stamp portrait of the actor or actress and the side selvage on the pane contained a scene from one of their seminal film roles. The Monroe stamp had been an anomaly because the estate, at the last minute, refused permission to use the classic Seven Year Itch scene of Marilyn's skirt blowing up over the sidewalk grating, deeming it as too "sexist." We were forced to use an enlarged version of the stamp art on the selvage in order to meet our print deadline, much to our chagrin.

In the case of the Peck pane, it was always assumed that the side selvage would feature a scene from To Kill a Mockingbird. Both meetings to review the new stamp included the trial scene from the film in the selvage, which was approved by everyone.

But that day, Veronique decided we should switch the portrait with the selvage. She and Cecilia's suggestion was to reproduce, in black and white, a still-frame closeup image of Gregory's face complete with the Atticus Finch glasses. Conversely, the side selvage would feature a black-and-white publicity photo of Peck—the man, not the actor. We argued against such a change but soon came to realize that Veronique doesn't know the word "no." In retrospect, we might have been partially to blame for the switch. We had shown Veronique a complete set of the Legends stamps, which included the upcoming Katharine Hepburn stamp which featured both stamp and selvage in black-and-white photos. That seemed to strike a chord with the two Peck women, which inspired them to rethink the entire concept.

Veronique proceeded to offer her rationale for the change. She said that Gregory had always considered the Atticus Finch role to be his best and that he felt closest to the character and embodied the beliefs of Atticus. He felt "intertwined" with Atticus, as if they were the same, as Veronique described it.

At this point in the meeting, Cecilia reached up onto the bookshelf and produced a book for me to look at. It was Gregory's original working script of Mockingbird. It contained numerous marginal notes in Peck's handwriting describing how to play a specific scene, where special voice inflections were important, and what the scene was really trying to convey. It was an incredible document, one that should be in a museum. As an avid film buff and bibliophile, sitting in a star's home reading his personal script from one of the greatest films of all time was an incredible experience.

Their "sell" job to convince me that using the Atticus/Gregory image as the stamp proved very convincing. I relented with the caveat that we needed to find just the right image.

Cecilia offered to work with Universal Pictures to access the original master print of the film to extract a few images to work with. We reluctantly agreed, and weeks passed before Phil Jordan and the staff at the Journey Group received the grainy images from which they had to manipulate a single frame to make it work as a stamp. Film technology has dramatically changed since 1962 when the film was made, making the conversion process extremely difficult. The images submitted were extremely grainy and would not hold up to six-foot enlargements that are normally produced for the unveiling and issuance. But the Journey Group staff did a great job computerizing and cleaning the art to make it presentable. As a result, a black-and-white stamp was issued, just as Veronique had requested. In retrospect, it's a nice stamp, but not what it could have been.

While New York City may not offer Hollywood's "tours of the stars' homes," there were a few meetings that were equally as memorable in the Big Apple.

The Belle of Broadway

Anyone who knows the theater knows the name Moss Hart, a prolific, prize-winning Broadway director and a writer and Hollywood screenwriter whose works spanned more than three decades including Broadway hits such as You Can't Take It With You, The Man Who Came To Dinner, My Fair Lady, Camelot, and many others. His autobiography, Act One, is considered the best autobiography to ever come out of the theater world. He was married to an equally famous singer, actress, and arts advocate, Kitty Carlisle. She began her career in opera before starring in films and on stage, including a role in the Marx Brothers' classic, A Night at the Opera. On TV, she made appearances on the very popular game show, To Tell the Truth.

My first meeting with Kitty followed her initial meeting with

Mike Owens of PhotoAssist, who had contacted her to obtain a range of images of her late husband from which to create the portrait. Kitty had graciously invited Mike to her home in midtown Manhattan, and that's where my meeting was to take place as well. Mike had warned me to be prepared for a real treat. A treat it was, and it was much more than I had anticipated.

Bill Gicker and I flew to New York and made our way to her apartment on the East Side for an 11 a.m. meeting. Upon entering the elevator, the operator asked who we were visiting. We told him "Mrs. Hart." No floor numbers. No apartment numbers. Just the name. As it turned out, no floor or apartment numbers were needed. When he opened the elevator door with his white-gloved hand and pulled the well-worn brass folding gate back, we found ourselves standing inside her apartment. Not in the corridor but in the outer room of her apartment.

We were immediately received by Mrs. Hart's personal secretary, who inquired if we were there to do an interview. Puzzled, we responded, "No. We have an appointment with Mrs. Hart to discuss a postage stamp for her late husband." She checked her calendar and found no such meeting listed. Somehow it had never been written down. She apologized and asked that we wait there while she spoke with Mrs. Hart.

Expecting to see the secretary return, we were instead greeted by Kitty herself, wearing a flowery housecoat and fuzzy slippers. She had been interrupted in her dressing for a luncheon, but she was not too proud to come out and greet us in that attire. Apologizing profusely for the mix-up, she said she had a previous engagement and would be unable to meet with us that day. After hearing her repeat over and over her sincerest apologies, we rang for the elevator and left empty-handed that day.

A few weeks later, we made the same trip to New York, hoping this time for better results. This time, the stamp's art director, Ethel Kessler, accompanied us. We were not to be disappointed. This time, Kitty was indeed prepared for us. Her secretary asked us to wait in the living room and that Mrs. Hart would be with us momentarily.

Glancing around the room, it was plain to see that this was no ordinary apartment, nor was it a small one. She later told us that she and Moss had lived there since the 1940s, which became evident as we noticed the numerous photos of her and Moss with famous

Broadway stars as well as a baby grand piano, the finest Oriental rugs, antique furniture, and other stately appointments. This was, indeed, one of those fabled East Side apartments of the wealthy.

We had just received that morning what we hoped would be the final art portrait by Tim O'Brien. Tim, also located in New York, gave us the painting in a carefully constructed deep box as the paint was not yet dry and he didn't want anything, or anyone, touching the surface. We jokingly noted that it reminded us of a small urn burial box, a joke we certainly were not about to share with his widow.

A few minutes later, Kitty swept into the room as only a 91-year-old theatrical actress could enter. No housecoat or fuzzy slippers this time. Instead, she greeted us warmly, donned in an off-white Chanel A-line dress, matching pillbox hat, and white gloves. We immediately wondered if she greeted all of her guests in her apartment this way. But, as we sound discovered, she was preparing to join a friend for lunch after our meeting.

Sitting on a large sofa in the living area flanked by Ethel, Bill, and me, Kitty shared her delight and anticipatory excitement about seeing the painting. Upon opening the box lid, she sat silently for a few moments, and then, as only a sophisticated lady could, reached into her purse, extracted a small, white linen handkerchief, and wiped tears from her eyes. It was one of the few times I had experienced such a moving response to artwork presented to a family member.

As you can imagine, she loved the painting and agreed to approve it without any changes, a rare occurrence. I always anticipated having to negotiate changes with family members, but not Kitty.

Kitty's demure stature belied her personality. She turned out to be one of the most entertaining and funny people I've encountered in all my stamp meetings. I should have guessed there would be a fun-loving and boisterous side to her. After all, anyone who could hold their own against the zany Marx Brothers for an entire film had to have spunk.

Once the official business concluded, she began to regale us with one story after another about her career, one more amusing than the last. Ethel asked her what she was doing in her retirement years. Her response was, "What retirement? I'm still going strong. In fact, I have a gig next month at a club in Manhattan singing the old standards." She added very quickly, "But don't tell my daughter, the doctor. She doesn't know, and she'd be very upset with me."

With that, she asked if we'd like to see the rest of the apartment. Mike had warned us to be prepared as he had received the same offer. We proceeded to move, guided by Kitty, from the living room into the dining room, which could seat twenty people comfortably at an enormously long, antique wooden table. Moving down the hallway, we were treated to a potpourri of movie and opera posters from her illustrious career. But of most interest were the original works of art interspersed among the posters.

Kitty casually pointed to a rather crude, dark painting of a single red rose in a dark vase, saying, "This one was done by Irving Berlin." Berlin's attempt at another form of art had been a gift to Kitty. We had no idea that this great Broadway composer had taken up painting in his spare time. But Kitty reassured us that it was one of a kind, and she had told him not to give up his day job. Fortunately for Broadway's sake, he took Kitty's advice.

Continuing down the long hallway, we were treated to original paintings by George Gershwin, Noel Coward, and even that zany ever-silent comic Harpo Marx, all very talented painters in their own right. All the paintings were personal gifts from the artists. It was a delight to be able to have the rare opportunity to see these works up close and in person.

Not wanting us to miss anything, we were shown out of the hallway and across the main room into Kitty's bedroom and even into her huge walk-in closet, stopping to chat in a side dressing room in which the walls were covered with photos of her with celebrities and politicians. Here was Kitty with Cary Grant, Richard Burton, the Marx Brothers, and on and on. As an advocate for the arts, she had met with presidents from both sides of the political divide, but when we noted that she was posing with then-current President George W. Bush, she scoffed, saying: "I don't like that one. I don't like him at all. But let's not talk politics." With that, we proceeded on through her personal bathroom and out again into the main living area. That was one of the most thorough home tours I'd ever been on, only to be matched by the Henry Fonda home tour a few months later.

While there were no more tours of homes or lavish apartments on our many trips to New York, I did have another very interesting meeting there the same year, 2002, that I met with Kitty.

Dancing to the Right Tune

The CSAC had chosen to honor four great American Choreographers in 2004, one of which was the talented African-American dancer and choreographer, Alvin Ailey. My wife Ann and I had the great fortune to attend one of his memorable performances of highly creative dance at the Kennedy Center years earlier.

Our visit to the Alvin Ailey Dance Company was the day after our meeting with Kitty Carlisle. Bill, Ethel, and I taxied over to the company's theater on the West Side of Manhattan late that morning to share the design Ethel had created using photographs of Ailey and a photo of one of his signature dances being performed by his troupe.

Shown into a rather bare, plain room with a worn wooden table and chairs, we were asked to wait there and Ms. Jamison would be with us shortly as she was still rehearsing the company. Until that moment I had no idea just who it was that we'd be talking to. We had not been informed of this by their offices. It certainly would have been helpful to have been given that bit of information prior to our meeting. Judith Jamison, at the time Ann and I attended the Kennedy Center performance, was Ailey's principal dancer and was widely considered to be among the greatest modern dancers of our time. Upon Ailey's premature death, Jamison was appointed head of the company. She would later go on to receive a National Medal of Arts for her contributions to the world of dance.

About ten minutes later, she entered the glass-enclosed room. Her size and stature gave her a commanding presence, and I knew instantly we were in the presence of a powerful individual who would not hesitate to share her real feelings, as I was soon to discover.

Ms. Jamison responded favorably to the working design. We then expressed our concern that the photo we were currently using depicted Ailey with what could be misconstrued as a stern or even mean look. We asked her if she could identify another photo we might consider, to which she replied that she was comfortable with the current photo. I pushed back, again asking if she didn't want to reconsider. Normally, I would have been thrilled to get an immediate approval, but members of the CSAC had expressed concern about the stern look. At that point, this towering woman, who dwarfed me even sitting down, turned and firmly said: "I don't think you are getting my point, Mr. McCaffrey. This photo is fine. It depicts him as he really was. He was not a nice man. Do you understand?" I understood. With that, we thanked her for her time and left. The Ailey stamp as printed and issued in 2004 carries that stern look of the "not very nice man."

It's one thing to discuss with families which reference photo to work from when developing stamp art. But it's another situation entirely to deal with feuding estates, especially family members. Two such families immediately come to mind when I think of feuding families that we, the Postal Service, somehow were caught between.

The Tough Guys

Individual members of the CSAC often made recommendations of subjects they had some knowledge, connection, or experience with. Such was the case for the Legends of Hollywood subject, Edward G. Robinson. Karl Malden was the "go-to guy" on the Committee when it came to suggestions for subjects for the series.

Karl recommended fellow actor, Edward G., whom he had appeared alongside in only one film, The Cincinnati Kid, some years earlier. Off-screen, however, Karl and Edward G. and their respective spouses were close friends. When asked to explain his choice, Karl cited the numerous accomplishments of his old friend, and that was enough for Committee members to recommend him for inclusion in the series, specifically as the 1999 honoree.

Work began on the portrait, which proved to be problematic from numerous standpoints. But before it could be finalized, another actor entered stage right and sought to step into the limelight for the 1999 issuance: James Cagney, a contemporary of both Malden and Robinson. Cagney's name was on a list of actors and actresses under consideration, but there was no agreement by the Committee to issue a Cagney stamp.

Our office received a call from a legal representative of the Cagney estate wishing to discuss the possibility of a stamp. Because James Tolbert, my supervisor, Kelly Spinks, our rights specialist, and I were slated to be in Los Angeles for other meetings, we agreed to work in a dinner meeting one evening after our other meetings had concluded.

Upon arrival at a Mexican restaurant in North Hollywood, we were greeted by two gentlemen, Jeff Lotman and his lawyer, who had made the initial contact. We were seated in an outdoor patio that we had to ourselves, primarily because it was only 5:30 p.m., an hour when only seniors dine in Tinseltown.

During the usual pleasantries, Jeff shared his background, which we found fascinating. His father made his fortune by selling beef to McDonald's. Jeff used a share of the family fortune to amass a collection of animation cels from classic films considered to be one of the largest and finest in existence. Jeff shared that his interests had recently turned to estate representation and that he now represented the estate of James Cagney. At that time, only a handful of firms represented estates, most of which we were already acquainted with, but Global Icons was new to us.

To dispel any concerns, we might have had regarding the legitimacy of their firm, Jeff asked that his lawyer share with us additional information related to estate dealings. At that point, amid our margaritas and Mexican food, the lawyer produced a copy of the last will and testament of one James Cagney. To this day, I still consider it to be one of the most bizarre meetings I have had. The complete will was read to us as we dined on enchiladas and rice. We reassured them that it wasn't necessary, but they insisted because of the controversy surrounding the will, and we soon discovered how this "controversy" was about to complicate our lives.

Cagney, in his later years, retired to a farm in Connecticut, where he lived out his remaining years. He became estranged from his daughter, Cathleen "Casey" Thomas, during that time. As he began to fit more comfortably into the Connecticut countryside and surroundings, he found company in Madge Zimmerman, the proprietress of a tavern down the road from his house. She befriended the retired actor and eventually assisted with his housekeeping and upkeep of the property. Their friendship was such that when Cagney passed, he left the bulk of his estate to Madge. As one can imagine, the Cagney family was unamused and contested the will, but failed to sway the courts in their favor. From 1986 on, there was bitter resentment in the words exchanged between the two parties.

This information was shared with us that evening with the caveat that they wanted the stamp issued in 1999, the one-hundredth anniversary of Cagney's birth. We shared that we had already slotted another actor for that year, and the time was very short in which to develop a new subject and issue it within that timeframe. But their persistence prevailed, so James, Kelly, and I agreed to put their request before the Committee, noting that the final decision was in the Committee's hands, not ours. At the next Committee meeting, they agreed to move Edward G. Robinson to 2000 and slot Cagney for 1999. But they turned to Karl first to make sure he was comfortable with the change, which he was.

The research and development process on Cagney went exceedingly well. Drew Struzan's portrait illustration was right on target, and the approval process went smoothly, with no hitches, glitches, changes, or rejections.

It wasn't until the first-day-of-issue ceremony in Hollywood that the family issues arose again. Fortunately, from my standpoint, I didn't have to worry about the family, but our Events staff did. Both Cagney's daughter Cathleen and Cagney's friend Madge were invited and accepted invitations to the event. A.C. Lyles, a living Hollywood legend who knew much of Hollywood's history and had lived it, was the presiding official. Before the evening event, the Events staff was tearing their hair out trying to appease the two warring factions. One family member said that if "they were going to be given time to speak during the ceremony, then we want equal time." Eventually, Cagney's daughter did speak, and Madge chose not to. Still, you could feel the tension in the audience. On one side of the auditorium sat Cagney's daughter, and on the other side sat Madge. Dirty looks were thrown between the two, especially during the daughter's blunt, pointed comments. The evening culminated with a showing of Yankee Doodle Dandy, the film for which Cagney received an Academy Award. Everyone felt relieved that no arguments had broken out before the event or afterward when reporters interviewed the two parties.

And now, back to Edward G.

Preliminary work had begun on Robinson's biographical information, photo research, etc. Howard Paine was assigned as art director and worked with illustrator Ren Wicks to develop the Robinson portrait based on a photo selected by the art directors at one of their monthly meetings. Upon completion of three sketches, the art was shared at the next CSAC meeting. The Design Subcommittee liked the art but held off approving it until Karl had a chance to weigh in. And weigh in he did.

Karl didn't like the portrait at all. In retrospect, we should have run our choice of photos by him before beginning work. Karl's reasoning was that the photo chosen did not convey the characteristics that one would associate with Robinson. Karl was looking for a portrait that not only conveyed the "tough guy" persona he was known for in many gangster films but also the gentler side that Karl and others knew off-screen.

At that point, before starting any new artwork, we sent reference photos to the two estate representatives, granddaughter Francesca Robinson Sanchez and film director George Sidney, a friend of the actor who married Robinson's widow. A third set was sent to Karl Malden. We hoped that all three parties could agree before further work began.

Reviewing the range of photos, the parties agreed on the appropriate photo for the illustrator to work from. In the interim, the original illustrator, Ren Wicks, suffered a bad fall and was unable to continue work on the project, eventually dying from those injuries. After conferring with Howard, he and I agreed on illustrator Thomas Blackshear to pick up the mantle and begin a new illustration. Blackshear's illustration produced the results everyone was looking for—everyone except Karl. His objection was that this Edward G. looked "too soft" and suggested we needed to "toughen him up a little." After making those changes, we were confident that we were on the right track.

Kelly Spinks and I flew to L.A. for a meeting with Robinson's granddaughter at our Santa Monica hotel. Our initial meeting with her was warm and cordial, giving us the comfort and confidence that this would be an easy task. But we were about to discover the history of bad blood between her and the other half of the estate.

Seated in a large, leather cushioned booth in the hotel bar, we shared with Francesca a copy of the approved portrait. She was so moved by the portrait that tears came to her eyes. (That made three weeping women: Fonda, Hart, and now Robinson. I never thought stamps could have such an effect on people.) We shared the fact that Karl had been personally involved in the selection and loved the art as well. Francesca spoke warmly of Karl and appreciated his involvement.

At this point, she dropped the bombshell on us. She asked if we had spoken with or shown the art to "him"—meaning George Sidney, the director known for such films as Kiss Me Kate, Bye Bye Birdie, and numerous other musicals and dramas. Her very tone of voice when uttering the word "him" gave both Kelly and I pause. We strongly suspected we were in for a bumpy ride.

We responded that we had not yet shown the art to "him," but that was our next step. Her response: "He won't like it." We inquired why, to which she replied that he would reject it merely because she had approved it. She chose not to go into detail about the relationship between the two halves of the estate but acknowledged there was conflict between them.

The next day, we called Karl and asked him to shed some light on the situation before we proceeded with the next approval step. Karl was more than happy to fill us in.

It seems that Edward G. and Sidney were very close friends for many years until one day Edward G. discovered that his good friend had been having an affair with his wife. Enraged and hurt, Robinson severed the relationship with his old friend and refused to speak to him again.

Upon Robinson's passing several years later, his widow married Sidney, much to the chagrin of the rest of the family. Some years later, the then Mrs. Sidney passed, leaving her portion of the Robinson estate to her husband, which, as can be imagined, upset the family even more. Silence and obstinacy became the hallmarks of the relationship between the two halves of the estate. This is what we were about to walk into the middle of.

After tracking Sidney down through his lawyers, Kelly sent a copy of the art to him at his Las Vegas address. Initially, it was returned unopened. After calls to his lawyer, because of his unwillingness to speak directly with us, we sent the art once again for his review.

Francesca was right. He rejected the art, saying it was the most hideous portrait he had ever seen, and refused to approve it. We shared his response with Francesca, and all parties (well, at least two of the three) decided we'd have to develop another portrait. We hoped that a second attempt would find approval from both sides.

Karl was involved again in helping to secure CSAC approval for this second attempt at an agreeable image. We then met with Francesca and again received her approval, just like the first time. Needless to say, we received the same response from Sidney too: rejection.

A third attempt was made with a new illustration and illustrator, Drew Struzan. It seems that while the two estates were clashing, illustrator Blackshear decided to remodel his home and studio. When contacted to begin a new illustration, Blackshear declined due to his studio being unusable. Struzan, a seasoned stamp illustrator, stepped into the breach and created an illustration that both the CSAC and Karl readily approved, not to mention Francesca, and after much stalling, a tacit approval came from Mr. Sidney, much to our surprise and relief.

Francesca was concerned that Sidney would attend the first-day event, which would only cause friction and potentially bad publicity. But she had nothing to worry about as he declined to attend the ceremony. To add to Francesca's frustrations over the entire process, we moved the stamp from 1999 to 2000 to accommodate the one-hundredth birthday of Jimmy Cagney. In the end, Francesca, Karl, and everyone else were pleased with the final results. It was the journey that had proved so difficult.

More often than not, family members are thrilled with the honor of having the U.S. Government select their loved one to be featured on millions of postage stamps. Most families understand the significance of this honor and are more than willing to work with our design team to develop an appropriate illustration. Sometimes, though, families have preconceived notions of how their loved one should be depicted, and they attempt to dictate the artwork.

Makeup vs. Mug Shot

One such instance is the Classic Movie Monsters series issued in 1997. Carl Burcham, our Stamps Marketing Manager, had suggested these stamps to the CSAC around 1995. The Committee gave the green light to develop four subjects: Frankenstein, Dracula, Wolf Man, and The Mummy. I assigned Derry Noyes as art director, and we agreed that Thomas Blackshear was the best choice to illustrate the monsters.

Over the next year, Thomas produced four great portraits, readily approved by the Committee. Then it was time to contact not only Universal Studios, which controlled the rights to the monsters, but family members as well.

This meant yet another trip to L.A. for my boss James Tolbert, Kelly Spinks, and me. I was delayed at the office, so I arrived the following day. I was told to meet them at Universal Studios, where we would be negotiating with the family members. Because James and Kelly had already rented a car, I didn't need one. Kelly told me to take a Super Shuttle van that would drop me off at the studio. I wish now that I had not taken her advice.

Upon arriving in L.A. at 11 a.m., I got into a taxi van along with five other people. For the next two hours, I was driven from one end of L.A. to the other. As I expected, I was the last to be dropped off. To make matters worse, they dropped me off at the entrance to the Universal Studios theme park, which was many blocks from the working studio. After frantic calls, I was able to figure out which building I needed to find.

I arrived at the meeting to find a long, narrow, dimly lit large conference room that smelled of pizza. It appeared that before my arrival, they had ordered in pizza and had left one cold slice for me. By this time, I was not only starved but in a frazzled state what with a two-hour taxi ride, delivery to the wrong location, and jet lag. Little did I know what further obstacles lay ahead.

In addition to Universal Studios representatives, there were three family members at the meeting representing the Boris Karloff, Bela Lugosi, and Lon Chaney, Jr. estates. We soon discovered those three knew each other very well and regularly negotiated contracts as a group. The main spokesperson for the group was Sara Karloff, Boris's daughter. Bela Lugosi, Jr., and Ron Chaney, the son of Lon Chaney, Jr., being the other two. Because of Sara's strong personality, she did most of the talking.

In my briefcase were copies of the four CSAC-approved Monster illustrations. At that point, none of the families knew we had already completed the painting. They believed that we were there to begin negotiations for the stamps. They also had a very different concept of what the stamps should look like.

Sara made a strong plea for us to consider honoring the three actors, not their famous monster roles. Immediately, I began to feel queasy. Things were going in the opposite direction from where I thought we would start. Not only did they want to see the actors portrayed sans makeup, but Sara had already chosen an illustrator to do the work. Things were going downhill fast.

The illustrator had created previous portraits for the families that had met with approval from all parties. While the illustrations were okay, they were not of the caliber and quality of the painting I had hidden away in my briefcase.

With my stomach growling (I chose not to eat the lone remaining piece of cold pizza) and my head swirling from all the roadblocks being thrown in our way, I knew we were in for a long afternoon—and long it was.

After three hours of negotiating, I felt I had to "fess up" and show our artwork. As I laid the art on the table, I could see that Sara in particular seemed upset that we had taken the project to such an advanced stage. I made my case for the illustrations and lauded Thomas's brilliant artwork. They all agreed the paintings were wonderful, but their concern remained that it commemorated the monster characters and not their fathers and grandfathers.

To complicate matters further, Ron Chaney made a surprise request. He wanted to add a fourth actor to the mix. He wanted his grandfather, Lon Chaney, Sr., included. He rightly pointed out that his grandfather had created some of the earliest film monsters, specifically, the Phantom of the Opera. It was hard to disagree with his request, and we agreed to consider adding a fourth image.

Discussions dragged on for another two hours before a very frustrated Bela suggested we adjourn the meeting and reconvene at a restaurant because he thought everyone might be as hungry as he was. I was the first to agree. He chose an Italian restaurant in Beverly Hills that he liked to frequent, and off we went.

For the next two to three hours, we feasted on wonderful Italian food and wines. Somehow, I got seated next to Sara. At first, I was a bit intimidated by her, but that wore off in short order. After a glass of vino, we began talking about her growing up as the daughter of Frankenstein's monster. We enjoyed many good laughs, and I learned how much she loved her father and what a kind, gentle soul he was. Laced throughout our conversations, though, she kept pressing for the actor, not the monster, to be portrayed. I could certainly see their point about their fathers, but the Postal Service's position was that the monsters would be much more popular, which would continue to be the main sticking point in reaching an agreement.

I shared with Sara the first time I saw her father's great performance in Frankenstein. I related that I was only about eight years old and had been allowed to stay up late on Saturday night to watch the Late Show on our local TV station. Back then, in the early 1950s, they telecast old movies late at night, and on that particular night, they were showing one of the greatest monster movies of all. I begged my father to allow me to stay up. He agreed.

Sitting in a dimly lit room with one lone floor lamp shedding a dusky yellow light, on a small, dark, wooden stool in front of my father's recliner, I was totally mesmerized watching a grainy television image of that stark black-and-white film. As the tension grew, so did my fear. My only hope was to seek protection. Slowly, my stool pushed back, closer and closer to my father, who was probably nodding off as he usually did. As the townspeople were storming the castle with their torches, I pushed up against my father's knees and stayed in that position for the remainder of the film. I knew I could count on my father to keep me safe. It left an indelible impression on me for years to come.

When I finished the story, Sara gave me a big hug and kissed me on the cheek, exclaiming, "That is one of the most beautiful stories I've heard, and I will always cherish it." Minutes later, Sara asked for everyone's attention. She said that she had reached a conclusion that they (she, Bela, and Ron) should acquiesce to our request and allow the Postal Service to use the monster illustrations, but with one caveat. We needed to find a way to honor the actors as well. Everyone agreed, leaving it to me to provide a solution agreeable to all parties.

Back at the office, a suggestion was made to use black-and-white photographic portraits of the four actors in the decorative selvage at the top of the pane of stamps, which proved to be an excellent solution. It received immediate approval.

The stamps were dedicated in an elaborate first-day ceremony at a theater on the Universal Studios lot, and the stamps would go on to be among the biggest sellers of the year.

Sara and I would go on to become good friends and saw each other frequently at stamp events held on the West Coast. I would have the opportunity to work with her again when we produced the

American Filmmaking: Behind the Scenes stamps in 2003. These stamps honored the creative talent behind the scenes. The Makeup stamp showed makeup artist Jack Pierce applying makeup to Boris Karloff as Frankenstein.

Thousands of individuals proposed over the years have failed to be selected for commemoration on postage stamps, resulting in a lot of disgruntled families. Oddly enough, there have also been numerous instances when the family took issue with their relative being depicted on a postage stamp.

Tall in the Saddle

In 1990, the Postal Service released a block of four stamps honoring four Classic Films of 1939, one of which was the classic Western, Stagecoach, which featured a prominent image of John Wayne. The Stamp Services staff managing the program at that time had obtained reproduction rights from the respective film studios. After all, the stamp was honoring the films, not the actors portrayed on the stamps. So, the images of Clark Gable and Vivien Leigh (Gone with the Wind), Gary Cooper (Beau Geste), Judy Garland (The Wizard of Oz), and John Wayne (Stagecoach) never required signed reproduction rights from their estates.

Upon the Stagecoach stamp's release, Michael Wayne, John's oldest son and manager of the Wayne estate, contacted Stamp Services. He insisted that rights needed to be obtained from the Wayne estate, and no amount of talking would change his mind. Additionally, no licensing could be done for the Stagecoach stamp without a signed licensing agreement. This caused a bit of heartburn for the office staff, who had to inform post offices nationwide that they were not allowed to create licensed products, i.e., T-Shirts, coffee cups, etc., depicting the Stagecoach stamp. The Marketing staff in many large post offices were naturally disgruntled but had no choice but to comply. That acrimonious relationship between us and Michael Wayne was a bitter pill to swallow for years to come.

Now, fast-forward twenty years to when the CSAC chose John Wayne for a future Legends of Hollywood issuance. Surely, by now, the animosity between the two parties must have faded. Right? Alas, that was not the case. Kelly Spinks contacted Michael Wayne and requested a meeting to discuss a stamp for his father. There was initial reluctance to even meet with us on Michael's part. But Kelly managed to convince him to meet at his Wilshire Boulevard offices in L.A.

Kelly and I were accompanied on this trip by our manager, James Tolbert, Jr. The initial reception was chilly, to say the least. Michael let it be known from the start that he was reluctant to participate in another stamp as he felt maligned by the previous issuance. We assured him that this was a new day, new staff, and new policies regarding reproduction rights.

The meeting started at eleven and, after an hour, Michael suggested that we discuss it further over lunch. We adjourned to his favorite restaurant across the street in a small alley, aptly called The Alley. Walking through the dining room to our table reminded me of classic movie scenes where movie moguls, sporting Italian-made suits and smoking cigars, walked through the room greeting numerous agents, producers, and stars. Michael did just that, stopping often to chat with several diners as we worked our way to our table.

Michael proceeded to order a large, high-calorie lunch and implored us not to tell his wife or daughter as they would have a fit about his diet. The lunch went well, and we relaxed and enjoyed each other's company. Upon returning to the office, Michael began to soften his position and entertained the possibility of reaching an agreement. He shared with us his father's sweat-stained cowboy hat, bandana, and six-shooter, all iconic objects his father had worn in numerous films, which we were allowed to handle. We left with the understanding that we would work on the rights agreement but that we could proceed with art. He insisted his father be portrayed in a cowboy outfit, which had also been our intention.

On the next visit to Michael's offices, we met with his assistant and her son, who had been working on cataloging and digitizing thousands of images of John Wayne, a daunting and endless task. Nonetheless, they were diligently working away at it. We were allowed to peruse the images in search of iconic poses that would best fit our needs. Art director Derry Noyes accompanied us to L.A. for the photo search. We came away with more than enough images to explore.

Drew Struzan was selected to create the portrait, and between Derry, the art directors, and me, we selected an image we thought would work best. The art Drew created from that selection was immediately approved by the CSAC some months later. In the interim, we met again with Michael to discuss rights issues. When the art was approved, we made yet another trip to L.A. to get Michael's approval. Much like other estate reps who feel compelled to ask for changes, he requested changes, all minor, but changes that had to be made, nonetheless. I believe the estates do that to ensure they are having some leverage in the process rather than being mere rubber stamps, which I completely understand so long as we could reach an agreement.

The revisions were made, and a copy was sent to Michael for final approval. At that point, everything went silent. We never received final approval of the art, nor did we get the signed agreement. All that we lacked were final signatures. But Michael was not talking to us. By this time, Kelly Spinks had left the Postal Service and was working at the Roger Richman Agency handling rights agreements for other stars, which left me to try to get Michael to talk to us.

For the next year or so, whenever I was in L.A., I would call his office and ask if I could stop by to chat. I was always told he was not in or unavailable. I resorted to stopping by his office unannounced, but never found him there. I even went across the street to his favorite restaurant hoping to catch him dining, but never found him there either. His assistant was very curt with me, which gave me pause. It was as if he had dropped off the face of the earth.

Then months later, I received word through mutual contact that Michael was ill and dying of cancer. In fact, he had been ill for months, and that was the reason we couldn't meet with him. A month or so after hearing this news of his illness, I read of his passing, at which point I suggested to the CSAC that we put the Wayne stamp on hold, which they agreed to.

Months passed until one day I received an unexpected call. On the other end of the line was Ethan Wayne, John's youngest son and the new manager of the Wayne estate. He said he had come across my business card on which Michael had handwritten "postage stamp." Ethan wanted to know what that was about. Containing my excitement as best I could, I proceeded to explain the status of the project. He expressed strong interest in making the stamp happen and immediately invited me to meet with him. "Could I be in L.A. tomorrow?" he asked. Bill Gicker and I boarded a plane bound for

L.A. the following day and drove down to his Newport Beach offices. No Wilshire Boulevard offices for Ethan. He was much more laidback than his older brother. We met in his office, which appeared to be a retail store in its previous life. Ethan came bouncing down the stairs from the open loft area and seated us in overstuffed armchairs in the middle of the empty showroom floor. It was in that sparse setting where we reviewed the art, which Ethan loved and immediately signed off on. He agreed to review the rights agreement and move it quickly. We cemented our friendship and stamp partnership over lunch at a popular, excellent seafood restaurant near his office. Within a few weeks, we had a signed agreement with the Wayne estate and moved the issuance back into the lineup.

On September 9, 2004, the Grauman's Chinese Theatre first-day-of-issuance event on Hollywood Boulevard was held. The ceremony took place in the outdoor plaza among all the famed footprints with the entire Wayne family in attendance. The ceremony was capped with a showing of clips from many of Wayne's classic films inside Grauman's Theatre. For me, it was yet another wonderful Hollywood event that made the small-town Minnesota boy in me burst with excitement.

Ol' Blue Eyes

Six years later, another prominent entertainer was subjected to the same discussion. Only this time, instead of a television star, it was a music legend. Frank Sinatra was selected by the CSAC for commemoration in 2007, ten years after his passing. Despite Sinatra's many film roles, the Committee felt his major contribution to the American arts was as a singer. The decision was made to feature him, not as part of a series like the Legends of Hollywood but as a single issue commemorative stamp.

Art director Dick Sheaff recommended Kazuhiko Sano to paint the portrait. Actually, Kazu had been in touch with me, literally begging me to let him do the portrait. He indicated he was a major fan of Sinatra's and would be honored to do it. Upon sharing this with Dick, we agreed Kazu could be the right person for the job.

As with Judy Garland's family, three siblings would have to approve the art: Nancy, Tina, and Frank, Jr. For whatever reason, their mother was not part of the picture. I didn't ask questions; I just agreed to work directly with Tina, who managed the estate on behalf of the family.

Bob Finkelstein, a prominent Hollywood agent, represented Sinatra along with numerous other famous personalities, including Gregory Peck, whose stamp would be issued a few years later. Bob and Tina shared workspace in a Tudor-style, two-story house. Bob's office was downstairs and Tina's upstairs.

My assistant Bill, my rights specialist, Layne, and I arrived for our first meeting with Bob and Tina. Bob greeted us at what was the back door to a small, narrow pantry entry next to the kitchen. The living room just beyond it was filled with books, photos, and wall posters relating to Sinatra. Bob called upstairs for Tina to come down: "The guys from the D.C. Post Office are here."

Bob was attired in an open-collar dress shirt, casual slacks, and loafers with no socks. I was to learn over the following years that this was his usual attire. Unfortunately, we three "D.C. Post Office guys" were dressed in suits. Tina bounded down the steps and greeted us warmly. She shared how excited she was by the prospect of having a stamp honoring her dad. So much so that when her mail carrier arrived at the door with a package, she brought this small Asian woman into the room and introduced us to her. It only took a moment for her to share the confidential information that her dad was going to be on a stamp. The letter carrier nodded, smiled, and said, "That's nice." She then quietly inched her way to the door with a quizzical look on her face as if to say, "What was that all about?"

That initial meeting consisted of exploring imagery for us to paint from. It was obvious that there was plenty of source material right in that room. But Tina, who had taken a liking to us immediately, decided to play with us. She jumped up from the chair she was lounging in and said, "I've got the perfect photo for you." She crossed the room and took down a large reproduction of the infamous photo of a very young Frank posing for his mug shot at the police station. He had been arrested on a minor charge, but the photo had gained notoriety over the years. We laughed and said that we weren't sure that that was the appropriate image. She chided us for being "stuffy D.C. bureaucrats" and said we needed to "loosen up." We did loosen up after that, but we all agreed that the police mug shot wasn't the one. But we did leave with a good range of more appropriate photos for Kazu to work from.

A few months later, we returned to work out the details of the contract with Tina and Bob. But this time, we chose to have a little fun with Tina. Bill had discovered online a black T-shirt with Frank's police mug shot on it. We immediately ordered three shirts for the trip. After arriving at the house and before Bob opened the back door, we slipped the T-shirts over our shirts (no suits and ties this time). When Bob opened the door, there stood three "D.C. bureaucrats" wearing the Frank mug shot. He broke into immediate laughter and yelled for Tina to come down immediately. Once she rounded the corner off the stairs and came into the living room, she stopped, stared, and broke into gales of laughter. She thought it was hilarious. That one gesture cemented our relationship and made the entire process much simpler.

Upon returning to D.C., we reviewed at the next art directors' meeting the art developed by Kazu. I was very unhappy with the look and feel of it. The colors were very moody, an effect that Kazu was going for. But I felt it failed to capture who Sinatra really was. Dick and I disagreed on it. Kazu was adamant that his approach was "cool, just like Sinatra," but the other art directors and I were reluctant to either support it or reject it. Both Dick and Kazu pressured me to send a copy of it to Tina for the family's review. Reluctantly, I did just that.

To no pleasant surprise, the family disliked it very much. They asked for an entirely new piece of art. This time, we encouraged Kazu to paint a more realistic portrait of Frank from the 1950s in his famous cocked hat pose.

New art was developed, and it was back to California once again. Until then, we had worked only with Tina, not Nancy or Frank, Jr. But this time, we assured Tina we had a winner, so she asked Nancy to stop by. Frank, Jr. was based in the New York area, so we had no direct dealings with him.

When we arrived, we were told that Tina would be down in a moment and that I could step into the other room where Nancy was waiting. As I approached the back room, I heard the distinct sounds of Nancy's big hit, "These Boots Are Made for Walkin'" coming from the room. Stopping in the doorway, I found her singing along with the music track on the sound system. No white go-go boots but dancing and singing her heart out. She was so intent on her singing; she never noticed me standing there. I was being given a personal, one-on-one performance by Nancy Sinatra of her smash hit. I was overjoyed but remained quiet until she was done. When the song ended, she turned, smiled, and said, "You must be Terry. I'm Nancy." What a way to start a meeting!

Eventually, we all gathered in the room: Bob, Tina, Nancy, Bill, Layne, and I. Tina was so nervous about seeing the art, she said she wanted to sit next to me on the sofa. Sitting close to me, Tina slipped her arm through mine and hugged me close in anticipation. Nancy sat opposite me on the other side of the coffee table. As I uncovered the art, Tina's first comment was: "It's perfect. That's Dad!" Nancy eagerly wanted to see it, and she agreed with her sister. In fact, she gave the art a big kiss of approval.

The first-day ceremony turned into multiple ceremonies. There were numerous discussions between our events staff and the Sinatra family as to the best location for the ceremony. The Sinatra's insisted the stamp be dedicated in Hoboken, New Jersey (his birthplace), Los Angeles, and Las Vegas. Surprisingly, the Postal Service, normally constricted by tight budgets, felt that Sinatra was important enough to warrant three separate ceremonies, so we acquiesced to the family's wishes. Nancy represented the family in L.A., Frank, Jr. in Hoboken, and Tina in Las Vegas. I chose to attend the Las Vegas ceremony because of my close working relationship with Tina and Bob.

The ceremony was held outside of the Bellagio Hotel and Casino on May 13, 2008, on a rather warm day even for Las Vegas. A green room had been set up in one of the hotel suites for the participants, and it was where we found Tina and Bob and other dignitaries, both Postal- and Sinatra-related. We had invited Kazu to attend at the request of Tina. As expected, Kazu was in seventh heaven. Tina seemed very nervous and gave me a big, long hug when I saw her. Her nervousness surprised me considering her strong managerial style coupled with her acting and producing background in Hollywood.

As the ceremony was about to begin, Tina came to me and asked that I join her in the dignitary section. I told her I didn't have permission to sit there, but she said: "You do now. Come with me. I want you by my side." Not wanting to refuse, I joined her and Bob in the roped-off area. She held my hand through most of the ceremony, which I found very touching.

These are but a few of the "family" memories I encountered over my twenty years in Stamps. Looking back over it now, despite any problems and pitfalls I might have encountered in developing these miniature works of art, I still feel fortunate to have been given the opportunity to work with families whose loved ones have contributed so much to our culture and history.

Chapter 8
The Big Show

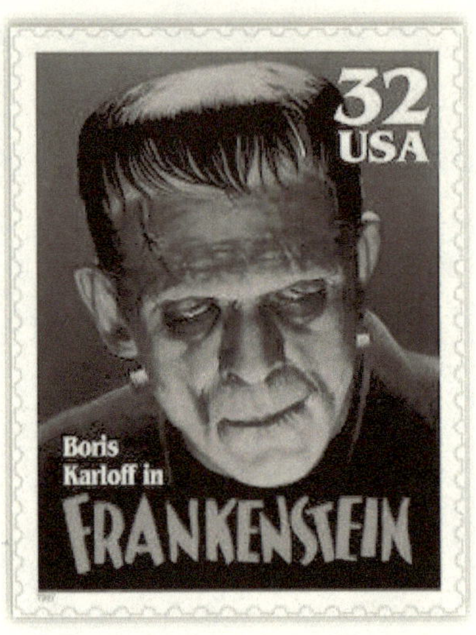

The Postal Service and its predecessor, the Post Office Department, have tried to maximize the awareness and sale of new stamps when they are issued. For many decades, as noted throughout the book, they have held what they have termed "first-day-of-issue" ceremonies.

What makes these events significant, especially for stamp collectors, is that the stamp is dedicated in an official ceremony in a predetermined location appropriate to the subject matter and often on a specific date relating to the subject matter, such as a birthdate, the anniversary of an event, etc. Families of the honorees and other officials are invited to speak at the ceremony. But of the most interest to the collecting community is that the sale of the new stamp is limited to that location on that one day only. Nationwide sales of the stamp begin the following day. That policy has changed in recent years with the stamps now going on sale nationwide on the first-day date.

The ceremonies range from small local events at stamp shows to major, star-studded events in Hollywood. What always struck me as odd was the actual "unveiling" of the stamp image. Virtually every ceremony I attended handled it in the same way. An enlargement was made of the stamp, and it was draped in a large cloth. At a certain point in the ceremony, usually after many (often bland and repetitive) speeches, the appropriate officials and family members were asked to assist in unveiling the design. Yanking the curtain aside to reveal the image always brought applause and even gasps of approval. The odd thing, from my perspective, was that everyone in the room already knew what the stamp looked like. In fact, they had already purchased stamps at the postal station set up in the lobby of the venue. I could never come up with a better way to dramatically issue the stamps, so I just accepted the hoopla of curtain unveilings.

A Philatelic First

My first appearance at a stamp dedication was on January 17, 1976, in Philadelphia at the B. Free Franklin Museum. I was still working in the Communications Department, not the Stamp Services Department, but I attended because it was my own stamp design—my first. The stamp commemorated the opening of what was at that time the largest philatelic exhibition in the world. The U.S. was chosen as the host because it was the Bicentennial year. The exhibition was named Interphil '76, an odd name for anyone outside the world of stamps but a moniker I was forced to work with in designing the stamp. Up to that point, I had had no experience dealing with stamp collectors. I was to get a real fast lesson in how avid their interest is in the world of stamps.

Shortly before the ceremony began, someone in the audience figured out who I was, which opened the floodgates. Word spread immediately, and collectors began passing me their ceremony programs and first-day-of-issue envelopes for my autograph. Moments later, I was overwhelmed by collectors. A Stamp Services staff member working the ceremony saw what was happening and came to my rescue, cutting off all autographs until after the ceremony. The collectors were dismayed but regrouped when the ceremony concluded, attempting to get autographs before I could be ushered to the signing table with the other dignitaries. Obtaining autographs of ceremony participants is regarded as a bonus for collectors. This experience was to be repeated often in the years to come.

Stately Events

Some first-days, while not as glamorous or exciting as some Hollywood events, can be memorable. And some politically-driven issuances carry overtones of "officialdom."

As each state celebrates the anniversary of its admittance to the Union, at fifty-year intervals, the Postal Service issues a stamp commemorating that event. Two statehood observances of special interest to me were the Wisconsin (1998) and Minnesota (2008) statehood anniversary commemorations. Having been born and raised in those states, I was very keen to participate in the events.

For the Wisconsin event, I took my entire family along with me, including our four-year-old grandson Nicholas. My sister Karen and her husband Jerry drove down from La Crosse for the event, and we spent quality time together over a few days. The stamp dedication was held on the grounds of the State Capitol. We arrived early and took our seats, right down in front. But I guess I didn't have enough clout because when we later returned to our reserved seats, we found that U.S. Senator Herb Kohl had moved in with his entourage and claimed them. By that time, the remainder of the seats had been taken, so we were all relegated to standing on the sideline. While the event proved to be rather typical of these events—lengthy and filled with long-winded repetitive speeches—it was nonetheless great to be back "home" with the family.

Ten years later, I attended a similar event, this time across the Mississippi River in St. Paul, Minnesota. For this occasion, I was able to convince my youngest sister Missy to make the trek south from her small town of Orr, near the Canadian border. My other sister, Karen, and her husband Jerry again joined us. But this time, I wasn't relegated to standing on the sideline during the event. My boss, David Failor, arranged for me to be the dedicating official, a role normally filled by a senior postal official, certainly higher up than me.

I was pleased and delighted to participate alongside former Vice President Walter Mondale and his wife Joan, who at the time was a CSAC member. Walter worked the crowd as if he were still running for office. But he was one of the most outgoing, pleasant individuals

I've worked with, as was his wife.

Like the Wisconsin statehood ceremony, this was an outdoor ceremony on the Capitol grounds. In my remarks, I remember addressing my complete innocence regarding the site depicted on the stamp. I discovered after Committee approval that the design, based on an aerial shot of the Mississippi River, was taken about twenty miles from my birthplace. I found it amusing, but a few wags in the collecting community questioned my impartiality in the selection.

A Royal Ceremony

While some stamp subjects are light and whimsical, the first-day ceremony doesn't always reflect that mood. One such subject was the 2006 Favorite Children's Book Animals stamps issued in conjunction with Great Britain's Royal Mail.

When it came time to organize the first-day event, the Brits and USPS officials decided that our set should be issued at the American Embassy in London. Once again, my boss David Failor recommended me as the dedicating speaker. I was thrilled, not only to visit London again but to be honored at such a formal event.

My trip to London was short. I flew out of Washington one evening, arriving in London the following morning. The dedication was set for that evening. I got some rest as I didn't sleep well on the plane and roused myself in the late afternoon to get ready for the event. As usual for London, it was raining that evening, and the makeshift wire-fence fortification around the Embassy was daunting. The cabbie dropped me off on the wrong side of the building, and I ended up walking in the rain, without an umbrella, around to the guard station on the other side.

Once inside, I spent time in the men's room attempting to dry off. As the ceremony began, the last of the wetness dried up, and I gave a speech prepared by our staff, which I don't normally like to do. I prefer to give my own remarks, but I got through it. Despite the whimsical subject matter, the entire affair was very formal—almost too formal. But I didn't have much say in the logistics of the ceremonies.

The following morning, I was off to Heathrow for the return flight. A too-fast trip for such a nice event but one I was glad to be part of.

United We Stand

Probably the most somber first-day event I attended was the "United We Stand" U.S. Flag stamp issued a mere six weeks after the 9/11 events of 2001. I had designed the stamp in a matter of days after the attacks, and we were able to find press time to print quantities for an October release.

The ceremony was held on the plaza in front of the Postal Headquarters in D.C. with numerous postal and federal dignitaries in attendance. The mood was very somber throughout the numerous speeches. As the designer, I had hoped for a small role in its dedication, but that wasn't to be. I was relegated to sitting in the back of the audience, where I could hardly hear what was being said. Despite the "snub," I felt honored to have been part of this important issuance.

Premiere Events

The Postal Service has made valiant attempts to make these ceremonies memorable, but occasionally they struggle with a particular subject, usually subjects of a serious nature. On the other hand, some were "naturals" for special treatment. Entertainment-themed subjects come to mind.

Grauman's Chinese Theatre was the site of three first-day events including Comedians (1991), Humphrey Bogart (1996), and John Wayne (2004). They were usually staged on a platform erected outdoors near the famed handprints of the stars. It was at the first of these Grauman's events honoring comedians that Postmaster General Runyon invited Karl Malden, who would later to join the CSAC and serve for nine very active years on the that Committee.

I was unable to attend the Bogart ceremony, but my boss James Tolbert, Jr. told me it was a great event. Bogart's widow, Lauren Bacall, attended and gave James the icy treatment. She was miffed when she finally saw the artwork for Bogie and shared her displeasure with us. She had wanted us to use the iconic black-and-white Philippe Halsman photo of Bogie smoking a cigarette. Despite her protestations, we refused to feature smoking on stamps. Surprised that she would share her displeasure at such a late date, we discovered that the stamp art had been reviewed and approved by Bogie's two children, who controlled his estate, and it had never been shared with Bacall.

At the John Wayne ceremony at Grauman's, the entire Wayne family was in full attendance to honor the "Duke." It, too, was held outdoors, but they did screen a compilation of clips from his many films following the ceremony in the theater.

All three ceremonies attracted not only the stamp collecting community but many star-struck tourists as well.

On two other occasions, Grauman's also played a role in stamps. In October 1997, we unveiled the Alfred Hitchcock stamp at the Hollywood Museum on Hollywood Boulevard. The ceremony took place in a downstairs room, and following the ceremony, all participants were invited to stroll down the boulevard to a special screening of the Hitchcock classic, *Psycho*. Dick Sheaff, the designer of the stamp, and I joined the stroll. To say the least, it was a special treat for me to be at that showing. *Psycho* is one of my all-time favorite films, and I am a major Hitchcock fan. So, to attend the screening and sit behind Janet Leigh and Patricia Hitchcock was a big thrill. If someone had told me the first time I saw *Psycho* that one day I would be seeing it again alongside the star and the director's daughter, I never would have believed it. The subsequent first-day event was held on August 3, 1998, at the Director's Guild of America auditorium. I attended the event and had the great privilege of meeting and chatting with another great film director, Robert Wise, whose career spanned from editing *Citizen Kane* to such great films as *The Sound of Music*, *West Side Story*, and too many others to mention.

The other Grauman's unveiling was in 2007 when the *Star Wars* stamps were first shown to the public. Just like the other events, it was held outdoors, complete with a multitude of people dressed as Princess Leia, Han Solo, and numerous other characters from the film. The stamp pane was unveiled by none other than R2-D2 and C-3PO. It was a casual, but fun, experience. As a big fan of *Star Wars* and as co-designer of the stamps, it was special. The first-day ceremony was held later that year at a major event in L.A. Unfortunately, we were featured for all of two minutes on stage. Our booth that sold the stamps was buried in a side room in the back of the theatre, which did not make us very happy. I guess there were other exhibitors that paid more money to be there and were capable of generating more licensing profits from their products than our stamps would. I was a bit disappointed by the whole first-day event. We had worked so hard on making the stamps exciting, so to have us sidelined didn't sit well.

Strike up the Music!

Los Angeles, especially Hollywood, is known for extravagance when it comes to promoting things. Star-studded film premieres are just one example. Even the stamp world gets caught up in some of the Hollywood hoopla. A case in point is the Henry Mancini stamp of 2004.

After all the back and forth between the CSAC and one of its members, Digger Phelps, in determining whether a Mancini stamp would ever happen and when it would happen, it became an event unto itself. Mancini's widow, Ginny, was known in Hollywood circles as a "mover and shaker." Jean Firstenberg, a member of the CSAC at the time, had arranged the meeting with Ginny and warned that we should be prepared to let her run with her thoughts on what the stamp ceremony should be. How right Jean was. We did step back and allow her to organize the event, and we were all the better for it.

The event was held on the plaza in front of the Dorothy Chandler Pavilion, the home for many years to the Academy Awards. To kick things off in a big way, she brought in the famed USC Marching Band to play a selection of her late husband's compositions; the biggest crowd-pleaser was his "Baby Elephant Walk" from the film, *Hatari!* On a "quieter" note, the brilliant flutist James Galway performed. It was a lavish affair that the Postal Service could never have pulled off on their own, let alone afford to produce.

Ironically, Digger Phelps was a no-show for the event despite his pressuring of the Committee to honor his father-in-law. Digger's reasoning, when pressed to explain his absence, was that he didn't want to be a hindrance and draw attention away from the event. In fact, he was no longer part of the family because he and Monica had divorced by that time. Despite the family drama, the stamp provided the stamp world with a spectacular first-day event.

But that midday ceremony was not the last of it. Ginny had

booked the newly-opened Disney Concert Hall that same evening and drew a sellout crowd for a concert honoring Henry. Cohosts of the event were none other than Julie Andrews and Senator John Glenn. Performers included Quincy Jones, Stevie Wonder, Michael Feinstein, James Galway, Andy Williams, and John Williams. Due to the cost of the tickets, only CSAC members, my boss Dave Failor, the stamp designer, Carl Herrman, and my wife Ann and I were given tickets by the Mancini family. The other art directors and researchers who normally attend CSAC meetings were left out in the cold, which upset me, but I couldn't convince the event organizers to rethink the invitee list. I must admit that the entire Mancini first-day had to rank as one of the most elaborate the USPS has seen.

First-Class Disney

Speaking of gala events, the Postal Service was privileged to participate in five annual issuances of the Art of Disney stamps between 2004 and 2008. As you can well imagine, Disney knows how to throw a party, and we were not disappointed with any of the events. True to Disney form, they offered to host and organize the events at their theme parks, complete with costumed characters, singers, dancers, and, yes, even fireworks.

Three of the first-day ceremonies were held at Disneyland in California (2004, 2005, 2008); the other two were at Disney World in Florida (2006, 2007). All were held outdoors in the parks, which in some instances made for rather toasty afternoons.

For all five issuances, the two individuals who developed the stamps were in attendance: David Pacheco, the Disney artist who provided the preliminary sketches, and Peter Emmerich, the illustrator who painted the final images. Following the ceremony for the first set of stamps, entitled Friendship, the three of us were whisked down Main Street by staff and set up in a room inside the Disney Collectibles Shop. We were asked to spend a few hours signing autographs. When we arrived, we were surprised to see a very long line. Many had been in line for hours. Once the doors opened, the flood of collectors descended on us. Our writing hands were numb after spending three hours giving autographs.

That scene was to be repeated for the next four years for the three of us. We developed a close friendship and had great fun kidding each other while signing our names on thousands of stamped envelopes and Disney memorabilia. The most difficult year was the event for the 2005 Celebration set issued in Florida. The autograph session after the ceremony was held inside an air-conditioned building. Because the first year's signing had been so successful, Disney asked us to sign autographs that year for two days, three to four hours each day. David, Peter, and I estimated that we signed more than seven thousand autographs apiece during those two days. We were exhausted but appreciative of the cool location.

A cool location would have been nice for the 2007 Magic set. The ceremony, once again, was outdoors, in an open-air theater by the lake at Epcot. With little or no air movement down in that pit, by the time the three of us were escorted to the location for autographing, we were drenched in sweat. We assumed we would be seated inside a nearby store. Wrong! They seated us immediately outside the store. The only cool air we felt for the next three hours was when each customer left the store, allowing the wafting of cold air onto our backs. By the end of the day, we were soaked through and exhausted.

The entire Disney collaboration was so positive that we didn't want it to end. So, we developed the two issuances of Pixar stamps in 2011 and 2012. I had retired from the Postal Service prior to the issuance of these two sets of stamps, but Disney asked me to attend the first-day event for the first set, entitled Send a Hello. I took my wife Ann and our sixteen-year-old grandson Nick with me on the trip. It was Nick's first time to Disneyland, so Ann and Nick "did the park" while I was at the ceremony.

David Pacheco was once again involved with the ceremony, but Peter was not. The Pixar art had been created by a different group within Disney. Peter was missed, but David and I had a good time. The big thrill for me was that John Lasseter, the Oscar-winning creative genius behind Pixar, agreed to attend the ceremony. The Disney team choreographed the entire ceremony. To our surprise, David and I were asked to participate and give a short lecture on how we developed the stamps, and then personally introduce Lasseter to the audience.

I had the privilege of meeting Lasseter in the green room before the ceremony as the Disney team was fawning over him upon his arrival. Attired in his trademark Hawaiian shirt, he was shown around and introduced to everyone in the green room. His entrance reminded me of *Simpsons* creator Matt Groening's arrival at Fox Studios for our interview in 2009. The Postal Service's Deputy Postmaster General, Ron Stroman, was there, but Lasseter spent little time with him. When we were introduced, he expressed interest in talking further with me. A little later, when he was asked to sit in the makeup chair, he asked that I sit in the chair next to him for my makeup so we could talk. He asked a multitude of questions about stamps and said he hoped we could chat again soon. I was thrilled to have the opportunity to sit and talk with him, but we've never had the chance to meet since then.

Back Lot Previews

The back lots of film studios are often the scene of special events hosted by the studios. This was the case for all of the Looney Tunes stamps issued between 1997 and 2001. Warner Bros. hosted the event for the Bugs Bunny stamp, the first of five classic Looney Tunes characters. A gigantic enlargement of the stamp was unveiled on the side of one of their largest sound stages. I never heard what the exact dimensions were, but I expect it was twenty to twenty-five feet tall. Everyone, me included, was duly impressed. The next four issuances were well-feted, too, but not as elaborately as the Bugs stamp.

Universal Studios hosted the issuance of the Classic Movie Monster stamps in 1997, the same year as the Bugs Bunny stamp. Their event was held in an auditorium on the lot. Each of the five monsters (Frankenstein, Dracula, Wolfman, The Mummy, and the Phantom of the Opera) was represented on stage by costumed actors. The most dramatic and memorable moment of the event was when the Phantom flew over the audience onto the stage suspended on a wire. The event provided an opportunity to connect with my new "best friends" once again—Sara Karloff, Bela Lugosi, Jr., and Ron Chaney—whom I had worked so closely with in developing the designs.

The Oscars

Aside from film studio lots and Grauman's Theatre, we found another "venue" conducive to our ceremonies: the Academy of Motion Pictures show, or as everyone knows it, the Oscars. A few times over the years, our Communications group made unsuccessful attempts to host an unveiling of a particular film-related stamp on the televised Oscar awards. But we were able to utilize their library on a few occasions.

The Motion Picture Academy Library was a relatively new addition to the Academy's properties, due in large part to CSAC member Karl Malden, President of the Academy. When he first accepted Runyon's offer to serve, we on staff fully expected to see him rarely, if ever, because of his other commitments. Having experienced member Larry King's tenure, when he never once attended, we expected Karl's membership might meet the same fate. To our surprise and pleasure, Karl rarely missed the quarterly meetings for the next nine years.

During his tenure as Academy President, Karl spearheaded a movement to create a library for the Academy that would house numerous items related to film. He worked to purchase an old waterworks on La Cienega Boulevard in Hollywood. The building was refurbished and became one of the crown jewels of the Academy. Subsequently, two stamp dedications were held there.

The first was the 2003 American Filmmaking: Behind the Scenes set of ten stamps. These stamps also carried the imprint of Karl Malden. The first-day event was held in the lobby of the library. While not a large event, it was interesting, nonetheless. Gena Rowlands, the Oscar-winning actress whose husband John Cassavetes was depicted on the Director's stamp, did attend the ceremony, accompanied by longtime friend and actor Robert Forster.

A much more elaborate Academy Library ceremony was held three years later, but that time it was outdoors in the garden adjacent to the library. The Hattie McDaniel stamp was dedicated on January 25, 2006, as part of our extremely popular Black Heritage series.

A large tent was erected and was soon filled with an overflow crowd. Numerous speakers were on the program, many more than usual. Every living member of the *Gone with the Wind* cast had been invited, and each wanted to say something about Hattie. But the person who spoke the longest and garnered the most attention was a politician: Maxine Waters, a California Congresswoman. She launched into an in-depth description of Hattie's entire life, including some rather surprising details, including her drug use. Many, me included, thought that was a bit out of line at an event praising her life and career.

Overall, the event was a success, paying tribute not only to a great actress but a social advocate as well. It continually amazed me throughout my career in stamps how much I learned about our history, its people, and our culture.

One other event was held at the Motion Picture Academy Library, but, sadly, it was not a first-day ceremony. Instead, it was a memorial service to honor our good friend Karl Malden, who passed away in 2009. I was honored to be invited to the memorial representing the Postal Service along with Jean Firstenberg, the CSAC Chair.

The small lobby space was filled to capacity with old friends paying respects to one of the most well-liked and respected individuals in a town noted for caustic, superficial, and difficult relationships. As everyone was finding their seats, I found myself sitting next to Ernest Borgnine and Kirk Douglas, both of whom I had met previously. Borgnine had served on the CSAC years before I joined the Stamps office, but he had been brought to the Communications art department to pose for pictures with me and my first stamp, Interphil '76, which were published in the Headquarters' internal newsletter. I had met Mr. Douglas at the dedication of the renaming of one of the Brentwood post offices in Karl's name. On the other side of me was Norman Lloyd, the great supporting actor who I remembered from the popular 1980s TV hospital drama, *St. Elsewhere*. I immediately shared with him that I could not see him without picturing him hanging by his fingers, about to fall from the Statue of Liberty in the 1942 Hitchcock film classic, *Saboteur*, to which he laughed and said that I must be the "Stamp Man" Karl always spoke of.

Kirk Douglas, a lifelong friend of Karl's, wasn't sure whether he was supposed to speak during the ceremony, so Jean asked that I check with Karl's widow, Mona. Her response was: "Of course. That's why I invited him!" When I relayed this information to Kirk, he asked at what point during the ceremony he was supposed to speak. Unable to get Mona's attention again, I asked Karl's daughter, Karla, who assured me that it was all under control, and Kirk would know when it was time.

After hearing comments and stories from Bruce Davis, the Academy Director, Eva Marie Saint, Karl's costar in the film classic *On the Waterfront*, and Carroll Baker, who costarred with Karl in *Baby Doll*, it was Kirk's turn. Because of his stroke, he was nervous about working his way through the tightly-knit crowd of chairs and asked for my assistance. Taking his arm, I escorted him to the stage, where he delivered a moving tribute to his dear friend. Kirk was followed by his son, Michael, who shared many memories of working with Karl on their TV series, *The Streets of San Francisco.*

The numerous other luminaries attending included Warren Beatty and his wife, Annette Bening. It was a wonderful tribute to one of the true gentlemen of Hollywood, who I was proud to call a friend.

Bungalow Soiree

The other event wasn't a first-day event but a reception on the evening before a stamp dedication. The Marilyn Monroe stamp, the first in the newly-created Legends of Hollywood series, was to be dedicated at Universal Studios on June 1, 1995. The event was fine with the exception of the gigantic stamp enlargement—a hideous interpretation of a beautiful painting by Michael Deas. But the most interesting event was that reception.

It was held at a small bungalow where Marilyn had once lived—not the one she died in but one of the many residences she occupied during her time in Hollywood. The bungalow is rented out for such occasions, so Azeez arranged the reception, complete with a jazz trio, hors d'oeuvres, and plenty of drinks.

Among the invited guests were Eli Wallach and his actress wife, Anne Jackson. Eli had starred with Marilyn in *The Misfits*. They were staying at the same hotel, and when Carl Herrman, the stamp's art director, and I were waiting for a cab to go to the reception, we met the couple. They were waiting for a limo to arrive to take them to the same reception. The limo arrived before our cab, so they invited us to join them. I can assure you; we didn't hesitate for a moment to accept their invitation. Both were very gracious and a joy to chat with. For those of you who are wondering—no, Eli's character is nothing like his role in the classic *The Good, the Bad and the Ugly* or any of the other colorful characters he's portrayed over the years.

Bette in Boston

The Legends of Hollywood issuances were not always held in Hollywood. Judy Garland's was held, as I mentioned, at Carnegie

Hall in New York City. Bette Davis's was held, of all places, in Boston, at the request of the family. I was asked to represent the Postal Service at the event, which I immediately accepted, having been a big fan of Davis.

I was delighted to share the stage with Bette's longtime friend and legendary actress Lauren Bacall. I did have a bit of hesitation when meeting her as I didn't know what to expect from her. Her outspokenness and demands were legendary, and she had not had a good relationship with the USPS when her late husband Humphrey Bogart's stamp was dedicated.

She turned out to be a delight to talk to, even though she gave off the airs of a diva. She arrived with her small dog, which was handed over to Postal staff to tend to while she was on stage. She spent a great deal of time chatting with Davis family members both before and after the ceremony. I was given the privilege of introducing her during the ceremony. To this day, I cannot remember what I ad-libbed about her as part of my introduction, which brought laughter from the audience. What I do remember is that deadly glare of hers when I turned to her. I almost panicked, thinking I had really put my foot in my mouth this time. But as she approached me at the lectern, her dour glare turned to a smile, and she immediately responded to my remark with a great comeback, drawing further laughs.

Before the ceremony, I was introduced to one of the rights holders of the estate, Ms. Davis's personal assistant, Kathryn Sermak. The staff asked if I would accompany her to the lobby so she could see the stamps, first-day covers, etc., for sale there. I gladly obliged but soon discovered why she wanted someone to accompany her. She feigned that she didn't bring her purse, so she had no way of paying for anything. Graciously, I offered to pay for her items, to which she immediately became like a child in a candy store. We, or I should say she, exceeded one hundred dollars in purchases that morning. Fortunately, I was able to be reimbursed. You would have thought that a social secretary to a legendary actress and heir to some of Ms. Davis's estate would carry at least some money. But apparently not.

Animals, Animals

Animals have played a key role in a few ceremonies. The most memorable for me was the Endangered Species ceremony at San

Diego Sea World in 1996. It was memorable in part because I never thought I would see the then-Chair of the CSAC sharing the stage with a trained seal. Virginia Noelke, one of the most delightful and fun-loving members of the Committee, was asked to be on stage for the unveiling alongside a trained seal. Her initial reluctance soon gave way to a more cavalier "whatever" approach, which resulted in her not only sharing the stage but getting splashed by the seal.

Not too many people would readily choose Bats as a good subject for a postage stamp, but we did issue a set of four American Bat stamps in Austin, Texas, in 2002. What made it so unique was that it was held at the Congress Avenue Bridge where thousands of bats hang out and make a nightly appearance for crowds of people, swooping and soaring over the downtown bridge and the Colorado River. We did discover too late that these bats were actually Mexican bats, not the American bats we were commemorating. Oh well, bats are bats to most people, so we chose not to share that tidbit of information with the public.

Sending a Little Love

A different kind of winged creature provided a personally memorable ceremony. This winged creature is far more attractive than bats. It's the cupid on the 1995 Love stamp issuance. I would venture to guess that most everyone has seen this cupid and its companion on coffee mugs, greeting cards, etc. They were the famed Sistine Madonna angels. I had always admired them and decided they needed to be on a stamp. The first-day ceremony staff found Valentines, a small town in southern Virginia, very near the border with North Carolina, in which to hold the ceremony. As the designer, I was invited to attend the ceremony.

My wife and I drove from our home in Northern Virginia down to Valentines that morning. But I had miscalculated how much time it would take. As we got closer, I realized we were going to be late, so I stepped on the gas. Taking a side road shortly after leaving Interstate 95, I floored it. Much to my chagrin, a State Trooper coming from the opposite direction happened to come around the bend at the same time. Of course, you know the rest. He turned his cruiser around, turned on his lights, and I ended up with a $100 speeding ticket and an additional twenty minutes of lost time. Now we were really going to be late.

We arrived minutes before the ceremony but had trouble parking. It seems that this ceremony was a big deal in that community, and hundreds of people were there. Many could not even get into the building for the ceremony. Ann and I had to park on the side of the road about two blocks from the event and rush to get there. We finally arrived, out of breath and sweating. I was immediately grabbed and pushed on stage. I lost sight of what happened to Ann but found her later.

Later, we were invited to the general store where the post office is located. While chatting with locals there, others came in, and before we knew it, there was a line of people requesting autographs. Of the many ceremonies I attended, this was one of my personal favorites.

Three months later, Ann and I traveled to the Pennsylvania Poconos to help dedicate the same Love stamps, this time released in a denominated version. The first version issued in Valentines carried no denomination because it was issued between rate changes. Those non-denominated issuances usually confused the public, a confusion that we were forced to deal with more frequently than we wanted.

The Poconos event was held in the Champagne Palace nightclub at Caesars Cove Haven Resort in Lakeville, Pennsylvania. The day's entertainment proved to be the most memorable moment for me. The local post office had worked with the resort to provide entertainment. The area's USPS Vice President agreed to participate in the ceremony. He had a reputation for being very stiff and formal, a no-nonsense man. During the ceremony, as a respite from too many boring speeches, the resort provided its version of entertainment. From backstage, a chorus of scantily-clad chorus girls appeared, singing and dancing to love songs. I found it kitschy and frankly quite comical, but the VP was not amused. His jaw dropped, and his face turned red. The staff standing near him realized the mistake they had made, but it was too late. I can assure you the VP shared his thoughts about it after the ceremony.

Out of This World

Even subjects as serious as science can result in interesting and entertaining events. I had designed a stamp to commemorate the Mars Pathfinder's landing on that distant planet. The CSAC had expressed an interest in commemorating this historic event in 1997, which meant a very short turnaround time in order to keep the issuance timely. The other six art directors were already overworked with projects, so I took on the task myself. Fortunately, I had access to NASA's photo files, located down the street from Postal Headquarters. The small, single-stamp souvenir sheet was produced in an incredibly short timeframe and carries the distinction of being the single largest stamp ever produced by the U.S. Postal Service (three inches in length).

As you might expect, the ceremony was held at the Jet Propulsion Laboratory in Pasadena. The ceremony was held outdoors, which proved to be a bit problematic for the event coordinators. It was an extremely blustery day, and the eight-foot-long cloth stamp enlargement acted like a sail on a yacht. It was tethered on poles, but the gusts kept tipping the enlargement, which was covered with a cloth. Doug Moyer, the event coordinator, eventually had to stand behind the enlargement gripping the pole with all his might to keep it from blowing over on top of the dignitaries on stage.

The best part of the ceremony, apart from watching Doug fight the elements backstage, was the unveiling itself. The JPL provided a model of the Mars Pathfinder for use at the ceremony. When the time came to unveil the stamp, a cord was attached to the Pathfinder model and, through remote control, was wheeled across the stage, gradually pulling the cloth cover aside. All the while, Doug was still at the other end, steadfastly holding on with all his might. For a "techie" type of subject, it was a fascinating and fun ceremony.

Azeez Jaffer hosted a dinner at the Huntington Hotel in Pasadena that evening following the ceremony. Invited guests included local postal and Jet Propulsion Lab officials. My wife and I sat at a table with three of the scientists who were instrumental in landing the Pathfinder on Mars. It was an honor to sit with them and hear of their experiences in getting the probe to the surface of Mars.

So, whether a subject was entertaining or serious, I could always count on an eventful ceremony filled with pageantry, speeches, and reminiscences each time the Postal Service launched another stamp in its long history.

Chapter 9
The Ones That Got Away

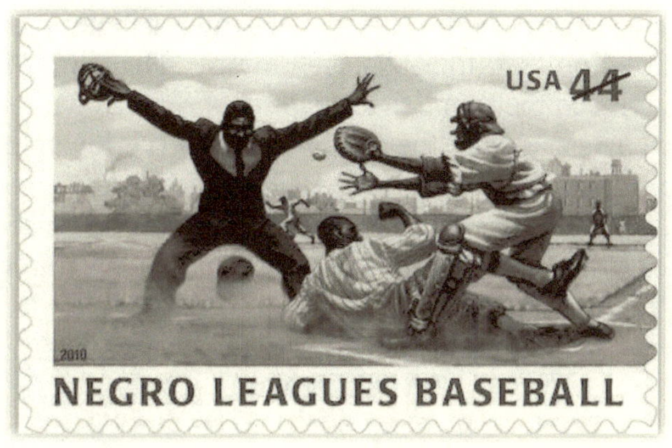

Over the course of my twenty years in Stamp Services, thousands of stamp designs were produced. Ideas generated by the CSAC, staff, and the American public were vetted, researched, negotiated, approved, printed, and issued. That number may seem huge until you realize that our office received many thousands of suggestions annually from the public, and only a small fraction of them ever saw the light of day. But there is one more facet of the stamp development process that hasn't been touched on, nor is the public aware of it, which is the stamps that were never produced. For one reason or another, they were never made despite being recommended for development by the CSAC, USPS officials, or the Stamps staff.

More often than not, the subject eventually was dropped due to differences between the estate and the Postal Service. Money was occasionally a leading factor in the breakdown of those negotiations, but not the only one. One of the more difficult aspects of the stamp development process is negotiating with the estates. Over the years, first Kelly Spinks and then Layne Owens of my staff spent countless hours working on these agreements. Frustration was a mainstay of their job. What most estates couldn't understand was why the Postal Service wouldn't pay the estate royalties on each stamp sold, much like other companies who licensed the likenesses of their loved ones. The Postal Service position was that, as a government agency, it wished to bestow one of the highest honors the U.S. government could give an individual by commemorating their relative on a postage stamp. Aside from portraits on currency, which are restricted to politicians, there is no other "official" tribute produced and distributed nationwide like postage stamps. That line of reasoning usually convinced the families to grant us the rights without payment of any sort. The one way the family can receive revenue is through licensed products associated with the stamp. Some products were developed by the USPS, but usually, a third-party licensee produced product featuring the stamp and made payments directly to the families.

Striking Out

Occasionally, an agreement could not be reached because the family held out for money. In other words, they weren't buying our "patriotic" line. One example stands out in my mind. The CSAC approved the development of a block of four subjects commemorating Negro League Baseball for a 2010 issuance. To identify the four best players to be included, PhotoAssist researched and provided a list of names, which the CSAC approved.

Design development began as Layne reached out to the four families for rights approval. One of the players' daughters insisted that she be paid royalties. No amount of discussion could persuade her to change her mind. Layne, at the same time, had reached out to the other three families. They too were concerned about payment but were willing to discuss the issue.

During discussions, the daughter I mentioned asked who the other three players were, which Layne shared with her. Sadly, she chose to contact two of the others (the fourth individual had no family) to encourage them to stick together and demand money, which they eventually did. Despite heroic efforts on Layne's part to persuade them otherwise, all three estates refused to sign the agreements.

Reluctantly, the decision was made to pull the plug on featuring those three players. Instead, two stamps, one honoring Andrew

"Rube" Foster, (the fourth player) known as the "father of Negro League Baseball," was featured alongside a scene of an umpire calling "safe" with a runner sliding home and the pitcher standing over him. This scene was meant to commemorate all players in the league. The resulting illustrations by Kadir Nelson captured the drama of the game and paid tribute to its founder. It was sad that we were unable to commemorate the other three men, but sometimes money speaks louder than honor.

Hold the Music

Money wasn't always the main factor in abandoning a stamp project. Even threats could change our minds.

As we developed the massive set of Legends of American Music stamps issued between 1993 and 1999, we worked from a comprehensive list of possible subjects provided by the Smithsonian's Music Division. One category, which was never included in the final package, was Rock. The first set, issued in 1993, was Rock and Roll/Rhythm and Blues. It included some of the early rock-and-roll stars such as Elvis, Buddy Holly, Bill Haley, and Ritchie Valens. Strong consideration was given to producing a set later in the series commemorating "rock" that might feature Jimi Hendrix, Janis Joplin, and others from the hard rock side of the music genre despite the CSAC's reluctance to consider these individuals because of their association with the drug culture. Lord knows, they swallowed a bitter pill when PMG Tony Frank insisted they issue Elvis as the leadoff stamp in the series. They really had trouble with this second rock group. But the Stamps staff sought to reach out to the families to ascertain their interest.

We got no further than Jim Morrison, lead singer of the Doors. PhotoAssist located his widow and gave us her contact information. A letter was sent to her requesting a meeting to discuss an agreement. We received a short reply stating that "Jim would not have liked the idea, and furthermore, if you pursue such a project, she, herself, would put a hex on the Postal Service." The USPS had enough problems without having a hex put on us, so we pulled the plug and took her answer as a "no."

It didn't take long for the plug to be pulled on the entire set of Rock stamps. Ironically, in the past few years, the USPS started another set of Music stamps and has issued both Jimi Hendrix and Janis Joplin stamps. It's amazing how a few years can change things. But still no Jim Morrison stamp. I guess the hex threat still stands!

Altered Patriotism

There are times when a design is developed, but for whatever reason, it fails to be issued as originally intended. One such design stamp that was given a second chance was the Patriotic Quill and Inkwell issue of 2011.

Azeez Jaffer, who at the time was Director of Stamp Services, asked us to develop a stamp for the Declaration of Independence. The CSAC questioned the rationale for such an issuance, noting that the document had been honored multiple times over the years, and there was no significant anniversary justifying another issuance. But Azeez, the ever-present and persistent marketer explained his rationale.

Norman Lear, the creator of *All in the Family* and other landmark TV shows, had purchased an authentic copy of the Declaration recently and wished to share it with the American public. I don't know whether Lear contacted the Postal Service or Azeez contacted Lear about partnering in this effort. My guess is it was the latter. Azeez's proposal was that the Declaration be housed in a Postal semi-truck and travel from city to city for a year. His pitch: "What better way to showcase the document than in a vehicle from the government agency that is as old as the U.S." He was right! Lear agreed, and the two of them developed an exhibit to be housed in the semi-truck.

Azeez believed that the perfect product to promote this venture would be a postage stamp. The CSAC reluctantly agreed, and I tasked Derry Noyes to work with Craig Frazier on developing the stamp. She returned to share with the CSAC a very contemporary interpretation featuring a quill pen in an inkstand with very elaborate, scroll-like calligraphy to suggest the original document. The CSAC immediately approved the design.

Before we could issue it, however, the plug was pulled on the stamp. Not the document tour, just the stamp. Senior management decided it was just too "self-serving" to issue the stamp promoting the tour. That rationale was the same used by the CSAC, which

Azeez had dismissed. Already burdened with too many stamps in the annual program, it was removed from the annual mix. Needless to say, Azeez was less than amused, but he had no choice but to comply with the PMG's decision.

The art lingered in the vault of unused images for many years. I maintained a book of color copies of all unused images in my office. When looking for a specific subject or theme, I would often reference that book to see if something would lend itself to our needs.

One of the mainstays of every annual program is a U.S. Flag stamp or some other patriotic symbol, such as the Liberty Bell or Statue of Liberty. I kept seeing the Patriotic Quill image over the years, and because I was partial to the design, I wanted to see it issued one day. A few years later, I suggested we consider using that art as one of the patriotic issuances.

The problem was that the original design was created in a commemorative format of approximately 1 x 1.5 inches. Our mail-use stamps are always in a one-inch-square format. Not to be dissuaded, I asked Derry to see if she could redesign the image to fit into the smaller format. Derry worked her usual magic and reworked the image in the smaller format. It was eventually issued a few years later. I personally still feel it is one of the more beautiful contemporary designs in either commemorative or definitive formats.

The Patriotic Quill and Inkwell wasn't the only "promotional tie-in" stamp Azeez promoted. But unlike the Quill stamp, there were others that we struggled with that never saw the light of day. One such project comes to mind.

A Strong Message

Growing crime rates in the U.S. in the 1990s were a topic of discussion among politicians, pundits, and the media. Azeez suggested to the CSAC that they consider a "message" stamp addressing the issue of violence. There was immediate skepticism among certain Committee members, but in his usual blustery style, Azeez pushed the members to develop a design. Rather than assign this difficult subject to one unwitting art director, I chose to ask all six art directors to explore concepts and present their ideas at a future meeting. Much to my surprise, most of them eagerly attacked the subject (no pun intended). One can only imagine the types of imagery one could use to depict violence. But, keeping in mind that the final design had to convey the message, be creatively dynamic in its visual presentation, and be compelling enough to attract purchasers to use it, it was a daunting task.

Between the CSAC and the design team, it was agreed that the overriding theme should be "Stop Violence." A Swedish stamp issued a few years before our attempts at the subject provided a source of inspiration for the design team. It depicted a revolver with the barrel twisted into a knot. A brilliant concept, but we couldn't use the same idea for our stamp.

Dick Sheaff, one of the six art directors, enlisted the help of an illustrator who developed his own concepts. The illustrator submitted one concept that struck us all as original and powerful. It depicted a body-chalk outline, typical of crime scenes on street pavement or sidewalk concrete, of the Statue of Liberty. The CSAC Design Subcommittee members and our design team felt it was the right solution. When Azeez stopped by the meeting to see how things were progressing, we shared the design with him. His immediate response was the usual flamboyant, bombastic reaction we'd all come to know. Without wishing to even discuss the concept, he said, "There is no %#$@%$&# way we're doing this stamp." Back to the proverbial drawing board!

Hundreds of sketches and concepts later, we finally found the solution. The word "Violence" was scrawled on a blackboard in chalk with an eraser wiping away a portion of the word. While I felt it was a satisfactory solution, I thought there were better concepts, but I was just one person in a complex bureaucracy where everyone has their say.

Looking for a Little Peace

And what about the "promotional tie-in" that Azeez was so fond of, well, promoting? He had been informed through his sources that none other than Stevie Wonder was producing an album tentatively titled Pageant of Peace. Azeez leapt at the opportunity and contacted Stevie's agent offering to partner with them. He indicated he could provide the "Stop Violence" stamp image for the cover of the album.

Stevie's agent was intrigued and eagerly awaited the final design.

On one of my frequent trips to Los Angeles, I was asked to bring along our final design. Azeez had arranged for James Tolbert, Kelly Spinks, and I to meet with Stevie's agent. The four of us met one evening in a small, crowded restaurant. I was scheduled to catch a redeye flight back to D.C. that evening, so my time was limited. Trying to balance a folder on my lap during dinner, which was served on a small circular cocktail table, I was asked to show the agent the design.

I distinctly remember the expression on his face when I shared it. He seemed a bit incredulous and hesitated for what seemed a long time before responding: "Stevie won't like this at all." It was obvious from the start that the stamp and the music album were being developed on two different tracks, so finding a design we could agree on was not in the cards. Leaving the design with the agent, I excused myself from the dinner to race to the airport and left James and Kelly to wrap things up.

We thought we had heard the last of the album/stamp project until about a month later when Azeez walked into my office with Stevie's agent. We briefly discussed making yet another attempt at a stamp design, one that Stevie could live with, which both parties agreed to pursue. But after discussing it with the CSAC, they stood firm that the current, approved design was the way to go, and the tie-in should not control our project. In an uncharacteristic move, Azeez quietly walked away from the entire project, blaming the design team for failing to come up with a workable design. The stamp was never issued despite all the time and effort expended on it. My recollection is that internal politics suppressed the issuance.

Family Feud

Sometimes, as was the case with the ill-fated "Stop Violence" stamp, we had to walk away from a particular project. Because of the time, money, and resources devoted to developing what we hoped would be a successful stamp, we were usually reluctant to abandon our efforts. But some projects just were not meant to be due to circumstances beyond our control. One such project was a Legends of Hollywood subject.

The CSAC, with the help of Karl Malden and Jean Firstenberg, had developed a list of potential names of famous stars to be included in future issuances of the Hollywood series. Jean and Karl's film industry expertise was invaluable in making the selections. One such star whom everyone agreed deserved recognition was Spencer Tracy. One bon mot thrown out at one of the Committee meetings was to pair Tracy with Katharine Hepburn, his great love. While it would have made an interesting issuance, many felt it would be difficult to sell the idea to Tracy's family. Little did we know at the time how difficult certain family members would become during the design development.

Art director Dick Sheaff initially submitted an early 1930s photo of Tracy, which was roundly rejected by the design team as being too young and not what fans would remember him looking like.

A newly commissioned 1950s portrait eventually found approval from the CSAC with little discussion. At that point, contact was made with Tracy's daughter, Susie, to arrange a meeting in L.A. to share our design for approval. Susie had already signed the rights agreement and repeatedly shared her enthusiasm about commemorating her father on a postage stamp. She suggested we meet at the John Tracy Clinic, named after her brother and established to help young hearing-impaired children and their families. It's where Dave Failor, Bill Gicker, and I eventually met with her and the director of the clinic.

Initially, Susie expressed some reservations about the image, but she was easily persuaded that it would make a handsome addition to the series. In retrospect, I believe she felt compelled to accept the design fearing that she didn't have the right to ask for changes that might jeopardize the project. Out of this concern, she gave us verbal approval to proceed with the project, assuring us that she had sole control of the estate.

Weeks later, I was back in L.A. for other meetings when I received a phone call that would be the beginning of what was to be a roller-coaster ride through the entangled life of the Tracy family.

That ominous call was from Spencer's nephew Joe, John's son. Actually, it was Joe's wife Cindy who called on her husband's behalf. At that juncture of the project, Joe was unknown to us. But they reassured us that he was one of the players in the contract and approval process. They insisted on meeting with us as soon as possible to discuss the project. Caught off guard, I suggested that we meet for a drink at a restaurant on La Brea Avenue where we had dined many times. On this trip, I was accompanied by Dave Failor, Bill Gicker, and Derry Noyes. We had attempted to contact Kelly Spinks back in D.C. to see if she could shed some light on this nephew and his claim to any legal estate rights, but because it was late in the afternoon when I received the Tracys' call, everyone in D.C. had left for the day. So, we went into the meeting not knowing what to expect.

Upon arrival at the restaurant, we glanced into the bar area to see if they had arrived, but much to our chagrin, we found them seated in the restaurant already perusing the dinner menu. So much for a quick drink!

Cindy did the majority of the talking. Joe seemed to be a very submissive individual, especially around his wife. We were informed, directly, that he controlled half of the Spencer Tracy estate on behalf of his father John. (John was deaf due to Usher syndrome, which eventually caused blindness, rendering him unable to handle legal affairs and giving Joe control.) The two of them insisted they had equal veto power with Susie despite not being able to produce any documentation at the restaurant showing such authority. They reassured us numerous times during the dinner, which they generously allowed us to pay for, that they would produce the documentation soon.

As if that weren't enough, Cindy turned to Joe and instructed him to "go out and get the portfolio." It seems that Joe is an artist, and they wanted to give Joe the opportunity to create the art. "It would be an added benefit to have the stamp art created by Spencer's nephew," they argued. Without further ado, Cindy flopped a large art portfolio onto the dinner table and asked us to "look at the wonderful art Joe has created over the years."

As I turned the portfolio pages, I saw pencil portrait drawings more appropriate for a boardwalk "sketch-your-portrait" booth than any postage stamp. Cindy played salesman and touted the expertise and talent of her husband while Joe remained quiet throughout the presentation. As I passed the portfolio to the other members of our team, we all had the same thoughts. We knew immediately that we were walking into a quagmire of creative trouble.

Cindy insisted that Joe be allowed to present art to the Committee before the final approval was given on the design. Reluctantly, we agreed to allow them to proceed. Pitting Joe's talent against the talents of Drew Struzan, one of the most talented and well-known illustrators in the L.A. film community, seemed almost too cruel, but Joe and Cindy were not to be swayed by the competition. Cindy insisted that Joe could do better, and he would start immediately. She was at least right about that as he did start immediately. The following morning, I was stowing my luggage in the overhead bin on the return flight home when Cindy called to reassure me that Joe was hard at work on the art.

Kelly Spinks, our rights manager, contacted Susie immediately to ascertain whether Joe's (and Cindy's) assertion that they controlled half the estate was accurate. Susie had insisted that *she* was the sole rights holder. We urged her to talk with Joe and work things out, which she said she would do. We heard through our West Coast sources that there was a lot of bickering between the two parties as Joe created his version of the portrait. Eventually, we heard that John had been moved to Joe and Cindy's ranch, where they took control of his affairs. It appeared that they gained control of half of Spencer's estate, thus giving them co-approval on the stamp. Susie kept insisting, however, that she had sole control. It was soon evident that there were differences within the family that no USPS legal document was going to resolve without them coming to terms among themselves.

Joe's version arrived in our offices a few weeks later. As we expected, it did not live up to the standards of quality illustration that we demanded in stamp design. But we had agreed to share it with the Committee. It took only a minute for the entire Committee to reject the art out of hand. The call to Cindy and Joe did not go well. Cindy was incensed that Joe's work was rejected, and they insisted they would get back to us and that we were not to proceed until further notice.

In light of the delay, Susie, feeling emboldened, asked that a new and different portrait be developed. She said she never really cared for the photograph we used to paint from. She offered a family photo she felt was a more pleasing likeness of her father. We agreed to review the photo before proceeding any further. Upon receiving it, we found it a pleasant, soft-focus photo, but not of the highest quality we were used to working with. When it was shared with the Committee, one member attempted to dismiss it, saying it was of poor quality and that Spencer "appears to be drunk." His view was noted, but the Committee agreed to allow a new image to be developed based on the photo.

We immediately had Drew create a second portrait, which he produced expeditiously. We showed it to Susie, who approved it without hesitation. But we were forced to meet with the dynamic duo, Cindy, and Joe, to get Joe's approval.

That meeting, which Susie insisted on being a part of, was held at the Hamburger Hamlet on Sunset Boulevard, the same tired old chain restaurant where we'd met with Shirley Fonda, Henry's widow, the previous year. I'm not sure what any of them saw in that place, but we weren't about to complain. We just wanted to meet to get final approval.

Cindy, Joe, and Susie were all ensconced in a corner booth of that dimly-lit restaurant when Bill Gicker and I arrived. They had not yet finished their lunch, and they asked that we sit in the booth facing them. It was a very awkward situation. Bill and I were well within earshot of their conversation, which didn't prevent them from talking openly about their displeasure with the entire process. Joe and Cindy liked the new resource photo better but still insisted that Joe could do better than Drew's new painting.

Once again delaying the entire project, we were forced to allow Joe to create a second "masterpiece." As one can only imagine, the second attempt was no better than his first. And, once again, the CSAC's review of the art met with a resounding rejection.

It was left for me to inform Cindy and Joe that Joe's work didn't meet our standards and that Drew's painting would be used once the agreement was signed by both parties. It would be an understatement to say that call was not well received.

Over the next two years, I received numerous calls from Susie pleading with me and even breaking down in tears as she begged us to proceed with the stamp. She so wanted the stamp to be released before she passed herself. We kept reassuring her that we would be delighted to issue the stamp but that first, she and her nephew had to settle their differences, and both sign the contract. Joe continued to refuse to accept the terms. Finally, we at the Postal Service gave them a deadline, after two years of wrangling, to come to an agreement or we would drop the stamp and move on to other film stars whose families would agree to terms.

Susie was distraught. Joe was adamant. The Postal Service stood firm. Spencer Tracy as a Legend of Hollywood stamp was never to be. I felt bad for Susie, and I was personally saddened that such a great talent—one of the greatest actors in film history—would be denied a stamp honoring his work, all because of family bickering. That stamp was truly "one that got away."

Chapter 10

Around the World in 8,000 Days

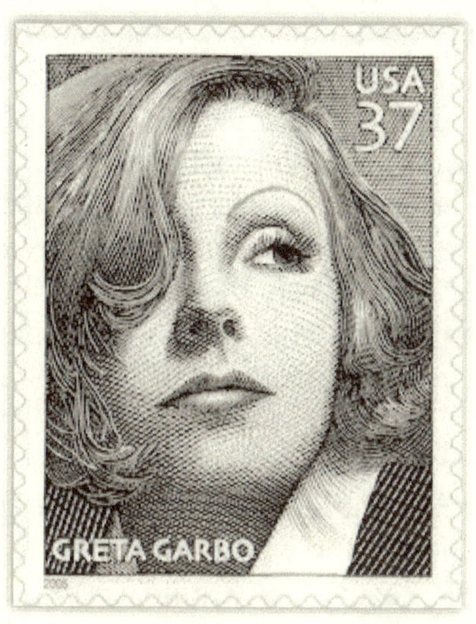

Unlike Phileas Fogg, the intrepidly confident hero of Jules Verne's classic *Around the World in 80 Days*, it took me a little longer to see other parts of the world. Approximately 8,000 to be specific. My first international trip took place in 1988 to the frozen world then known as the Union of Soviet Socialist Republics. It was a fascinating, bizarre, and unproductive trip that solidified my suspicions that Cold War adversaries are really just the politicians running the respective countries, not the general populations. That ten-day, bitterly cold visit halfway around the world would only serve to whet my appetite for more international travel on behalf of the Postal Service.

To Russia with Love

While still working in the Communications Art Department in 1988, I became involved with a book unlike any other I would work on in either Communications or Stamp Services in my career. This book was one I had little control over, unlike *An American Postal Portrait* a few years later and stamp albums. It wasn't going to be filled with wonderful images, beautiful layouts, or even colorful prose. It was to be a scientific journal filled with patents of postal equipment from around the world. Not the most exciting project for a designer, but it did allow me to embark on a journey of a lifetime.

The project itself was unique, even for the Postal Service. It was to be a first-ever joint venture between the U.S. Postal Service and the USSR PTT. The "PTT" stood for Post, Telephone, and Telegraph, a common title throughout Europe as these agencies usually managed all three services—unlike the U.S., which has separate agencies overseeing the three services. Gary Herring, a manager from the Postal Technology Center, who headed up the project, and I were thrilled to be approved to make the trip. We were to be the first official representatives of the U.S. Postal Service ever to enter Russia.

The objective was to receive patents from all foreign postal administration members of the Universal Postal Union, which meant virtually every country in the world, for the book. The patents would be sent to the USSR Post, which would, in turn, organize them into assigned groups. At that point, the USPS would provide design support in developing the layout and cover of the book.

Remember that in 1988, the world was just beginning to embrace the computer culture, which has since become part of everyday life. But at that juncture in time, it was a relatively new phenomenon.

Upon mutual agreement of the design format, the USSR PTT would electronically scan the thousands of submissions, complete with drawings and diagrams, and feed them into the layout. Upon completion of the final product, the Soviets would transmit, via satellite, the electronic document to the U.S., where the book would be printed. It was very high-tech for its day but very primitive by today's technological standards.

Over the next few months, Gary handled all the preliminary procedures, and I just waited anxiously. Finally, the word came from the Soviets. We should plan on arriving in Moscow in late November for our meetings.

Just days before we were scheduled to depart, we received an abrupt, terse message from the Soviets: "It is not a good time to come. Please wait for a new date." No explanation. No apology. Nothing. Very typical of the Soviets. We canceled our flights and began waiting.

Approximately a week later, we received a second terse message: "Please arrive in Moscow around December 10." Again, no explanation or apology. But at least we had approval to enter the country. We rushed to rebook our tickets. As planned, Gary flew to Germany to visit his daughter, and I booked a flight from D.C. to Moscow through London. I must admit I was a bit apprehensive about traveling alone to such a dark, forbidding country where I didn't know the language.

To make matters worse, Gary said that he was given no instructions on where to go when arriving in Moscow, but he assumed that someone would meet me. He hoped to be in Moscow by the time I arrived but didn't know whether he'd be allowed to meet me at the airport. I flew blind into Moscow, not knowing the names of any individuals I would be meeting, where I would be staying, or any other details of the trip. It seemed that the Soviet way of doing things was for them to determine the hotel. The choice was not ours to make. The standard depiction of Soviet society being very secretive certainly was proving true in my case.

I arrived in Moscow at 4:30 p.m. on Saturday, December 10, amid snow and a typical bleak, gray day. The sun had set half an hour earlier, but I was still able to see the city as the plane approached. Upon my arrival, the international terminal was dimly lit, bleak, and blandly gray, much like the weather outside. The most startling sight was machine gun-toting Soviet military personnel stationed at intervals along the corridors as we paraded, single file, down to Customs. At that point, my stomach started to churn with apprehension.

The following morning, after a rather sleepless night in a single bed with a thin, board-like mattress and no box spring, Gary and I met our very distinguished hosts for the Moscow portion of our trip, Mr. Botenko and Mr. Vassiliov, the number two and three PPT officials, respectively. Because it was a Sunday, their intent was to take us on a tour of Moscow.

Most of the day was spent touring parks, the Kremlin, Russian Orthodox churches filled with incredible icons, and the Arbat Street shopping district. All this in twenty-two degrees and snow. Late that afternoon, we were driven to the famous Moscow TV tower, at one time the tallest structure in the world, housing an observation deck and revolving restaurant. While we were allowed to take photos on the ground, we had to relinquish our cameras, for security purposes, when we ascended the tower. As if my little camera was going to capture any secret Soviet installations! I'm sure our satellites had already discovered all of those sites. But we turned in our cameras, nonetheless.

The head of the TV tower greeted us and escorted us to the observation platform 337 meters into the snowy sky. Fortunately, despite the light snow, we were able to admire wonderful views of the Moscow skyline as the sun was setting. We then proceeded upstairs to the restaurant called "Seventh Heaven," or "Sky" as our guides called it. We had heard other dinner patrons while we were in the observation area, but when we arrived at the restaurant one level down, patrons were being led out of the area. It seems our hosts had reserved the entire restaurant for our visit. Four men, at one table, in a vast revolving restaurant! We felt privileged yet a bit foolish that such extreme measures were taken for our visit.

Our assumption the following morning, Monday, was that we would begin discussions with our PTT counterparts. Not quite yet. Alex and our newly assigned interpreter, Anya, escorted us to the thirteenth-century Danilov Monastery, founded by Prince Danilov, the son of Alexander Nevsky.

Then it was off through the bitter cold (ten degrees) on windy, snowy streets to meet our business partners. But not to work. Lunch first. We met Mr. Kokorov, the head of research at the PTT, who immediately took us to a "cooperative" restaurant for a two-and-a-half-hour lunch complete with vodka and wine of course. After our marathon lunch, Alex and Anya took us on a tour of Red Square.

After all of those scenic diversions, it was back to the PTT where a brief discussion about our formal business agenda was held prior to breaking for, what else, another meal: a three-hour dinner at an Uzbekistan-cuisine restaurant in a private dining room complete with lavish multiple courses and, you guessed it, vodka, wine, and for toppers, cognac.

The next morning, we were off to PTT for one last visit with Mr. Botenko, Mr. Vassiliov, and Mr. Kokorov. Little substantive business was discussed. They were more interested in exchanging gifts. After an hour of very diplomatic discussion and an exchange of gifts, we were whisked off to ride the Moscow subway before heading to the airport.

Flying Aeroflot is an experience—one I'd rather not experience again. It was crammed, and I happened to be the last person to board. I went to the last seat available in the last row. Because of the lack of luggage space, I had to put my carry-on bag under my feet, so my knees were almost to my chin. As if that wasn't bad enough, my seatmate was a Pakistani businessman who reeked of spices. To my disbelief, as the plane was taxiing and taking off, the lone stewardess was walking through the aisles checking on passengers. Once aloft, she passed out small, shallow bowls of water. Gary and I looked at one another, not knowing whether it was a finger bowl for washing our hands before eating or what. To our surprise, we saw other passengers drinking from the bowls. It was our in-flight beverage service. Fortunately, it was only an eighty-minute flight.

The second leg of our Russian trip and the primary business portion of the trip took us to Leningrad. Still known then by its Communist name, the city of St. Petersburg is truly one of the most beautiful and fascinating cities I've ever visited.

Upon arrival, we were greeted by our hosts, Mr. Uzilevsky, the head of the Technical Institute, the Postmaster of Leningrad, whose name I cannot remember, and Rumia, our interpreter for this leg of the trip. The weather was the same as in Moscow. Cold! A frigid ten degrees was the norm in that area. The hotel chosen for our stay was the Moscow, located across the street from the Alexander Nevsky Monastery.

Mr. Uzilevsky put us situated in our rooms and then asked that we meet him in the lobby at six p.m. Upon arrival in the lobby, we were greeted by Mr. Uzilevsky, three of his assistants from the "Problems Laboratory" (the term we were told), the Postmaster and two of his assistants, and of course, Rumia, our interpreter, who would prove invaluable to Gary and me.

We had assumed that we would be taken out to dinner, but instead, Mr. Uzilevsky had arranged a dinner in the hotel dining room of this very ornate old-world hotel. Upon entering the dining room at the top of a small, curved staircase, Gary and I were struck by the sheer size of the room. It must have seated more than three hundred people. All of the tables were occupied with the exception of one large table in the exact center of the room. It quickly became very obvious that it was meant for us. A clue was that there were American and Soviet flags as centerpieces on the table. As we arrived at the table, we could hear hushed murmurs from the crowd: "Americanskys." Many of the patrons turned to stare at us as if we were from another planet.

We were soon to discover that there is an intense rivalry between Moscow and Leningrad on many fronts. Residents of Leningrad have held a grudge since the capitol was moved from there to Moscow, triggering the competition between the two cities. Because Gary and I had first traveled to Moscow, the staff in Leningrad were not to be outdone by their archrivals. The dinner was to be only the beginning of efforts by the "Problems Laboratory" staff to outshine Moscow.

The dinner—banquet would be a more appropriate term—was big and lavish, complete with numerous bottles of Stoli vodka, Georgian white wine, and of course, "Peep-si," all served in champagne buckets. Numerous toasts were made celebrating the newfound relationship between the two postal administrations. A few toasts included locking arms with our hosts and downing shots of vodka. Being seated in the center of the room made us the center of attention for the other diners, but after a few shots of vodka, our concerns and inhibitions loosened.

Approximately two-and-a-half hours after being seated, we were served dinner. Typical of a Russian banquet, there were many courses of meats, cheeses, fish, etc., with pork as the main course. When the pork was finally served, a floor show began on stage consisting of a twenty-piece orchestra, ten dancing girls, two acrobats, and a juggler. Only in Russia!

Midway through the show, Rumia interrupted our conversation with a plea to pay attention to the orchestra conductor. He said he was pleased to introduce two distinguished visitors from the United States and proceeded to give our names, which came as a surprise to Gary and me. He then proposed a toast to the mutual friendship of the two countries and, at that moment, every person in the room stood and toasted the two of us. It was a moment I will never forget. We quickly asked Rumia if we should respond with a toast, and she said, "Most assuredly, but you must go on stage to do it." So, there went two vodka-weary Americans to the stage, where we proposed a toast honoring our Cold War-thawing friendship. Again, the entire audience rose and toasted us.

As if that weren't enough, when we returned to our table, Rumia told us that the conductor had informed the crowd that they would play a musical tribute to "our American friends." The orchestra launched into a medley of American tunes, starting with "Yankee Doodle Dandy," continuing with numerous Glenn Miller hits, and ending with a portion of Gershwin's "Rhapsody in Blue," all of which was accompanied by ten chorus girls costumed in red, white, and blue outfits and waving small American flags. Gary and I were flabbergasted.

After the show, the conductor was invited to our table, and we had a very animated discussion about American music, especially jazz. The evening finally ended at 11:30 p.m. after five-and-a-half long, exhausting, but exhilarating hours. It was truly one of the most memorable evenings of all my days of travel both then and in the years that followed.

The next morning, we were whisked by private car to the "Problems Laboratory," where we were given a tour of the labs. There was a good exchange of information about the mailing processes of our two agencies. After lunch at the hotel, Gary and I found time to walk across the street to the Nevsky Monastery despite the heavy snowfall. It was like something out of *Dr. Zhivago* as the blowing snow and dim streetlights illuminated the beautifully carved tombstones of such renowned Russian artists as Tchaikovsky, Rimski-Korsakov, Borodin, Gogol, and Dostoevsky. Then it was back to the lab after that brief respite. We drafted language for a joint agreement statement of purpose for the meetings. On our second full day in Leningrad, the morning was devoted to touring the main post office and the airport. Our hosts showed us their version of letter-sorting machines, which surprised both Gary and me when we observed their primitive mechanics. Gary whispered to me: "It's so 1930s!"

Not wanting to "overburden our guests," as Mr. Uzilevsky put it, many of the days were broken into part work and part recreation. The afternoon was devoted to sightseeing with Rumia as our guide and Alexander "Sasha" Steimack, a professional photographer hired by Mr. Uzilevsky to follow us around to record our visit. In talking with him, we discovered that he was an employee of *Izvestia* (The News), one of the largest Soviet newspapers.

The following Saturday, our hosts devoted the day to relaxing events. After picking up sandwiches, we drove out to Pushkin Palace for a private tour. This was another magnificent structure filled with breathtaking amounts of gilt and gold. We walked around the snow-covered grounds and then drove on to Pavlovsk Palace, stopping near the palace to eat our picnic lunch in the car. After touring yet another incredible building, we came upon two boys throwing snowballs at one another as even more snow fell to the ground. Gary and I joined them in the snowball fight. Our hosts weren't sure what to make of two grown businessmen in suits frolicking with children, but we enjoyed ourselves despite the frigid temperatures. We were disturbed, however, to hear the news our host shared with us when we returned to the car to warm up.

Gary and I had repeatedly requested that we discuss in detail the plans for sending the files via satellite to the U.S. for printing. Our hosts sidestepped the issue each time we mentioned this. It wasn't until we were pressed shoulder to shoulder in that small black Russian sedan, munching on our sandwiches, that Mr. Uzilevsky made his confession. Despite his country's boasts of advanced technology, the Soviets did not possess, at that time, the expertise to fulfill their half of the agreement. Obviously, Mr. Uzilevsky was embarrassed to share this information, but after much discussion, it was roundly agreed that it was out of our hands. Alternative solutions were proposed, but in the end, we were forced to resort to a tried-and-true (and appropriate) method: the mail. Some months later, the Soviets unceremoniously mailed the files to our headquarters. The resulting book, though it will never be included in the annals of good design, eventually saw publication and its rightful place in oblivion.

On Monday, it was back to work. At the "Problems Laboratory," Gary and Mr. Uzilevsky signed the agreement followed by a lunch prepared by members of the staff, consisting of borscht, fish pie, pickled mushrooms, assorted vegetables, meat-filled pastries, tea, and chocolates. But before lunch was served in the bomb shelter below the building, Mr. Uzilevsky produced a special bottle of Ukrainian vodka, and numerous toasts were offered, meant to solidify our newfound friendship and cooperative partnership. After lunch gifts were exchanged between our groups, Sasha, the photographer, gave us albums of photos he had taken during our visit. The remainder of the afternoon was spent fielding questions from laboratory staff members, then it was back to the hotel to begin packing for the trip home.

Our last night in Leningrad would prove to be memorable. Mr. Uzilevsky, Rumia, Vladimir, Sasha, Gary, and I were driven out to a pre-Baltic restaurant on Vasilevsky Island on the Gulf of Finland. Entertainment during our twelve-course dinner was provided by twelve Russian Gypsies, including a belly dancer, performing folk songs and dances. The usual round of toasts, involving much vodka, white wine, and "Peep-si," were made. We left the restaurant at midnight to be chauffeured back to our hotel to get two-and-a-half hours of sleep, only to be awakened at 3:15 a.m. to leave for the airport at 4 a.m., as usual in falling snow. During my entire trip to Russia, I saw only two hours of pure sunlight. The long, dark, gray winter nights of Russia began to wear me down. I could see why the Russians spend so much time drinking. The weather can make you very depressed.

With one last round of bear hugs, we were off for home carrying with us many fond memories of great friends, food, libations, and sights. This trip would be the first of many I would be making over the next twenty years, some as unique and exotic as this one, and many others in the States that were less exotic but still interesting and memorable.

Would You Like Egg Rolls with That?

My next foray into international travel would be to a far warmer and more exotic locale: China.

When I joined the Stamp Development team in late 1990, the wheels were already churning to develop a joint issue stamp with the People's Republic of China. Don McDowell, a senior manager in Stamp Services, made the first of what would be three trips to China taken by our team. Don's goal was to establish a relationship with our counterparts in China Post.

Don's initial trip paved the way for Joe Brockert, the manager of Stamp Development, to be the second U.S. Postal person to make the very long flight to Beijing. Joe was my immediate supervisor when I made the move to Stamp Services and remained so until reorganization by incoming Postmaster General Runyon in 1993 saw

Joe and I trade jobs.

In 1992, Joe met with his China Post counterparts in Beijing. His mission was to identify a common subject both groups could be comfortable with, which was not as easy as one would assume. Pandas would be the most popular and natural choice, but both administrations had already issued such stamps, thus removing the subject from the mix.

Joe called me from Beijing one day to ask me to research a particular subject from an American standpoint: cranes, specifically endangered cranes. What information I could find on short notice was faxed to Joe. An agreement was reached shortly after that. Endangered Cranes it would be.

For the third trip, I was chosen to wing my way to Beijing. Joe had negotiated the terms of stamp development: Each country would develop design concepts for mutual review and selection. Because we were now entering the design phase, Joe ceded the role to me.

In 1992, the USPS had issued its first Lunar New Year stamp designed by Honolulu-based designer Clarence Lee, one of the leading Asian-American designers. Lee was immediately considered to develop the Endangered Crane concepts for the joint issue. To simplify logistics on both projects, I took over as art director for the remaining eleven Lunar New Year stamps as well as the joint-issue Crane stamps. Dick Sheaff, the initial art director for the Lunar series, was not happy about it, and in retrospect, I can understand his frustration. But when one is tasked with overseeing more than 125 designs at the same time, expediency and duplicity play a role in decision-making.

Turning the calendar page, it's now April 1993. After much back-and-forth logistics, working through translators, we were formally invited to Beijing to share our designs. Clarence and I had developed our concepts from our respective locations via phone, fax, and emails. Until the trip, I had never met Clarence face to face.

My flights on April 10 took me from D.C. to Beijing with transfers in Los Angeles, Honolulu, and Tokyo. After the five-hour flight to L.A. and another five hours to Honolulu, I spent the night at Clarence and Elsa Lee's beautiful apartment overlooking downtown Honolulu. The following day, Clarence and I departed on our long, long journey: an eight-hour flight to Tokyo, a three-hour layover, and then a six hour flight to Beijing.

We were greeted outside the Beijing terminal amid a sea of people, cars, taxis, and bicycles by our host, Mr. Chen, and interpreter Kathy Yu, who was waving a handmade sign with our names.

To China Post's credit, they decided we would benefit most by being housed in a hotel in Old Beijing rather than a large Western-style hotel. The Qian Men hotel was less than a mile from Tiananmen Square and the Forbidden City. To add to our exhaustion, Mr. Chen, through an interpreter, gave us a complete rundown of our busy itinerary for the next eight days.

After breakfast in the hotel the following morning, interpreter Kathy Yu met us, and our driver took us to the Ministry of Posts and Telecommunications for our first meeting. It would not be stereotyping to describe their offices as bleak, stark, and bland. But then, I've seen some federal offices in D.C. that could be described in the same way. The room where we met was what I would describe as an interrogation room. It was small and gray with blank concrete walls, and to top it off, it was very cold, which didn't do anything to ease our sense of apprehension and intimidation.

The initial meeting was very formal. Mr. Chen, head of the Stamp division, introduced us to Ms. Zhao from Stamp Design and Madame Cheng from the Stamp Design unit of the National Philatelic Corporation. After reviewing the agreement negotiated by Don McDowell and Joe Brockert in previous meetings and going over the design timetable, it was time to get down to the nitty-gritty. Let's see the artwork.

They laid out on the table six sets of illustrations of two different endangered cranes, each by a different artist. Clarence and I countered with four sets of design layouts, more graphic in nature, unlike the watercolor illustration concepts they displayed. Much discussion ensued, and it was finally agreed that we would use one of the six illustration sets from China Post, and the USPS contribution would be the design and typography. But which illustrations? That was the big question.

At that point, the China Post team excused themselves, saying they had previously agreed before this meeting which artist they wished to use. Now it was up to Clarence and me to make our choice. As Kathy so ably translated for Mr. Chen: "We hope you choose the right one." No pressure there!

Left alone in that small, dank, stark, cold room, Clarence and I looked at one another with trepidation. The pressure was on. Which one had they picked? Would we pick the same one? We decided that all we could do was to choose the one we liked best and hope that we would all agree. If not, it could mean hours cooped up in that cold room.

We analyzed what we saw and finally reached a decision, asking their team to rejoin us to hear of our choice. I felt like a contestant on a quiz show that, with great hesitation, gives their "final answer" only to have to wait in prolonged suspense before the emcee shouts, "You're correct!" Fortunately, we chose the right one. Beams of smiles immediately crossed their faces when we pointed to our choice. Their response: "It was the only right choice to make." I couldn't tell whether their response got lost in translation or they truly felt there was only one choice. Whatever. We were very relieved to have made the "right" decision.

That "right" decision was an illustration by Mr. Zhan Gengxi, one of the most revered nature artists in China. In fact, many of his works hang in the Great Wall of the People and other governmental buildings in Beijing. Both parties agreed that the Whooping Crane illustration was perfect, but his Black-Necked Crane needed to be reworked. Mr. Zhan was contacted and arranged to meet us that afternoon.

The afternoon meeting at our hotel was like something out of a B-movie. We sat in large, overstuffed, deep-red armchairs that one could sink into, complete with a tea service. The only thing missing was Mao-style uniforms. The meeting was very productive considering it was between two very bureaucratic governments, resulting in a deadline of one month for final art. A lavish sixteen-course feast at a local restaurant in downtown Beijing culminated a long day.

The next afternoon, we were taken to the National Philatelic Corporation headquarters to meet with three of their Design staff, one of which was a woman. She was very quiet during most of the meeting. Despite her reticence to speak, we spent a fascinating and insightful two hours exchanging our views on design. We discovered that despite the cultural differences, both groups had to deal with the same types of problems when designing stamps. To help bridge the cultural divide, I presented everyone with "Elvis" stamp pins, which they were thrilled to receive.

The meeting was followed by another massive sixteen-course dinner at Beijing Duck, the oldest and most famous restaurant in the city. This time, the emphasis was on duck dishes, including their famed Peking duck, all of which were delicious. I was seated next to the woman designer during dinner, which surprised me a little. Diplomatic protocol would normally dictate that my counterpart would be seated next to me. I was stunned to learn during the dinner that this woman was indeed my counterpart. I found it perplexing why she was so quiet and shy during the afternoon meeting, but at dinner, she relaxed, and we enjoyed a wonderful conversation about our similar jobs. I discovered that she was the first female designer in the government since the Revolution. The evening concluded around nine p.m. after much food, great conversation, and numerous *"Gan Bei"* toasts.

Our meeting the following morning focused on details of the designs and schedules. Our hosts said they would allow us to explore Old Beijing at lunchtime on our own. That afternoon, we walked off our large lunch by visiting Tiananmen Square and the Forbidden City with our interpreter, Kathy. She shared her personal story of the bloody uprising in the Square some years earlier. She was a student and had been in the square protesting like thousands of others. She awoke in her sleeping bag one morning to hear a strange sound. Looking up, she saw a helicopter hovering overhead. She sensed something bad was about to happen. She quietly rose, rolled up her sleeping bag, and left the square. It was shortly after that when the tanks rolled into the square and changed the course of Chinese history.

The must-see thing to do when visiting China, of course, is the Great Wall. We were not disappointed when we were told that we'd be visiting there the next morning.

We were picked up at eight a.m. by Madame Cheng and her daughter, Jane Song, who acted as interpreter for us, while Kathy stayed behind with Mr. Cheng to work on creating the agreement between the two postal administrations. Packed into a small sedan alongside a humongous driver who reminded me of "Oddjob" from the classic James Bond movie, *Goldfinger,* we headed out for the ninety-minute trip through rugged mountains. The petite Madame Cheng sat in the front seat with the burly driver while Clarence,

Jane, and I were tucked into the back seat.

Upon arrival at the Wall, we discovered that it was the first day of the Spring Festival complete with musicians and people costumed in ancient robes. Despite the crowds, it really brought the history of the Wall to life for us. The Great Wall is not to be missed by anyway exploring China. It was truly one of the most awe-inspiring sights I've seen. The steps are not for the weak-hearted but worth the strenuous workout.

After such strenuous and demanding "work" on this fascinating trip, our hosts insisted we needed two days of R & R. We were flown first-class on China Air ninety minutes south to Hangzhou, which the Chinese refer to as "Paradise on Earth." While the city itself is rather industrial and dirty, filled with a few million people and an abundance of smog—almost as much as Beijing—it gets its descriptive name from the West Lake District that abuts the city.

Without the able assistance of Kathy, our interpreter, we were forced to pantomime a lot with Mr. Chen on the trip to Hangzhou. Upon arrival, we were met by Mr. Yang, the Deputy Director of Posts and the Manager of Philately for Hangzhou. They brought their own interpreter, Mr. Lu, a young employee of the city post office who assured his bosses that he could converse in English. Such was not the case as we were soon to discover. Clarence and I struggled with Mr. Lu, but somehow we managed to understand one another. It turned out he was more interested in currency exchange in order to make a "big killing" off the two Americans and their dollars. We politely declined his monetary offers.

The following day, Sunday, we were taken to a tea museum outside the city. After trying numerous teas in the tearoom, Clarence and I were allowed to walk among the tea fields where women were harvesting the tea leaves. They seemed bemused by the presence of two Westerners and watched us with cautious eyes. Clarence and I attempted to communicate with a few of the women, but the language barrier was too much. But we did convince two ladies to lend us their cone-shaped straw hats to try on for photos. This silly move was greeted by the usual quiet titters, so typical of the Chinese culture.

After lunch, we were told we were going to meet with some local stamp collectors in downtown Hangzhou. To be quite honest, neither Clarence nor I were thrilled with the idea, but we had little choice in the matter. We expected a short visit with a bunch of elderly men, figuring that Chinese philatelists were no different than philatelists worldwide.

To our surprise, when we arrived at the philatelic offices and whisked to the second-floor conference room, we were greeted by applause, TV cameras, and a large audience. There were older serious collectors as expected, but also schoolchildren. It seems that our visit was so special that the local TV station was on hand to interview us for the evening news. Unfortunately, our so-called interpreter was not up to the task. He was very nervous in front of the cameras and had difficulty translating into Chinese some very simple answers I gave to the reporter's questions. Despite that, we had a wonderful time. We were introduced to a 93-year-old collector, the oldest in China, in addition to young students who presented us with drawings they had made for the occasion. Those two hours proved to be far more exciting and entertaining than Clarence and I could have imagined.

I have always enjoyed Chinese food, but it wasn't until I actually went to China that I realized just how different, and simple, the Americanized version of Chinese food is. In Beijing, I feasted on duck web, tripe, sea cucumber, and even the traditional Peking duck, but this duck came complete with its bill—all of it edible, I was told. Not to mention roasted squab, or as I later referred to it, "bird on a stick." But I had no idea just what was in store for me the next two days.

The first night in Hangzhou, we dined at the famed Tianxianglou seafood restaurant where former Chinese leader Chou En-Li dined regularly with guests. Our Hangzhou hosts were not to be outdone by the Beijing bosses. We were to dine on twelve courses during the evening, complete with wine—lots of it. "*Gan Bei*"! Some entrees included a large whole fish in sweet and sour sauce; snails in wine; whole baked chicken in clay molds which were broken open at the table; whole large frog; and numerous other more traditional foods such as beef, pork, vegetables, and shrimp.

The following night, our last in Hangzhou, we dined at the Louwailou seafood restaurant. During the banquet, we were to sign the official agreement between the two nations. I only hoped that my head would be clear enough after numerous "*Gan Bei*" toasts to be able to read the document. A private dining room was reserved for the event.

As guest of honor, I was seated at a large round table facing the door at the opposite end of the room. The lazy Susan on the table displayed each new entrée as it arrived. After we viewed each dish, it was removed and returned evenly portioned out on each diner's plate. As the evening progressed and multiple varieties of seafood courses were devoured, I learned that the local officials were rarely treated to such dinners and they were taking advantage of the opportunity, ordering the most expensive and lavish dishes on the menu. This I learned through broken English from our so-called local interpreter.

I was then asked to try one more dish. I should have known something was amiss when the Chinese officials pulled out their cameras and began to titter, covering their mouths with their hands. The door at the rear of the room opened and a waiter approached carrying a large, octagonal glass-covered dish. The dish immediately reminded me of a cut-glass dish that my grandmother used to keep candy in for us kids. I sensed by the reaction of the Chinese officials that I was not about to be offered candy.

Our interpreter told Clarence and me that the dish was called "drunken prawns." Clarence immediately reacted, saying, "Oh, Terry, you are going to love this. I had this dish in Hong Kong last year." I've always loved shrimp, so I thought I was safe trying this dish.

Then they lifted the lid off the dish. Awash in a thin, brown wine sauce were very large prawns literally jumping up and down. They were still alive! It seems that the prawns were cooked at a high temperature, causing them to jump around to avoid the heat. So there I was, facing giant live prawns—head, shells, and tails waiting for me to eat one.

I almost freaked out, but Clarence kept reassuring me that I could do it and that it would be disrespectful to our hosts to not at least try one. Sensing my dread, my hosts put down their cameras, spun the lazy-Susan table around, and proceeded to give me a demonstration on how to eat this delicacy.

Grabbing the moving object (prawn) by the tail, the host proceeded to bite the head off, spit it onto a side plate, and inserted the remainder of the body, shell, and all, into his mouth. He then very adroitly peeled the shell with his tongue (something Chinese are taught from an early age), spit the shell and tail out onto the plate, and then ate the body. So easy! Once the demonstration was over, the Lazy Susan was once again spun back to my side. It was now my turn.

Cameras once again raised. Everyone was ready for me to eat a live shrimp. As I was still reluctant, Clarence reassured me I could do it. Maybe it was all the alcohol that fortified me and convinced me I could really do this. Reaching into the dish with my chopsticks, I picked up a prawn, but he wasn't about to be cooperative. He slipped out of my grasp, flopped onto the table, and flip-flopped around, much to the amusement of my hosts. Putting down the chopsticks, I picked up the reluctant participant, put him in my mouth, bit his head off, and spit it out onto the side plate, just as I had been instructed. Not even wanting to attempt to extract the shell with my tongue, I quickly peeled the shell by hand and popped the meat into my mouth. To my delight and relief, it was delicious. Then I made the unfortunate choice of glancing down at the side plate only to see the head still moving. It was everything I could do to keep chewing the body, but somehow I managed to swallow it, avoiding any further glances toward the plate. Cameras flashed, and people laughed and applauded my "bravery." A great sense of relief came over me after surviving the ritual. So much so that I subsequently ate five more prawns. The last one was dead by the time I ate it. I guess it was exhausted from all that jumping and gave up the ghost. That poor thing was not as tasty as his four other friends, but it was still an unforgettable gourmet experience.

The following day, we were treated to a first-class seat on China Air for our return trip to Beijing for what was to be our last day in China. The last afternoon was spent touring the magnificent Temple of Heaven and its many buildings and beautiful gardens. The last night's dinner was a more casual affair in our hotel's "hot pot" restaurant. The evening was spent getting to know one another on a more personal level, setting aside all the business formalities. We left China the following day knowing we had made good friends who would live on in our memories far into the future.

China had to be the most "exotic" trip of my career, but it was not to be the last international trip I was to make on behalf of the U.S. stamp program. But before I venture to describe another trip, I need to mention that we arranged a second meeting with our China counterparts eight months later to finalize the designs for the two Endangered Cranes stamps to be issued in 1994.

The exotic Hawaiian Islands were the site for the second design meeting between our two nations in January 1994. I chose Hawaii for several reasons. Because Hawaii is the approximate midpoint between the two countries, it would cut down on the extremely long flight to the U.S. for the Chinese delegation. Secondly, Clarence was based in Honolulu, and thirdly, Hawaii would be a great locale where everyone could relax. I discovered during the course of the meetings that the Chinese were not entirely happy with my site selection. To them, Hawaii was still part of the Orient, and they had their hearts set on a trip to Washington, D.C., where none had ever visited. But as the meetings progressed, they had to agree that Hawaii was, indeed, a wonderful choice.

Accompanying Mr. Chen was the artist, Zhan Gengxi, the Chinese stamp engraver, and our favorite interpreter from Beijing, Kathy Yu. Numerous meetings were held discussing various aspects of the art, engravings, and production techniques; all interlaced with time to visit the sights of the islands of Oahu and Maui in an attempt to match the Chinese hospitality shown to us the previous year.

The joint issue of the Endangered Cranes stamps was unveiled on October 9, 1994, in both Washington, D.C., and Beijing, culminating the three-year joint venture.

Way Down Under

The Stamp Services offices routinely received requests from other postal administrations worldwide suggesting joint issue stamps between our countries. These joint issues are not usually financially feasible for the U.S. Smaller countries often benefited more from the purchase of our stamps. They required a purchase of far fewer U.S. stamps to manage the needs of collectors in their country. In contrast, in the U.S., we had to purchase much larger quantities of their stamps to meet the needs of the larger collecting base in all fifty states. Most requests were turned down, but occasionally we felt there was merit in taking on what could become a three- to five-year project. Negotiations, contractual agreements, and cultural differences between nations, not to mention finding a subject matter that relates in some way to both nations, could make the project more difficult than it was worth.

The New Zealand Post officials contacted us in 1999, five years after my Chinese trip. Their proposal was to create a joint issuance commemorating the America's Cup yacht race to be held in New Zealand the following year. After discussing it internally, we chose to accept their offer. It meant that I was to make another long, arduous plane trip to another "exotic" locale: New Zealand.

The almost 24-hour multiple plane trips proved to be one of those "trips from hell." After delayed departures, mechanical difficulties, "dinner" at midnight, and having orange juice spilled over me at breakfast, I was ready to arrive in New Zealand.

After that eventful trip, our meetings almost seemed anti-climactic. But the beauty of New Zealand proved to be so stunning that the arduous trip seemed almost worth it. I was met in Wellington by Kelly Spinks from our office and her boyfriend Andrew. They had arrived a few days before me to explore the South Island. Over the next two days, we met with three women from New Zealand Post: Wendy Riley, Viv Beck, and Deb de la Haye. Professionally, Deb was my Kiwi counterpart.

The one day of meetings went well, and everyone was very enthusiastic about the joint issue prospects. We were shown around the beautiful city of Wellington, its harbor, and hills, which are reminiscent of San Francisco. The following day, Kelly, Andrew, and I rented a car and drove from Wellington, located at the south end of the North Island, to Auckland, at the north end of the island.

Two tall people (Kelly and Andrew) and one shorter person (me) in a Ford Fiesta, along with all of our luggage crammed into the back seat next to me, set off on what we were told would be an eight-hour trip. Two things we hadn't factored in: 1) stopping every so often to marvel at the scenery: black-sand beaches, lush green hills (often topped by one lone tree), volcanoes, rugged coastlines, herds of sheep everywhere (they outnumber people), and even snow in July (it's winter that time of the year); and 2) the very small, narrow, two-lane roads we took. In many places, the lack of guardrails gave us pause as we traversed hills with precariously steep and deep ravines.

The trip took fourteen-and-a-half hours rather than eight. Longer than the flight from L.A. to Auckland! But it was worth every second to see the country.

The next day, despite being tired and cramped from the long road trip, Kelly and I met with Scott Chapman, an America's Cup official whose offices were located on the waterfront in downtown Auckland. It overlooked the Cup's "village" as it was being readied for an October kickoff. The event would run through the following February. Our meeting with Scott lasted two hours, after which we were shown the yacht that won the Cup in 1995 for New Zealand. We also saw a crew working on the USA entry, "America", captained by Dennis Conner.

To our dismay, and after all the effort, the America's Cup project was canceled. Surprisingly, it was the New Zealand Post that decided to withdraw from the project, which stunned us all. The reasons they gave were numerous. The officials we had met with were all very apologetic but had no choice but to pull out of the agreement. In the end, a trip of a lifetime resulted in a lost opportunity for a beautiful joint issue. But ironically, the cancellation of the project proved to be fortuitous for us. The American entrant failed to make the finals, thus avoiding Postal Service embarrassment in issuing a stamp commemorating a race the U.S. failed to finish.

Adventures in ABBA land

Among foreign nations requesting joint issue stamps with the U.S. Stamp Services, Sweden has probably been the most active group, issuing six joint issues over the years. One would think that larger countries, more comparable in size to ours, would have expressed more interest, but that was rarely the case.

Because of this continual interest in joint issues, I would make not one but two trips within a three-year period to that beautiful country. The first trip, in 2000, was to explore the possibility of commemorating the one-hundredth anniversary of the Nobel Prize with the intent to honor its founder Alfred Nobel in 2002. The second trip, in 2003, was to develop a commemorative stamp honoring the 100th birthday in 2005 of the great Swedish actress Greta Garbo, who had found great fame in Hollywood between the 1920s and 1940s.

Due to time constraints, we were required to make the Nobel trip in March 2000, not exactly the ideal time to visit a Scandinavian country unless you are planning a ski trip or just love the snow and cold. Having been born and raised in Minnesota you would have thought I would feel right at home, which I did to a certain extent. But it was still cold! I was accompanied by Kelly Spinks and James Tolbert, our manager, who was experiencing his first international trip.

We were greeted warmly by our Sweden Post hosts, Sales Manager Hans Nyman, Lead Designer Stephen Fransius, and Stamps Manager Ingegerd Mattsson. Like my Beijing hosts, the Swedes arranged for us to stay in the oldest part of the city, which meant the Gamla Stan district of Stockholm, at a sixteenth-century Inn. Fortunately, the rooms had been modernized with twentieth-century furnishings. The rooms were especially small, even by international hotel standards, but comfortable and quite charming.

The design for the Nobel stamp had been in the works for months between our two offices. It was when we had agreed upon a common design that a meeting was arranged with the Nobel Foundation. During the visit, we were taken on a tour of their facility and shown their display cases housing artifacts of many Nobel Prize recipients. Of most interest to me were the numerous first-edition books by many of my favorite authors.

The Nobel officials reviewed our proposed design depicting the Nobel Medal but rejected it, asking for an alternative, which threw us for a curve. Their rationale was that there was a Nobel policy against depicting the medal by itself. We had not expected such a reaction. The following day, we met at the Sweden Post offices and collaborated with one of the designers who made the requested revision, incorporating a portrait of Albert Nobel. Our plans called for us to depart Sweden the following day, so time was of the essence.

We scheduled a second meeting with the Foundation for the following morning. That meeting went much better than the first, and our revised design found approval, giving Kelly, James, and I just enough time to rush to the airport.

The second trip three years later was to develop a more "glamorous" stamp. The subject: Greta Garbo.

For this trip, I was accompanied by my coworker, Bill Gicker. We worked again with Stephen Fransius, but Hans Nyman had since retired, and there was a new manager of Stamps, Brett-Inger Hahn. We were booked into the same sixteenth-century Inn, mere blocks from the Royal Palace, which gave us a real taste for the Swedish culture. We found ourselves wandering the quaint narrow streets of the old city having coffee or drinks in charming cafes. One major difference between this trip and the previous one was the weather. Bill and I made the trip in June 2003, during the "white nights," which proved to be interesting.

The first morning after our arrival, I awoke to bright sunlight and immediately assumed that I had overslept. Jumping out of bed in a panic, I started to get dressed, stopped, and looked at the clock, which read: 4:00 a.m. Getting back to sleep was difficult after that. But Bill and I adjust quickly to the long nights of light.

Not having a family or estate to meet with, we were taken by our Swedish hosts on a Garbo tour one day. We visited her home in the morning and her gravesite in the afternoon. The cemetery was beautifully serene, filled with large shade trees. Despite having a map of the cemetery, we were hard-pressed to locate Ms. Garbo's gravesite. Hans eventually found a caretaker who directed us to the grave, situated on a slightly raised mound with a simple headstone.

One of the primary reasons for visiting Stockholm, as opposed to communicating through the mail, email, and phone calls, was to meet with the world's greatest stamp engraver, Mr. Czeslaw Slania, renowned in the philatelic world for his masterful engravings on many stamps from numerous nations, including the U.S. Mr. Slania had expressed interest in creating the portrait of Garbo, so it was our mission to sit down with him and discuss the image we had agreed to work from.

Art director Carl Herrman, who had been assigned to create a separate version of the Garbo stamp, selected a beautiful black-and-white closeup photo of her. It depicted her signature hairstyle, tilting down over one eye. It was provided to him by our research team at PhotoAssist. The photo was so stunning that not only the Stamps design team but also the CSAC members insisted we use the photo and not engrave the stamp as was suggested by Sweden Post. Many of Sweden's stamps are engraved, so it was only natural that they would recommend this complex printing process. Unlike Sweden, the U.S. stamp program had shied away from engraved stamps for budgetary and production reasons.

I'd had the privilege of meeting Mr. Slania a few times before at events such as stamp shows but sitting down to actually work with the master was a distinct pleasure. A small, frail bald man in his eighties with black-framed glasses, he could be mistaken as a nondescript bank clerk. But his genius lay in his hands and the ability to etch into steel plates, at actual stamp size, exquisite stamp images. His demeanor was that of a quiet unassuming gentleman. He spoke little English, preferring his native tongue. Sitting with Hans, Stephan, and Bill in a small, stuffy overheated room that day in June, I was about to receive a little lecture from the master.

We shared the photo with Slania, which thrilled him. He expressed his appreciation for choosing such a beautiful image. At that point, I had to drop the "bomb" on him and the Sweden Post staff. I shared the consensus of our staff and Committee that we, the U.S. Postal Service, wanted to reproduce the photo rather than create an engraving. Our rationale was that it would showcase two different approaches to the same subject, rendered in two different print methods, making it a unique, first-of-its-kind issuance. We added that it would delight collectors. At this point, Mr. Slania sat, stared, shuffled in his chair a little, and began to show a bit of sadness, frustration, and disdain for our suggestion. I could tell that I had offended him, which was the last thing I wanted to do.

A consummate gentleman, he quietly gave me a "tsk-tsk" with a shake of his head. I responded with a perplexed look of not understanding him. His reply, in English: "You will be so sorry if you do that. My engraving will be so far superior to your photo reproduction that yours will pale in comparison. But it is your choice." I immediately agreed that his work would be superb, but I attempted to convince him of the unique opportunity to do something different with a joint issue. I failed to convince him, so we left it at that.

Before we left Stockholm, one of the most beautiful cities I've ever had the privilege of visiting, Brett-Inger Hahn hosted Bill and me on an evening cruise through the Archipelago islands outside Stockholm. We dined well and soaked up breathtaking views of hundreds of islands both large and small. It was a perfect way to end a business trip, spending time with the good friends we had made at Sweden Post.

We became concerned when many months had passed after our Stockholm visit without seeing any results from Sweden Post and Mr. Slania. Numerous inquiries were made, but we were repeatedly told that it was "in the works" and that we would "see something soon." More months passed before Stephen called to inform me that Mr. Slania was unable to complete the engraving due to poor health. It seems that he had cancer and was unable to complete any of his projects. I did eventually see his initial attempts at the Garbo portrait, but it was obvious that his illness prevented him from creating his last masterpiece. Mr. Slania passed away on March 17, 2005, before the Garbo stamp issuance on September 23 of that same year, concurrently in New York City and Stockholm.

Sweden Post recommended that one of Slania's fellow engravers, Piotr Naszarkoswki, be given the chance to create the engraving, which we readily agreed to. Piotr created his engraving, which was shared at a CSAC meeting in Washington months later. We extended a formal invitation to the Sweden Post staff to visit D.C. in return for hosting us in Stockholm, which both Brett-Inger and Stephen agreed to.

Normally, visitors are not allowed to attend the closed-door deliberations of the CSAC. But they agreed to allow Brett-Inger and Stephen to observe the workings of the Committee and make a formal presentation of the final engraving of Garbo. When the time arrived for us to review the engraving, Stephen produced from his coat pocket an Altoid tin. Inside was a small, actual-size stamp proof of the engraving, which was passed around to the members and staff for review. It was a stunning engraving, one of the best we had seen.

After reviewing the engraving, they all turned in my direction for my thoughts. I swallowed my pride, and remembering the admonishment from Mr. Slania, I recommended that we print the engraving for both countries' issuances, which was readily agreed upon by all.

I'm sure Mr. Slania was looking down on us at the point, seeing how we had finally come to our senses. Although it was not his engraving, knowing that one of his top assistants had created such a work of art would be enough for him to think, *I told you so*, surely with a slight smile on his face.

Hopping the Pond

During my twenty years in Stamp Services, I "crossed the pond," as the saying goes to London a total of four times. England had always had an allure for me. The very first international trip I ever took was in 1984 with my wife and two children. We spent two weeks visiting London and driving around the English countryside, staying in B&Bs, inns, and even the White Cliffs Hotel in Dover. Knowing the language of an international country certainly helps, especially if it is your first trip abroad. The trip was memorable for all of us, and we still reminisce about it to this day.

I was given the opportunity again in 1997 to cross the pond for meetings with my Royal Mail counterpart. We had been conversing over the years through the mail, email, and phone, but we decided it was time to actually meet. The offer was extended for us to visit their offices and observe one of their stamp committee meetings. By "us," I mean Virginia Noelke, then-Chair of the CSAC, and Cindy Tackett, the Committee's logistical coordinator.

Our meetings with Royal Mail Stamps officials proved to be very fruitful. As with my counterparts in Beijing, Wellington, and Stockholm, we found that despite cultural and language differences, we shared many commonalities: frustrations and roadblocks in developing designs, delicate negotiations with estates, and certainly not the least of these, challenges in dealing with internal bureaucracy.

Their stamp committee was similar in structure, but their quarterly meetings lasted only one day, unlike our two-day sessions. One of the more interesting aspects of their process was their ability, both creatively and monetarily, to develop multiple approaches to a single subject. There have been only a few instances when the U.S. has been able to do that. The Elvis and Marilyn Monroe stamps are among only a handful that involved multiple design concepts by different artists.

Our discussions were productive and cemented a friendship and good working relationship among us for many years to come. The year following our visit to London, the head of Royal Mail Stamps called to ask if he could send Jane Ryan, their lead designer, to Washington to spend time in our offices learning more about our stamp development process and to observe one of our CSAC meetings. I was delighted to host Jane later that summer for four days. Our friendship and respect for each other's knowledge and expertise were to prove beneficial in the coming years as we worked toward a first-time joint issue between our two nations.

In early 2004, I received a call from Jane inviting me along with Dave Failor and Bill Gicker to visit London to begin discussions on subject matter for a joint issue. Upon arrival in London, we met with the Royal Mail design team and researchers to begin the process of identifying subject matter that both countries could justifiably commemorate. That task proved much more difficult than either of us had anticipated. Both groups presented possible subjects, but none seemed to pass the test. Either one or the other of us had already commemorated subjects put forth, or the subject had little or no relevance to the other party.

We did have one subject on our list that we were very excited to propose: The Beatles. For the U.S., one of the hurdles was how to depict the Beatles even though both Paul and Ringo were still alive, thus breaking our rule of not commemorating living people on stamps. We felt we could find a solution if our two groups approved the concept, but we were met with a simple "no" from the Brits. We were sure it would be a winner for both parties, but for some reason, they expressed total disinterest in exploring the Fab Four. It was not that many years later that Royal Mail did, indeed, issues Beatles stamps. Our suspicion was that they were contemplating the issuance when we arrived on their doorstep proposing the same subject. But they felt the subject would prove to be a blockbuster for them, so they played their cards close to their vest and never let on what their plans were. I can't say I blame them. But it would take another fourteen years before the U.S. Postal Service would issue a stamp commemorating John Lennon in 2018. To our credit, though, we also issued a Beatles-related stamp five years earlier, depicting the Beatles' Yellow Submarine as part of the 1960s decade stamps in the Celebrate the Century series in 1999. There are always ways to get around the system when one shows a bit of creativity!

After returning from London in February 2004—and after little or no progress was made on subject selection during many chats between Jane and me—we were asked to make one last trip to London to find a solution. Bill, Dave, and I made the trip in December 2004, ten months after our first meeting.

This time, maybe due to the pressure we felt to make it work, we agreed on a solution. We collectively wanted a subject that would be of interest to all ages, and Favorite Children's Book Animals was our solution. Working with London-based researchers and

PhotoAssist back in the States, we were able to agree on eight subjects from classic children's books that would be whimsical and fun. Once the animal selections were made, it was not difficult to develop a set of fun, colorful stamps, which were issued in January 2006 concurrently in London and Findlay, Ohio.

Oh, Canada

Once the Royal Mail project had progressed to the point where we could concentrate on other joint issue proposals, Stamp Services agreed to a proposal from our northern neighbors, Canada.

The U.S. Postal Service was about to mount what was billed as the Washington 2006 World Philatelic Exhibition, the largest stamp exhibition in history. Years in development, we were about to host numerous postal administrations from around the world at the Washington Convention Center in D.C. at this two-week extravaganza.

Canada Post proposed a joint issue to be issued during the exhibition. They had already begun issuing a series of Exploration stamps and felt a stamp in that series honoring Samuel de Champlain would be an appropriate subject.

What had to be one of the shortest international flights I experienced in my years with Stamps was in the winter of 2005 to frozen, frigid, icy Ottawa to meet with Canada Post officials. To maintain the continuity of design in their already existing series, they proposed having their designers/illustrators create the stamp while the U.S. developed a design for the souvenir sheet that would house the stamps. I personally accepted the responsibility of designing the souvenir sheet to simplify the design development process rather than involving one of the six art directors.

Unlike the multiple layers of design development, I had experienced with China, Sweden, and Great Britain, the joint Canadian/American process went very smoothly, making multiple trips unnecessary. The souvenir sheet honoring the 1606 voyage of Samuel de Champlain was issued at the end of May.

From Sea to Shining Sea

While the international travel was often "glamorous," I spent hundreds of hours airborne over our great United States.

Press inspections, design conferences, speaking engagements, rights approval meetings, and design meetings, not to mention quarterly CSAC meetings, were but a few reasons I found myself alighting in most major cities in the U.S., not to mention small towns such as Paducah, Kentucky, and Columbus, Wisconsin, to name just a few. Flights stretched from Anchorage to Miami, Boston to San Diego, and St. Paul to New Orleans, with numerous stops in between.

I am eternally grateful to the Postal Service for the many opportunities it provided me to have so many wonderful experiences when traveling as a representative of the U.S. stamp program.

Epilogue

The Long and Winding Road

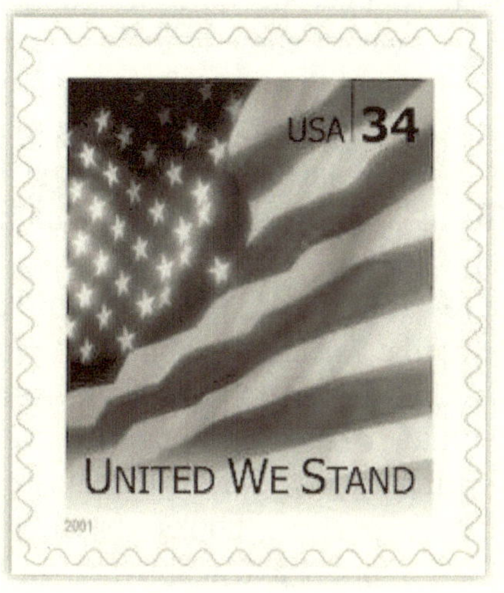

Forty years. In one sense, it seemed like an eternity, and yet in another, it appeared to rapidly fly by. If someone had told me when I graduated from art school that not only would I pursue a career in the federal government, but I would stay in it for four decades, I would have dismissed their prediction as ludicrous and preposterous.

Having tasted the bureaucratic world of government when my aunt Elva prodded me to apply for intern work at the Department of Agriculture, where she had made a good career for herself, I rapidly discovered that government office work was not to my liking at that point in my life. A second opportunity to join the ranks of government arose when I was encouraged to apply for a position in the Bureau of Engraving and Printing art department. The drab, bureaucratic surroundings I would have to work in day after day reminded me of a prison. Again, I shied away from the bureaucratic life.

Those two "tastes" of government life influenced my thinking for ten years. But when one is faced with losing one's job and having to turn to options other than the private sector, the government doesn't look so bad after all. That wake-up call changed my life forever. As anyone who has experienced being laid off from their job, you feel it's the end of the world. Bitterness and depression soon overtake you. But, as most people soon discover, a new position offers the opportunity for new and exciting challenges, and things generally work out for the best. That certainly was true in my case.

So, as my forty-year career came to a close and I stepped into the world of retirement, I found time to reflect not only on the events of those four decades, which I have detailed in these pages, but also the benefits bestowed on me, starting with my first days as the Postal Service's first "official" graphic designer and culminating in my role as Manager of Stamp Design years later.

One of the most rewarding and lasting benefits to come out of this illustrious career was the formation of many friendships. Countless fellow workers, whether designers, writers, or staff secretaries, have enriched my life with their knowledge, talents, and most importantly, their selfless dedication to working as a team to create a pleasing final product, whether posters, books, brochures, magazines, or stamps. Without their support and teamwork, my career would not have been as successful as it was.

Recognition for one's work has always been a hallmark of a designer's career. Design is present in virtually every aspect of our daily lives. Look around you, and you'll see it reflected in our homes, offices, signage, reading material, TV, and film, to mention only a few. To stand out in this very crowded field is especially rewarding to a graphic designer.

I was blessed to be honored numerous times for my work in magazine and poster design during my first twenty years in the Communication department. Both the Washington, D.C. Art Director's Club and the short-lived Federal Design Council honored my work with gold and silver medals. Nationally, my *Postal Life* employee magazine designs were recognized for design excellence by several national design competitions.

Upon moving to Stamp Services, I continued to receive recognition, along with my team of talented designers, illustrators, and photographers, from such national organizations and publications as the Society of Illustrators and the American Institute of Graphic Arts (AIGA), along with awards from communication arts and regional design print magazines and regional awards from art directors' clubs. Over that twenty-year period, we were recognized with nearly 350 awards.

Two awards that I am most proud of were bestowed on me by my peers in the design community.

The first was the "Distinguished Leadership Award" from the Art Directors Club of Metropolitan Washington, given to me in 1997 for my work on the stamp program. Fittingly, the evening's event was held at my alma mater, the Corcoran Art Gallery adjoining the School of Art.

The second, awarded a few years later, was the American Institute of Graphic Design's "Fellow" Award. This prestigious award is presented to designers within their respective chapters nationwide. It is the second-highest award given by the AIGA. I was the third designer awarded this honor after the D.C. Chapter began awarding its designers.

Heading up the Stamp Design group gave me numerous opportunities to share our achievements through the media over the years. I was privileged to give lectures on the design process to groups ranging in size from six avid philatelists who met in church basements on weeknights to lectures before thousands of graphic designers assembled for the annual AIGA national conference and multiple meetings and conferences of all kinds in between.

One of the most prestigious recognitions our Stamp Design group received was a half-hour documentary detailing the design process. Twenty2 Productions, a small filmmaking group from San Francisco, heard about the process and were intrigued enough to want to develop a series of half-hour films about each of the art directors and myself. In the end, budget limitations forced the duo to compress all of the filming into one documentary. They were able to promote the film to PBS, which aired the film nationwide numerous times over a one year period. Eventually, it would come to rest, where else, but on YouTube. You can still find it there to this day. Just type in "American stamps" to find it.

I also had the honor of being interviewed for a Smithsonian Postal Museum film about stamps, which has been shown in continuous loops in a small theater in the museum since it was first produced in 2000. It can also be found on YouTube under the title "Stamps: An American Journey."

Not to be outdone by TV and film, radio personalities have sought interviews to discuss the design process. Most notably, I was interviewed by Tavis Smiley about the Black Heritage stamp series. Local news media got into the act as well with on-the-spot interviews at first-day ceremonies. Anything we could do to help promote the stamp program was a win-win situation for us.

Apart from awards, recognition for one's work can be exhibited in other forms. In my case, the word "exhibited" can be taken literally. With the continued recognition for quality design and illustration shown on postage stamps over the years, it was only natural that other organizations would reach out to us to display these works of art.

The first such group was the Norman Rockwell Museum in Stockbridge, Massachusetts. Stephanie Plunkett, Associate Director for Exhibitions and Programs at the museum, contacted me in 1999 to discuss the possibility of an exhibition of stamp art at the museum. After meeting and showing her examples of stamp art available for display, organization of a major exhibition began in earnest. The result was a magnificent exhibit entitled "Pushing the Envelope: The Art of the Postage Stamp," which displayed framed original stamp art at the museum from November 2000 to May 2001.

The Smithsonian's National Postal Museum was impressed with the exhibit and, after the exhibition closed, sought to launch a similar exhibit in their Washington, D.C. museum. I had been a Postal Service liaison to the National Postal Museum exhibition staff for a number of years, so it fell to Patricia Burke, the Exhibits Director at the Museum, and me to begin discussions to make such an exhibit a reality.

Having firsthand knowledge of the entire canon of stamp art, I was asked to function as the guest curator, an honor I was humbled by. Working for many months with the museum staff, a revised and updated version of the Rockwell exhibit opened in D.C. on July 30, 2003, the tenth anniversary of the museum's opening. The exhibition was very well received and, to this day, is considered one of the most popular exhibits produced by the museum.

Building on the success of that exhibit, Patricia and I began development of a second stamp art exhibit. It would eventually be titled: "Trailblazers and Trendsetters: Art of the Stamp." Again, I was assigned the role of guest curator. That popular exhibit ran from

November 2006 to August 2008.

I was continually reminded during curatorial meetings how fortunate I was to be involved with exhibitions from one of the greatest museums in the world. When growing up in a small Minnesota community, I never would have imagined such a thing could happen to me.

Knowledge was certainly one of the key benefits of my career. Knowledge gained regarding design and color while creating hundreds of posters, books, magazines, brochures, and yes, stamps played a key role in making my life as a designer continually exciting and rewarding. My creative instincts were continually challenged by endless ideas. A constant interchange of ideas between me and my fellow designers, illustrators, photographers, and researchers proved to be the spark that kept the fire alive through all those many years.

Selecting subjects and designing stamps gave me the opportunity to gain knowledge about subjects I was unfamiliar with. Our research team proved indispensable when it came to this critical aspect of stamp development. The educational aspect of developing stamps broadened my knowledge of whom and what had most impacted our great nation.

One's legacy is an important aspect of anyone's life, I believe. We all would like to be remembered when we pass on for who we were or what we accomplished while here on earth. Certainly, one's family is by far the most important legacy one can leave behind. But it can also be good to know that you have accomplished something good during your time that may live on after you.

So, speaking as a professional graphic designer, I am thankful to the U.S. Postal Service for giving me the opportunity to play a key role in developing more than 2,500 of those miniature works of art during my twenty-year tenure with Stamp Services. As it was pointed out during my retirement ceremony, approximately half of all the stamps produced from the advent of the first stamps in 1847 to my retirement were produced under my direction. I was stunned to hear that statistic read aloud that evening and equally humbled by the honor.

Stamps have always been a part of my life, just as it has for most Americans—that is, until today's generation, who have little or no idea what a postage stamp is.

Thinking back to my youth in rural Minnesota, I recall making occasional trips to our local post office to purchase stamps or mail letters for my mother and grandmother. I can still picture the old lodge building that housed the post office: well-worn wooden floors, a wall of dull brass post office boxes with their numbered dials, and the clerk's window with bars covering the top half of the opening. The three-cent Statue of Liberty stamp was the stamp of the day. How ironic that my career in Stamps would, almost sixty years later, culminate in a controversy surrounding the same subject.

I owe a debt of gratitude to those individuals who supported me, mentored me, taught me, traveled with me, laughed and enjoyed life with me, and continued to spark my creativity during those forty years. Without their love and support, I would never have been able to accomplish the things I did.

Even more importantly, I can never express enough love and gratitude for my wife and children. My dear wife Ann has stood by me, supported me, and encouraged me through even the darkest days of my career when even the sparks of creativity were threatening to die out. My children have been equally supportive and gave back so much love over the years. Without my family behind me, I would be nothing.

So, as I close this chapter in my life, I look back on my life and realize that life is in the details, large or small. Stamps are the same way. They may be small, but it's the details that count. The next time you have the opportunity to see, or hopefully use, a postage stamp, stop for a moment and reflect on how much time and effort went into making that little piece of paper we are fond of referring to as our "nation's calling card."

Acknowledgments

Recalling memories of a forty-year career could not have been possible without the assistance of coworkers, philatelists, friends, and family. For his assistance in helping me recount stamp events of the past in this book, I am indebted to George Amick and his in-depth reporting on every stamp issued during that period for the *Linn's U.S. Stamp Yearbook.* Those countless hours spent talking into his pocket tape recorder, sending me home at night with a raspy voice, proved to be indispensable as I wrote this book.

Being given the opportunity to work with some of the most talented and creative people in the graphic design field was a gift that keeps on giving.

Without the diligent work of the PhotoAssist research team, I would not have been able to manage the monumental task of developing those thousands of stamps.

I would have been lost without the able assistance of my staff. Their dedication and devotion to supporting the stamp program have been invaluable.

My thanks also to the many families and organizations that partnered with us to create lasting images for the collecting public, and to the stamp collecting community who always kept my job interesting, for better or worse.

My appreciation to my editor Robert Cooper, whose expertise, guidance, and good judgment have made invaluable contributions to this book.

Last, but certainly not least, I owe an incalculable debt to my family, especially my dear wife Ann, whose strength and positive outlook sustained me through both the highs and lows of my incredible career, and to my children and grandchildren, who were always there for me. Without every one of them, this book would not have been possible.

About the Author

Terry McCaffrey is a national award winning graphic designer whose career spanned over 5 decades. Upon graduating from the Corcoran School of Art and Design in Washington, DC, he began a career in graphic design and for the next 40 years worked in that capacity for the U.S. Postal Service. His work included hundreds of lobby and workroom posters, magazines, brochures and stamp products and promotional material. The last 20 years of his career was spent as design director for the stamp program. During his tenure he oversaw the development of all stamp and stationery items issued which numbered in excess of 2,500, approximately one half of all stamps issued from its inception in 1847. An independent documentary film featuring him, and his design staff, exploring the stamp development process, was produced, and aired nationwide on PBS stations. The stamp images produced under his direction have been honored with numerous museum exhibitions nationwide, including the Smithsonian Institutions. After residing for over 60 years in the Washington, DC area, he and his wife, Ann, retired to New Braunfels, TX.

www.ingramcontent.com/pod-product-compliance
Lightning Source LLC
LaVergne TN
LVHW041157150826
845673LV00001B/199

* 9 7 9 8 2 1 8 3 3 3 5 6 0 *